Additional Praise for *The*
English Theology

"In this engaging study, Inman shows how in the nineteenth and early twentieth centuries, theology emerged from its status as an 'architectonic science' framing the whole of Oxford University education to become a specialized subject. Distinct for historical reasons from arrangements for theological study in Germany, Scotland, and the United States, theologians at Oxford strove to be part of the university yet root the discipline in worshipping communities. The combination of biblical criticism and the influence of 'Nonconformist' faculty and students, Inman argues, pushed Oxford toward a new environment for theological education that was variously furthered or impeded by strong-minded professors and graduates. *The Making of Modern English Theology* is a welcome addition to the growing body of scholarship on how 'religion' became an academic discipline."

Elizabeth Clark, Duke University

"Daniel Inman has written an important and engaging book. Anyone interested in understanding the historical forces that have shaped modern English theology and its institutional environment will find much of value in this fine study."

Thomas Albert Howard, Gordon College

The Making of Modern English Theology

The Making of
Modern English
Theology

God and the Academy at Oxford, 1833–1945

Daniel Inman

Fortress Press
Minneapolis

THTE MAKING OF MODERN ENGLISH THEOLOGY

God and the Academy at Oxford, 1833–1945

Cover design: Laurie Ingram

Cover image: UK, England, Oxford, Univerisity of Oxford, Bodleian Library. © Alan Copson/JAI/Corbis

Library of Congress Cataloging-in-Publication Data is available

Print ISBN: 978-1-4514-6926-4

eBook ISBN: 978-1-4514-8957-6

Manufactured in the U.S.A.

This book was produced using PressBooks.com, and PDF rendering was done by PrinceXML.

IN MEMORIAM
Mark Thurston Inman
(1981-2003)

Contents

Acknowledgments

This book is a development of a DPhil thesis gained within the Faculty of Theology and Religion in the University of Oxford, entitled "God and the Academy: The Practice of Theology in the University of Oxford, 1850-1932." Prof. George Pattison and Dr. William Whyte were exemplary supervisors, and their encouragement and advice since the completion of the doctorate has been superb. I am also grateful to my examiners, Dr. Jane Garnett and Prof. Stuart Jones, whose comments aided the preparation of the thesis for publication.

Throughout this project, I have benefited from the professional excellence of the librarians and archivists of the Bodleian's Special Collections, the Oxford University Archives, the Cambridge University Archives, Lambeth Palace Library, and the Oxford colleges. My thanks to Penelope Bulloch, Elizabeth Boardman, Judith Curthoys, Cliff Davies, John Davies, Lynette Dobson, Cara Downes, Colin Harris, Sue Killoran, Oliver Mahony, Alice Millea, Anna Petre, Robert Petre, Michael Riordan, Anna Sander, Amanda Saville, Tessa Shaw, Verity Westgate and David Wilson. Fr Barry Orford of Pusey House was also very helpful in navigating me through their collections. The Principal of Harris Manchester College, Ralph

Waller, kindly made available the records of the Society for Historical Theology.

My bishop, Colin Fletcher, and vicar, Hugh White, were very generous in allowing me time away from my parish during my curacy to complete this. I am particularly grateful for the advice and support at various stages from my parishioners, my colleagues at Queen's, Sarah and Marius Apetrei, Andrew Atherstone, Catherine Bradley, Peggy Chadwick, Mark Chapman, Paul Fiddes, Sarah Foot, Anne Geniets, Robert Gilbert, Leslie Houlden, Diarmaid MacCulloch, Judith Maltby, Charlotte Methuen, Colm Ó Siochrú, Justin and Sarah Pottinger, Geoffrey Rowell, Chris Rowland, Graeme Salmon, Katrina Sheldon, Simon Skinner, Peter Southwell, and Johannes Zachhuber.

Michael Gibson and Marissa Wold have been incredibly helpful editors, and I am grateful to all the staff at Fortress for being so accommodating, imaginative, and encouraging.

My father and stepmother have been unfailingly supportive, and I dedicate this book to the memory of my brother, Mark, whom we miss.

DDI
Oxford, July 2014

Introduction

Theology and the Modern University

During the final stages of the Terror in Paris in September 1793, the National Convention abolished all the universities and colleges of *ancien régime* France. By doing so, the Convention was beginning a process that would directly or indirectly revolutionize the university as a European institution and the practice of theology as a university discipline. The French universities, some of the oldest and most venerable on the continent, had been the training grounds for those defending the religious and political orthodoxies of the eighteenth century and even the fall of Robespierre could not alter the secularist Republic's underlying conviction that the university "had no more place in the new age than monasteries, serfdom or slavery."[1] Those who were planning the new terrain of higher education in France admired theology as the 'queen of the sciences' as much as they had admired Marie Antoinette, and by the time of Napoleon's concordat with Rome in 1801, theology had been exiled from the new central institutions of higher education in France to seminaries.

This might have signalled the end of the university as a modern European institution. As we shall see, the survival and development

---

1. L. Brockliss, "The European University, 1789-1850" in *The History of the University of Oxford,* (8 vols., Oxford, 1988-2000), 6:93.

of the university was in many respects surprising and the inclusion of theology within the modern university perhaps even more so. The genealogy of the discipline has become of crucial significance in recent years, since, while theologians in the West today do not face the violent rejection that their forbears encountered in late eighteenth-century France, many will describe their continued presence in universities as being comparable to a Babylonian captivity. The Enlightenment university, it is claimed, has programmatically driven theology either to extinction or into the more secularly respectable – and less sectarian, it is assumed – study of religion. These anxieties over the pursuit of theology are framed by a wider confusion over the condition of the humanities in the university, and the very purpose of the modern university. The celebrated mid-twentieth century president of the University of California, Clark Kerr, famously described the university in 1963 as "a series of faculty entrepreneurs held together by a common grievance over parking" and his coinage of the term "multiversity" to describe the disparate aims of modern higher education in the West remains germane.[2]

Determining how theology has reached its current state in the Western university is a harder question to answer. It is persistently asked in contemporary theological circles, where the loss of territory within the university and the retreat of the churches from the academic sphere have been a cause of acute concern. Is it the result of the seemingly unstoppable process of secularization? Was theology ruined by its own methodological collusion with the social sciences? Or is theology's decline just one aspect of the technologically driven collapse of the humanities within our universities? All these answers

---

2. Clark Kerr, *The Uses of a University* (Cambridge, MA: Harvard University Press, 2001), 15. See also Stefan Collini, *What Are Universities For?* (London: Penguin, 2012); M. Nussbaum, *Not for Profit: Why Democracy Needs the Humanities* (Princeton: Princeton University Press, 2012).

have been offered, and yet within each response there is a lack of historical context that should be worrying to scholars who are otherwise so sensitive to such detail. This book seeks to begin the work of providing that historical definition to theology's contemporary predicament. As the first book to provide an account of theology's modern institutional origins in an English university, it will, it is hoped, underline the phrase oft-repeated by Karl Barth, 'Latet periculum in generalibus'.[3]

This is not a work of historical theology, but an account of how theology was practised in an English institution that was converted from an ecclesiastical seminary on the Thames into a globally influential research university – open to all denominations and none – by the beginning of the twentieth century. As we shall see, it is not a purely local account; despite their isolationist tendencies, even Oxford and Cambridge could not fail to be envious of the fruits of research emanating from German universities during the nineteenth century or be affected by the changing fortunes of France and the United States. Nonetheless, the effects of continental developments and, in particular, the influence of the University of Berlin, can be overstated for contemporary thinking about how theology has come to be practised in the European university. Theologians at Oxford and Cambridge came to model an idiosyncratic paradigm of theological practice in the way they negotiated relationships between the churches and university, between theology and the study of religion, and between 'scientific' theology and ministerial training.

What follows are two assertions. Firstly, although Berlin – and particularly Schleiermacher's importance to its foundation – is undeniably influential for the making of modern theology, it is suggested that certain readings of Humboldt's masterly creation have

3. "Danger lies in generalizations."

come to dominate, sometimes unhelpfully, the historiography of modern theology. The second assertion challenges the first by suggesting that the English university has, largely through its reaction to continental political developments, evolved with significant differences from continental, Scottish, and North American institutions. By analysing theology's place within the University of Oxford during a period of extensive reform, this development of this distinctive paradigm is introduced as an alternative way of thinking about theology's institutional development since the Enlightenment.

From Paris to Berlin: the Origins of the Research University

The decisions adopted in France during the Revolution were so significant for the history of the modern European university since the institutional models that were established in their place in the Republic were soon being exported across Europe by the French bayonet. In place of these formidable ecclesiastical foundations, the Thermidorean administration founded a series of specialist *écoles,* set alongside the research-directed *académies,* that would offer a more focussed professional education to students in contrast to the old universities' diet of classics and theology. Although several of Europe's 'enlightened despots' had attempted to reform the curricula and administration of their universities in the face of declining matriculations and mismanagement, it was the advance of Napoleon's troops that ultimately provoked the greatest changes to the operations of Europe's oldest universities.[4] His protégé monarchs shut such prestigious institutions as Louvain, Wittenberg, and Halle (the last

---

4. It should be noted, however, that the success of such initiatives was limited due to conservative religious forces within the universities. One exception was Joseph II of Austria who successfully rationalized the number of universities, made German rather than Latin the official language, and compelled the universities to admit Jews and Protestants. (L. Brockliss, *ibid.,* 89)

having only been established in 1694) and even where the university survived, such as in Bologna, Padua, and Pavia (which came under the control of Napoleon's stepson Eugène de Beauharnais), the faculties were reconfigured with theology excised. In the few institutions where the old higher faculties did survive, such as at Turin, the funds available were so reduced by the Napoleonic war machine that the university was effectively crippled.[5]

This assault on Europe's universities and their theological faculties was not simply the result of Jacobin anti-clericalism. At the heart of these changes was a desire to introduce Enlightenment methodologies to higher education. Influential French thinkers such as Charles de Talleyrand and Nicolas de Condorcet perceived the pursuit of truth not as the reverential reception of dogma and the defence of orthodoxy but the hard labour of inductive study, and universities – if they were to survive at all – ought to exist for the expansion of human understanding. They should not perpetuate and defend aristocratic and ecclesiastical interests. From as early as the end of the seventeenth century, extra-mural academies had been founded to foster research in the natural sciences and natural philosophy and the Revolution only confirmed a well-established instinct that it would be these academies, rather than the inherited universities, that would become the primary seats of higher learning in enlightened Europe.[6]

How then did the university survive as an influential institution of modern Europe? It can be attributed only indirectly to the French. After Napoleon defeated the Prussians in the battles of Jena-Auerstedt

5. D. Outram, "Military Empire, Political Collaboration, and Cultural Consensus: The Université Imperiale Reappraised: The Case of the University of Turin", *History of Universities* vii (1998), 287-303.
6. M. Purver, *The Royal Society: Concept and Creation* (Cambridge, MA: MIT Press, 1967); J.E. McClellan, *Science Reorganized: Scientific Societies in the Eighteenth Century* (New York: Columbia University Press, 1985).

in October 1806, with territory ceded west of the Elba to the French, the future seemed bleak for German scholars. Theodor Schmalz, a professor of jurisprudence from the suppressed university in Halle, approached Friedrich Wilhelm III with a plea endorsed by other members of his university for a new location for studying and teaching. In response to their plea, the king is reported to have said to Schmalz, "That is right, that is commendable. What the state has lost in physical strength it must replace with intellectual strength."[7] Friedrich Wilhelm seems to have recognized immediately that a new university could restore national pride in the face of defeat and be a means for the Prussian civil service to realize their progressive social vision.[8]

In 1808, with the Francophiles in the Prussian government diminishing in influence, the senior civil servant Wilhelm von Humboldt followed the jurist Karl Friedrich Beyme as the minister responsible for public education and culture in the Prussian Ministry of the Interior. In this role he enthusiastically assumed the task of founding a new university in Berlin, drawing upon the *Bildungstheorie* emerging from post-Kantian idealism. This was a vision of education that saw every member of the university as a participant in a unified theory of knowledge, termed *Wissenschaft*. For a subject to be *wissenschaftlich* required that it be philosophically coherent both internally and in relation to other disciplines, and that both professor and student were committed to working for

7. Rudolf Köpfe, *Die Gründung der königlichen Friedrich-Wilhelms-Universität zu Berlin* (Berlin: Gustav Schade, 1860), 37; quoted in E. Lawler, "Neohumanistic-Idealistic Concepts of a University: Schelling, Steffens, Fichte, Schleiermacher and von Humboldt", in *Friedrich Schleiermacher and the Founding of the University of Berlin: The Study of Religion as a Scientific Discipline,* ed. H. Richardson(Lewiston, NY: Edwin Mellen, 1991), 2.
8. *Wissenschaftlich* is usually translated, unsatisfactorily, into English as 'scientific'. See Matthew Levinger, "The Prussia Reform Movement and the Rise of Enlightened Nationalism" in P.G. Dwyer, *The Rise of Prussia 1700-1830* (London: Longman, 2000), 259-77; Thomas Albert Howard, *Protestant Theology and the Making of the Modern German University* (Oxford: Oxford University Press, 2008), 150ff.

the systematic unity of knowledge which was ultimately deemed possible by the transcendental principles of idealism.[9] Drawing upon the writings of J. G. Fichte, Friedrich W.J. Schelling, Heinrich Steffens, and Friedrich Schleiermacher, Humboldt created an institution in a matter of months that would come to be admired across the world by the end of the century, both for its wealth of research and as a model of higher education that other nationalist governments eagerly desired to emulate. Contrary to expectations at the beginning of the nineteenth century, by its end it was the reconceived idea of the university mastered at Berlin, rather than the French *école,* that was internationally more influential.

Berlin's foundation and success was also an important new context for theological life. For, while rejecting the ecclesiastical foundations of the medieval university, the University of Berlin still invited the scholar to raise his eyes to a lofty ideal: the unity of all knowledge, discerned through universally rational frames of reference. It has remained a matter of interest and historical significance, therefore, that theology was included in the foundation of the new university. In the context of widespread revolt against what was perceived as obscurantist confessionalism across Europe, how did there emerge a new theological faculty in an institution that was so imbued with the principles of the Enlightenment? Although one might have assumed the zealous bureaucratization of Prussian education and religion in the early nineteenth century to have happily coincided at Berlin, the reason for theology's survival as a university discipline on the continent is more complicated. As will now be shown, it was as much the result of outstanding persuasive arguments as it was pragmatic necessity.

9. J.G. Fichte, "Deduced Scheme for an Academy to be Established in Berlin (1807)", tr. G.H. Turnbull, in Turnbull, *The Educational Theory of J.G. Fichte: A Critical Account, Together with Translations* (Liverpool: University of Liverpool, 1926), 170-265

Schleiermacher and the Making of Modern Theology

Theology's surprising inclusion at Berlin has been widely attributed to the brilliance of Friedrich Schleiermacher in an unsolicited paper he sent to von Humboldt in 1808 regarding the foundation of a new university, *Occasional Thoughts about Universities in the German Sense.* Fichte had argued against ecclesiastical involvement in the new institution, following Kant's strictures in *The Conflict of the Faculties* that the university must stand only under the jurisdiction of reason, rather than the government or the church. "A school", Fichte wrote, "of the scientific use of reason presupposes that whatever is given to it may be understood and penetrated down to its ultimate ground; accordingly, something which proscribes the use of reason and puts itself forward *a priori* as an unfathomable mystery, is in the nature of the case excluded from such a school."[10] According to Fichte, as theology's content was delivered by special revelation and contained within certain sacred books, it was evidently incompatible with the *wissenschaftlichen* criteria of study at Berlin. Along with medicine and jurisprudence, he considered it a largely practical science and what little of theology that could reasonably be considered 'scientific' ought to be apportioned to the departments of history, philosophy, and philology.

It was this second reproach to theology's place in Berlin that Schleiermacher specially attacked in his *Brief Outline on the Study of Theology* and in his own paper on the foundation of the new university, *Occasional Thoughts.* In the latter document, in particular, Schleiermacher articulated a broader account of *Wissenschaft* than Fichte. To hold a belief in the transcendental condition of the unity of all knowledge required more than just the bare logical principles

---

10. J.G. Fichte, "Deduced Scheme", 198.

of rational coherence; for him a "strictly empiricist approach would reduce the person, the state, and science to mechanisms"[11]. Rather, the scholar and the university must adopt a *Weltanschauung* - a comprehensive perspective that included the aesthetic and the moral alongside the purely noetic. Therefore, Schleiermacher suggested, the philosophical faculty was rightly the first faculty, as it nourished this "science of the whole".

Within this richer vision of human reasoning, however, Schleiermacher averred that religion had its own position as a tradition that contributed to the overall, rationally meaningful, exploration of human understanding. Even when, as he accepted, theology was included as one of the *Spezialschulen* that had been included because – like the faculties of law and medicine – it met social demands, this did not diminish the possibility of its inclusion in the university. While theology operated as a "conceptual skill governed by practical aims", *positive Wissenschaft,* the new German university existed to unite both research and teaching, including teaching for the public professions.[12] To place such a premium upon the practical was particularly relevant for theology because, for Schleiermacher, theological language "functions as part of the web of relations constituting the community of which it is a part", and the university ought to exist for both the descriptive in human reasoning as well as the explanatory.[13] In the end, von Humboldt included theology in his plans for the university, accepting that the university must also exist for practical ends in the grand enterprise of *Wissenschaft.* Even if it was the considerable cultural influence of the Protestant church in early nineteenth-century Prussia rather than theology's *wissenschaftlichen* components that ultimately affected

11. Lawler, *ibid.,* 27.
12. Hans Frei, *Types of Christian Theology* (New Haven, CT: Yale University Press, 1992), 114.
13. Frei, *ibid.,* 115.

Humboldt's decision, the inclusion of theology at Berlin as it opened its doors to students on 6 October 1810 seems to have been secured, in large part, through the influence of Schleiermacher.

Wissenschaft and the Science of Religion

The position for theology that was secured – theology as both *wissenschaftlich* and oriented towards practical aims – has, however, been perceived by subsequent generations as less than satisfactory for either the academy or the church. In particular, the "relativizing consequences of historical ways of thinking" that dominated the academic culture of Berlin presented a challenge to the privileged position of Christian theology in the university.[14] As Johannes Zachhuber has shown in his study of theology as *Wissenschaft*, while Schleiermacher wrote in *The Christian Faith* that the "utter novelty of a historical movement, which cannot be deduced from previous events, is the only reasonable meaning the word 'revelation' could possibly have", this at once exposed theology to the iconoclastic forces of modern historical study.[15] Christianity's intrinsically historical character may seem self-evident to theologians today, but the relocation of theology's primary residence from the philosophical to the historical sphere in the nineteenth-century university was foundationally destabilizing in ways that Schleiermacher could not have anticipated.

Theology's vulnerability to the historicist techniques became particularly apparent as the century progressed. As Zachhuber has demonstrated with admirable detail, alternative visions of theology as *Wissenschaft* become more prominent as the historicist-idealist mode of theology embodied in the work of Ferdinand Christian

---

14. T.A. Howard, *ibid.,* 379.
15. Johannes Zachhuber, *Theology as Science in Nineteenth Century Germany* (Oxford: Oxford University Press, 2013), 16.

Baur gave way to the thoroughgoing 'presuppositionless' historicist theology of the Ritschlian school from 1850 onwards. Alongside changing understandings of what constituted *Wissenschaft*, Thomas Albert Howard has indicated how the study of religion in the second half of the century also dramatically shifted the nature of theology's position in the university. Although the *Religionswissenschaft* was poorly represented in the German theological faculties, the new availability of Eastern texts, the development of philological study, and German colonial expansion all contributed to an enthusiasm for what was becoming known as the 'History of Religions' (*Religionsgeschichte*). Friedrich Max Müller who, though German by birth, spent the vast majority of his scholarly life in Oxford as Taylorian Professor of Modern Languages, has been seen as the founder of this new 'science of religion'; his 1873 *Introduction to the Science of Religion* is considered a founding document of the discipline.[16] University chairs and lectureships were established in the subject across Europe, America, and even Japan in the thirty years after its publication, in addition to those that were already established in the 'history of religion' at Basle, Lausanne, and Geneva. Unusually, however, the German theological faculties resisted their establishment as confessional departments of theology: a fact that increasingly became a cause for criticism.

In the same year as Friedrich Max Müller published his *Introduction*, two German scholars published damning critiques of the condition of German university theology. Paul Lagarde, a nationalist philologist and Old Testament scholar at the University of Göttingen, published his essay *On the Relationship of the German State to Theology, the Church, and Religion*, arguing that the theological faculty was, as a

---

16. *Introduction to the Science of Religion* (London: Longmans, Green & Co., 1873), cf. T.A. Howard, *ibid.,* 382-33.

semi-confessional body, in need of replacement with a department of the comparative study of religion in order to avoid the confusion of *Wissenschaft* with ecclesiastical influence.[17] Believing Christianity as expressed in the Protestant churches to be redundant, he believed that a more truly scientific account of religion would help nurture his nationalist vision for a new Germanic religion.

Also in 1873, the Basle church historian Franz Overbeck published his own criticism of contemporary academic theology, *Über die Christlichkeit unserer heutigen Theologie*. Emerging from the same publisher as that of his housemate and friend Friedrich Nietzsche, Overbeck opined that the desire to make theology scientific had been inimical to Christianity's eschatological character. This was a religion, he argued, that in its essence denied the powers of this world, including those of learning, and Overbeck was confident in his assertion that "the antagonism between faith and knowledge is one that is permanent and thoroughly irreconcilable".[18]

The work of the faculties to analyse Christianity scientifically in its various parts had, Overbeck claimed, categorically misunderstood its radical centre. Friedrich Nietzsche advanced the same conclusion in his consideration of the dominance of historicism in German culture, and the "annihilating" judgment of "historical justice". "A religion," Nietzsche wrote,

> which is intended to be transformed into historical knowledge under the hegemony of pure historical justice, a religion which is intended to be understood through and through as an object of science and learning, will when this process is at the end also be found to have been destroyed…The reason is that historical verification always brings

17. P. Lagarde, *Über das Verhältnis des deutschen Staates zu Theologie, Kirche und Religion* (Göttingen: Dieterich, 1873).
18. Franz Overbeck, *Über die Christlichkeit unserer heutigen Theologie*, reprint of 2nd edn. (Darmstadt: Wissenschaftliche Buchgesellschaft, 1981), 22; quoted in Howard, *Protestant Theology*, 389.

to light so much that is false, crude, inhuman, absurd, violent, that the mood of pious illusion in which alone anything that wants to live can live necessarily crumbles away.[19]

The confidence of the theologians in the work of history to reach pure knowledge about Christianity was, for Nietzsche as much as Overbeck, a misunderstanding of the power and nature of religion, which was closer to art than science. Life that is "dominated" by science, he wrote, "is not of much value because it is far less *living* and guarantees far less life for the future than did a former life dominated not by knowledge but by instinct and powerful illusions."[20]

Thomas Albert Howard has shown how the impact of Lagarde, Overbeck, Nietzsche and the growing methodological influence of the *religionsgeschichtliche Schule*, largely based around the University of Göttingen, all signalled a fracturing of Schleiermacher's settlement for the German theological faculty and his own concept of *Wissenschaft* in the final decades of the nineteenth century. Despite Adolf von Harnack's impressive defence of the twofold character of theology in the university in his rectorial address to the University of Berlin in 1901, 'The Task of the Theological Faculties and the General History of Religion', Albert Schweitzer's *Quest for the Historical Jesus* (1906), and the turmoil that engulfed Europe in 1914 onwards cast doubt on Harnack's refinement of the Protestant religion through critical-historical study.[21]

The most influential post-war critique of university theology, however, came from the young Swiss pastor of Safenwil, Karl Barth.

19. Friedrich Nietzsche, "On the Uses and Disadvantages of History for Life" in *Untimely Meditations,* trans. R. Hollingdale (Cambridge: Cambridge University Press, 1997), 95-97. This 'meditation' was published on 22 February 1874. See also his first meditation on "David Strauss, the Confessor and the Writer", published 8 August 1873.
20. Friedrich Nietzsche, "On the Uses and Disadvantages of History for Life", 97.
21. Adolf von Harnack, *Die Aufgabe der theologischen Fakultäten und die allgemeine Religionsgeschichte* (Giessen, 1901). Later reprinted in Harnack's *Reden und Aufsätze*, 2. Auflage, Band 2, (Giessen 1906), 159-187.

He had come to believe that academic theology was failing to meet the demands of his parishioners and had been appalled by the support of German university theologians for the Kaiser's war aims as signatories to the 'Manifesto of the Ninety-Three' in 1914. Barth had been as a student one of the leading defenders of Harnack, but war and his parochial work compelled Barth to think more deeply about the nature and position of theology in the university.

In his 1922 lecture, "The Word of God and the Task of Theology", Barth asserted that theology had failed to act as the "signal of distress" (*Notzeichen*) within the university:

> ...the existence of theology in the academy...is justified and established, as is the existence of the Church in society, out of a notion that is not its own. It is paradoxically but inevitably true that theology has *no* right to exist in the academy the way other sciences do. It is a completely unnecessary duplication of a few disciplines that belong to other faculties. A *theological* faculty has a reason to be in the academy only when it is charged with the task of expressing that which the others dare not say under the circumstances, or say it in a way that is not heard, or when it at least signals that such things *must* be said.[22]

Existing "beyond the bounds of scientific possibilities", the dialectical revolutionaries believed that the historicism of German liberal theology had not, as Harnack believed, grasped the kernel of Christianity, but rather merely reflected the *opinio communis* of the academic guild, confusing the object of religion with the object of theology: namely, God.[23] "We ought to speak of God", Barth insisted, and "To speak of God in all seriousness would mean to speak on the grounds of revelation and faith."[24]

---

22. Karl Barth, *The Word of God and Theology* (London: Continuum, 2011), 181.
23. For more on the incongruity between Barth's and Harnack's theological methodology, see their correspondence from 1923, an English translation of which can be found in H. Martin Rumscheidt, *Revelation and Theology: An Analysis of the Barth-Harnack Correspondence of 1923* (Cambridge: Cambridge University Press, 1972); cf. T.A. Howard, *ibid.*, 413-14.
24. K. Barth, *ibid.*, 185.

Barth's plain rejection of Schleiermacher's and Harnack's defence of university theology as 'scientific' was not merely an institutional complaint about the failure of theologians to speak prophetically in a crucial period of German history. Barth's post-war writings, and most famously the second edition of his *Epistle to the Romans* has been widely regarded as the beginning of a new movement in western theology that unequivocally rejected the Liberal Protestant pursuit of *wissenschaftliche Theologie* that had been pioneered at Berlin and across Germany.

Berlin as a Post-Liberal Paradigm

Although a full treatment of dialectical theology's beginnings in the period following the First World War is not possible here, it is important to note that Karl Barth did not outwardly reject the institutional status quo – he would spend the rest of his working life in academic positions in Germany and Switzerland and argued strongly for the public character of theology and against its replacement with the study of religion in his writings. Nonetheless, Barth and his disciples argued that theology had conceded too much to the historical-critical method in its bid to be deemed *wissenschaftlich* and that theologians needed to attend less to ever more sophisticated philological, textual and historical techniques and draw nearer instead to the object of their discipline, namely God and the means by which he is known – the Word of God.

That critique of Liberal Protestant theology has, arguably, been so compelling to the theological community since the early twentieth century precisely because the model of the research university pioneered at Berlin has been so influential. By the end of the nineteenth century, few institutions across Europe or America could claim to have been untouched by Humboldt's creation, and advocacy of the research university had become the hallmark of political liberalism by the middle of the century. Also, as Lawrence Brockliss has indicated, Germany's success in the natural and philosophical sciences in the first half of the nineteenth century also entailed that "no country in the culturally competitive age of nationalism could afford not to have a research-oriented university system" and such a system became only more desirable with the cultural, economic, and military success of Bismarck's Prussia.[25] By the eve of revolution in 1848, the university was no longer susceptible to dismissal as it had been after the French Revolution, and where the Humboldtian model was not in place, revolution or nationalist competition was hastening its incorporation into European educational systems.[26]

Germany's influence over the university and the practice of theology was also recognizable in American colleges and the new universities of the nineteenth century. As Elizabeth Clark has shown through her study of six American seminary professors in the early nineteenth century, Germany played "a double leading role, as tutor and villain".[27] The Berlin model found transatlantic admiration most famously in the foundation of John Hopkins University in 1876, but Germany's academic strength was recognized long beforehand, with nearly ten thousand Americans travelling to Germany between 1815 and 1914 to hear lectures from the leading professors of the day.[28] Their experience transformed their own ideas of university education in a nation that was dominated by a handful of private colleges for most of the nineteenth century, which were themselves based on the ideals of the collegiate English universities. By the end of the

25. L. Brockliss, "The European University 1789-1850", 6:115.
26. See Christophe Charle, "Patterns" in Walter Rüegg, ed., *A History of the University in Europe* (4 vols., Cambridge: Cambridge University Press, 2004), 3:33-75.
27. Elizabeth A. Clark, *Founding the Fathers: Early Church History and Protestant Professors in Nineteenth-Century America* (Philadelphia: University of Pennsylvania Press, 2011), 3.
28. George M. Marsden, *The Soul of the American University: From Protestant Establishment to Established Nonbelief* (New York, NY: Oxford University Press, 1994), 104-5.

nineteenth century, however, the transformation of those colleges into universities, the foundation of new institutions such as Cornell University in 1865 and the University of Chicago in 1890, and the 'Germanization' of such institutions as the University of Michigan, all signalled the transatlantic acceptance of Humboldt's model.[29]

It is not surprising therefore that Humboldt's model should, for so many contemporary theologians, have become paradigmatic for their understanding of theology's genesis and development as a modern university discipline. Each generation of theologians since Berlin's foundation seems to have grappled with the existence of the discipline in the context of the research university and Schleiermacher's Berlin has invariably been employed as the interpretative key, usually unfavourably.

The Berlin paradigm has been especially significant for post-liberal considerations of the secular university as a context for the practice of theology, the most celebrated perhaps being some lectures delivered by the Yale theologian Hans Frei, included in his posthumously published *Types of Christian Theology* in 1992. In this dense exposition of Schleiermacher's idea of the university, Frei explored the debates around Berlin's foundations, the challenge of integrating theology with *Wissenschaftstheorie,* and how observing the behaviour of Christian theology in the university context can itself suggest a helpful typology for theology.[30] Despite Frei's careful elucidation of Schleiermacher's insistence that history and God could never be equated, the prominence that Berlin and its theological faculty gave

---

29. Cf. Richard J. Storr, *Harper's University: A History of the University of Chicago* (Chicago: University of Chicago Press, 1966); Morris Bishop, *A History of Cornell* (Ithaca, NY: Cornell University Press, 1962). Henry Tappan, chancellor of the University of Michigan from 1852 to 1863, has been called "the John the Baptist" of the American university, heralding the arrival of the German model at Ann Arbor. (G.M. Marsden, *The Soul of the American University,* 103). He was eventually deposed by his own colleagues, in part because of his European proclivity for taking wine with meals and not objecting to students drinking beer (Marsden, 110).
30. Hans Frei, "Appendix A: Theology in the University" in *Types of Christian Theology,* 95–133.

to the study of the 'scientific' and historical data of the Christian tradition has been understood by several leading theologians, largely under the influence of Karl Barth, as methodologically suicidal.

Stanley Hauerwas, for example, in his collection of essays, *State of the University* (2007) invoked Frei to speak of theology's compromised position in the contemporary secular university, arguing that his essay "is the necessary place anyone must begin who wishes to wrestle with the question of theological knowledge."[31] Frei, Hauerwas wrote, describes the development of a university that is not only "religiously neutral" but also "prohibited any allegiance from inhibiting the free exercise of critical reason". "Under such a regime", Hauerwas claims, "theology could only be a university subject by being transformed into a historical discipline."[32] Although Hauerwas clearly had a limited exposure to Howard's important study of the German university (and so lacks some historical nuance around Berlin's foundation), he is no less certain that "the attempt to make theology a subject among other subjects cannot help but make theology something it is not. Theology properly understood as knowledge of God means theology cannot be restricted to 'one field.'"[33]

George Marsden, the American historian of Evangelicalism, similarly argued in his 1994 book, *The Soul of the American University,* that the triumph of Liberal Protestantism and the influence of the Humboldtian model in the universities of North America resulted in the elevation of non-sectarianism and methodological neutrality which, in turn, began to consider non-belief as the only acceptable academic perspective.[34] From an altogether different angle, the

---

31. Stanley Hauerwas, *The State of the University: Academic Knowledges and the Knowledge of God* (Oxford: Blackwell, 2007), 4.
32. Stanley Hauerwas, *ibid.*
33. Stanley Hauerwas, *ibid.,* 6-7; cf. James Stoner, "Theology as Knowledge: A Symposium," *First Things* 163 (May 2006): 24-6.

British theologian and leading figure in the 'Radical Orthodoxy' movement, John Milbank, has argued that the "free, rational inquiry" that was the hallmark of the Humboldtian ideal handed over "the whole realm of the substantive to the play of agnostic forces":

> Enlightenment, therefore, is bound to evolve into the postmodern mixture of the purest, most unbounded and therefore most rigorous logic, plus the most untrammelled sway of vanity and fashion. In many ways a "religious studies department" is well adapted to our era. But we should be warned: the point of fashion is to change, and religious constituencies may well yet further wither away, or more probably mutate and take their custom elsewhere, far away from the universities (or what future will remain of them).[35]

Milbank argues that the specialization of the Enlightenment university, unloosed from the 'substantive' (that is, theology), led inevitably to the 'utter incoherence' of the postmodern university. It is not surprising that Hauerwas sees the Catholic order of learning articulated by John Henry Newman in *The Idea of a University* (1873), offering a healthier mould for the university. If a university is less concerned with shaping character and one's habits of mind than the pursuit of *Wissenschaft*, then that university will disintegrate. Newman asserted that "to withdraw Theology from the public schools is to impair the completeness and to invalidate the trustworthiness of all that is actually taught in them": a suggestion that secularist admirers of his *Idea* tend to view as symptomatic of "its remoteness, its opacity, and, above all, its overriding dogmatic

34. George M. Marsden, *The Soul of the American University: From Protestant Establishment to Established Nonbelief* (New York, NY: Oxford University Press, 1994), 408-429.
35. John Milbank, 'The Conflict of the Faculties: Theology and the Economy of the Sciences' in *Faithfulness and Fortitude: In Conversation with the Theological Ethics of Stanley Hauerwas,* ed. M.T. Theissen and S. Wells(Edinburgh: T&T Clark, 2000), 40. See also Edward Farley, *Theologia: The Fragmentation and Unity of Theological Education* (Philadelphia: Fortress Press, 1983), which likewise complains that the idea of theology as 'habitus' has long since given way to a desire for technical skills of ministry and disciplinary fragmentation.

intent."[36] For Newman, certainly, "admit a God, and you introduce among the subjects of your knowledge, a fact encompassing, closing in upon, absorbing, every other fact conceivable": a theological worldview naturally places theology at the heart of the system of study, and as the 'science of sciences'.[37]

Similar unease with the pervasiveness of 'the Berlin effect' for modern British theological life can be identified in the writings of the Aberdeen theologian John Webster, and, in particular, his inaugural lecture as the Lady Margaret Professor of Divinity in the University of Oxford in 2003, "Theological Theology". The modern university, for Webster, keeps theology in exile, unable to attend to its true sources (the revelation of God) and methods (worship), and thus leaves the discipline fatally compromised by its obligations to the secular academy. In the modern *wissenschaftlichen* university, Webster claimed, "we tell ourselves we argue not *from* but *towards* authority, and so only as free enquirers."[38] Whereas theologians in Britain, as elsewhere, have secured their place in the university by "conformity to an ideal of disengaged reason",

> the most fruitful contribution which theology can make to the wider world of learning is by demonstrating a stubborn yet cheerful insistence on what Barth called 'the great epistemological caveat...[T]he way of thought [of theology]...is not secure except in the reality of Jesus Christ and the Holy Spirit.'[39]

The belief that theology has been sullied by its collusion with the Berlin model, derived in large part from Barth and Frei, has thus evidently become a shibboleth of theological orthodoxy for many

36. J.H. Newman, *The Idea of a University Defined and Illustrated,* ed. I. Kerr (Oxford: Clarendon Press, 1976); Stefan Collini, *What are Universities for?,* 44.
37. J.H. Newman, *ibid.,* 38.
38. John Webster, "Theological Theology" in *Confessing God: Essays in Christian Dogmatics II* (Edinburgh: T&T Clark, 2005), 16.
39. John Webster, *ibid.,* 27, quoting Karl Barth, *Ethics* (Grand Rapids: Eerdmans, 1981), 98.

prominent Christian thinkers both in Britain and the United States. For such as these, Berlin and her imitators have discouraged theology from being theological enough, and both the university and those theological faculties will eventually disintegrate for the lack of "shared attention" to the source of all being, God.

Rethinking Theology's Institutional History

Berlin may yet have its defenders. Mike Higton in his recent book, *A Theology of Higher Education,* has recovered how *Wissenschaftsideologie* drew upon Judaeo-Christian theological concepts of sociality and freedom. Even in the writings of Fichte, Higton reminds us, the life of the *wissenschaftliche* 'Socratic school' was to be held together by love.[40] The dialectic that was the art of philosophical construction in the Romantic university was, Higton argues, the recovery of the 'sociality of reason' from the medieval tradition of the University of Paris. Even if that 'sociality' was divorced from any actual church, this was not without good reason. Kant's *Conflict of the Faculties* was, Higton reminds us, written in the context of a police state in which the church acted as censor-in-chief. The University of Berlin, finding its guarantee of freedom in the enlightened state rather than the church, was thus a recovery of a Christian educational tradition: "in their advocacy of fully public conversation they saw themselves as raising that theological inheritance to a new level, freed from particularism and conflict."[41] Although that investment of trust in the state proved to be deeply problematic in the long term for the German university, the founders of Berlin – and especially Schleiermacher – were nonetheless convinced that *Wissenschaft* was a moral pursuit, leading the state

---

40. Mike Higton, *A Theology of Higher Education* (Oxford: Oxford University Press, 2012), 58.
41. Higton, *ibid.,* 65.

beyond its narrow interests. Upholding "good judgment, [it] is untainted by special interest, and gradually roots out petty passions and prejudices".[42]

If that moral vision was blurred by an oppressive bureaucracy that scrutinized every aspect of the university's life and led to the "proliferation and fragmentation of newly professional discrete disciplines…with carefully policed boundaries, and well-understood criteria for what counted as an acceptable contribution", Higton does well to remind us of the very different intentions of Berlin's theorists. These men had sought to build a university for the sake of the 'church' – "a re-thought Body of Christ, the community of free giving and receiving, of participation in and anticipation of the absolute or universal community of knowing" – in the stead of "the fractious and cacophonous ecclesiastical form in which that tradition came to them".[43]

Even if Berlin cannot necessarily be reclaimed as an altogether nourishing model for theology in the university, Higton's and Howard's exploration of its origins and subsequent influence has highlighted the complex relationships that have existed between German theological faculties and the national church, the interests of the Prussian monarchy and an expanding bureaucratic state, and a wider society that was convulsed by revolution and war. Moreover, as both Zachhuber and Howard have stressed, by 1909, the character of *wissenschaftliche Theologie* in Berlin was theoretically and institutionally dissimilar to Schleiermacher's faculty a century earlier, the result of, *inter alia,* changing emphases within German theology, colonialism, the intervening rise of the natural and physical sciences, and newly discrete disciplines in the humanities.[44]

42. F.D. Schleiermacher, *Occasional Thoughts,* 7; quoted in Higton, *ibid.,* 71.
43. Higton, *ibid.,* 77.

Given the historical complexity of Berlin and the development of German theology, can that paradigm be sufficient for thinking about theology's institutional development in other European nations and in the United States? For instance, are the divinity schools and seminaries of the United States or France really comparable, where a constitutional separation of church and state has resulted in an altogether different institutionalization of theology and religious studies from that of Germany? As David Ford has commented with regard to American institutions, "the most obvious feature is the diversity, reflecting as in Britain a complex history of power struggles and negotiation, and resisting a resolution of the debates in favour of one conception or the other."[45] Those private universities that have retained theology are inclined to see it as a purely professional activity within the graduate divinity schools, whereas the English context is described by Ford as "a process" that has been "*ad hoc, diverse, experimental*" with "locally negotiated settlements among stakeholders."[46]

Ford is almost alone among commentators in emphasizing the importance of local history for theology's various evolutions internationally. Recognizing that the diverse relationships between church, society and university have had a profound impact upon the way theologians have practised their discipline across Europe and North America since the early nineteenth century, it is not surprising that Ford contends that the 'new theology and religious studies' found in the universities of the United Kingdom is distinctive and emerges out of a very particular interaction between theologians, their university contexts, the British churches, and wider society.

---

44. The use of the word *Wissenschaft* by Adolf von Harnack, for instance, is significantly different from that of Schleiermacher. This is of significance for Barth's own frustration with the German theological faculties and interpretation of *Wissenschaft*.

45. David Ford, *The Future of Christian Theology* (Oxford: Blackwell, 2011), 160.

46. Ford, *ibid.,* 158.

If these British 'settlements' are indeed so complex, so diverse, and *ad hoc,* is it not then peculiar that theologians have been content to interpret the history of their institutions with an historical model derived from a single institution in early nineteenth-century Prussia? Even if many leading British theologians agree with Karl Barth and his successors that the Berlin model proved, ultimately, deeply noxious for the health of European theology in the late nineteenth and early twentieth centuries (and Howard offers some reason for us to do so), this book begins the work of finding a thicker historical description of theology as an academic discipline in the British Isles, and in particular, England.

The Making of the English University

Those seeking to gain an understanding of the local history of British theology from the beginning of the nineteenth century will be disappointed by the resources to hand, there being no available account of theology's institutional development in modern British academic life.

The only book to engage seriously with historical analysis of the university in relation to theology in recent years has been Howard's study of the German context in the nineteenth century and, in relation to the British context, Mike Higton's *Theology of Higher Education.* The latter is primarily a theological vision for the secular university, but does devote its first section to an historical examination of Paris, Berlin, Dublin, and Oxford, recognizing each institution as particularly influential in forming a theological account of a university. Oxford and Dublin are considered in a distinct chapter, but Higton focuses not so much with the institutions themselves as with Newman's own vision for the university emerging from his involvement with both universities. This is an important and valuable theological account of higher education, and Higton naturally does not explore in depth the development of British theological and university life beyond some short reflections upon Newman's time at Oxford prior to his conversion in 1845. Indeed, even while Newman's *Idea* continues to exercise remarkable influence well beyond the theological sphere, only a few scholars, notably Mark Chapman, have begun to define the origins of that magisterial vision of the university in the distinctive *ethos* of early nineteenth-century Oxford.[47]

There are, however, strong reasons to promote closer investigation of the UK context and not just as an exercise in British exceptionalism. By the middle of the nineteenth century, the British universities, and Oxford and Cambridge in particular, were institutional anomalies in Europe. This was in large part the result of the isolation of Britain from continental revolution. As it was the French Revolution that had prompted the wholesale dismantlement or reconstitution of the traditional university on the continent, so Great Britain's isolation from these turbulent events resulted, paradoxically perhaps, in the consolidation and nurturing of the corporate, collegiate character of its universities.

Oxford had been a candidate for reform in the late eighteenth century as a resolutely High Church Tory institution that stood in opposition to the dominant Whig and latitudinarian culture. Its motto, *Dominus Illuminatio Mea* ('The Lord is my light'), the opening verse of the twenty-seventh psalm, speaks to this day of an institution with an unmistakable Christian heritage. Moreover, during the upheavals of late eighteenth century Europe, the Church of England's 'possession' of the English universities was cherished rather than

47. Mark Chapman, "Newman and the Anglican Idea of the University", *Journal for the History of Modern Theology,* 18 (2011): 212-22. Cf. J. Pereiro, *'Ethos' and the Oxford Movement* (Oxford: Oxford University Press, 2007).

rejected; the deep shock of revolution from across the Channel led to a swift reaction against both revolutionary and Idealist educational philosophies, and the English gentry began sending their sons in increasing numbers to Oxford and Cambridge. Institutions that had been previously scorned as bastions of religious and political obscurantism became, within a generation, important defences against a British guillotine. Better, Britain's landed classes thought, to have their sons read Homer and Virgil in the context of what were still considered to be seminaries of the Church of England than risk their exposure to seditious ideologies. Only Russia, interestingly, showed comparable enthusiasm among the other nations of Europe for the sustenance of the corporate university; tellingly, perhaps, both tsars Alexander I and Nicholas I received honorary degrees from Oxford.

Unlike the Scottish universities, Oxford and Cambridge are institutionally interesting because they also largely resisted utilitarian impulses to offer explicitly professional education for undergraduates. In England, lawyers were recruited through the Inns of Court rather than the universities and medical training was provided in the London and provincial hospitals. Even as the civil service expanded, specialist training was avoided, leaving the primary seats of learning in England with robust faculties of arts and weaker higher faculties. A classical education had become the distinctive mark of the English university in revolutionary Europe, and was defended from attacks in the *Edinburgh Review* most famously by Edward Copleston of Oriel College in 1810.[48] Indeed, the complex development of institutions in Great Britain in the early nineteenth century meant that even those who were dissatisfied with this consolidation and strengthening of the confessional status quota Oxford and Cambridge could always

48. See Asa Briggs, "Oxford and its Critics, 1800-1835" in *History of the University of Oxford,* 6:134-145. Copleston's defence of Oxford was echoed in Newman's *Idea* decades later.

send their sons to Scotland, and Nonconformists could attend their own colleges or, from 1826, University College London. Those Anglicans unable to meet the high costs of Oxford or Cambridge could in due course go to St David's, Lampeter (in Wales, founded 1822), King's College, London (founded 1828-9), and Durham (1832).

Accordingly, political momentum ensured that Oxford and Cambridge were not compelled by Parliament to be reformed into the likeness of Berlin or the French *Université* during the first half of the nineteenth century.[49] Instead, a relative lack of state intervention alongside the creation of new universities and colleges resulted in a more diverse settlement for English higher education during the nineteenth century. The relative freedom from the state enjoyed by Oxford and Cambridge have, and remain, crucial to their self-understanding; the preservation of ancient endowments allowed both universities to remain independent, corporately governed institutions that were, in essence, free from governmental interference until the need to expand scientific research during the First World War invited state investment.[50] Even as funding from the British government increased during the twentieth century as a proportion of university income, the self-governance of these collegiate research universities has been considered by many to be so integral to their success that, even in recent years, attempts to bring greater external influence to bear upon university governance have been regarded with intense suspicion and, in 2006 at Oxford, rebellion in its governing assembly.[51]

49. L. Brockliss, ibid., *History of the University* 6:131.
50. It could thus be argued that it was global warfare, rather than either the growth of the professional middle class or a secular mindset, that was the greatest catalyst for any unravelling of the liberal educational ideal at Oxford and Cambridge.
51. In that instance, Congregation (the University's parliament) defeated the Vice-Chancellor John Hood's attempts to introduce two positions for external members on the Council of the

While this autonomy of the academic guild averted the uncomfortable (and, at points, disastrous) Germanic equation of the university professoriate with the state civil service, this independence also resulted in the retention of the medieval collegiate structure. For most of its modern history, the heads of the colleges at both Oxford and Cambridge (and especially the former) have wielded more influence than the professors. These self-governing bodies within the corporate university retained their wealth and authority despite efforts at centralization: an aspect of university life that remains a source of frustration as much as pride; the dispersed nature of authority in the university has complicated and slowed the process of reform, even as it has arguably preserved the university from despots. More significantly for Oxford's theological life, as we shall see, it also enabled the colleges to prioritize the education of undergraduates over the advancement of research for most of the universities' modern history. The tutorial, so cherished by Newman as a distinctly pastoral and religious office, has consequently remained a distinctive aspect of this 'Oxbridge *Bildung*', despite the immense changes and funding challenges to higher education in Britain during the twentieth century.[52]

Interestingly, too, the preservation of the tutorial as a feature of university life did not suffer from the increasing influence of the German research ethos in the latter half of the nineteenth century. As Brockliss has commented, this integration of research into Oxford and Cambridge was "relatively painless" since "the research emphasis in the Western world in the late nineteenth century focused on just those areas – philology, mathematics, history and natural science – to which the University [of Oxford] after 1850 devoted its teaching

University. This was, in part, a reaction against the growing influence of corporate business interests in higher education that was being encouraged by central government.

52. W.P. Neville, ed., *Addresses to Cardinal Newman with his Replies, 1879-81* (London: Longmans Green, 1905), 184, quoted in M. Chapman, ibid., 223.

resources."[53] Paradoxically, Brockliss argues, as undergraduate education was weakened in the German universities in the latter half of the nineteenth century, the collegiate structures and tutorial teaching of Oxford and Cambridge allowed the English universities to model Humboldt's combination of research and teaching almost more convincingly than Berlin by the turn of the century.[54]

The Making of Modern English Theology

If the claim of educational historians that Oxford and Cambridge, and arguably British universities more generally, have modern genealogies that are distinctive from their continental counterparts is true, what might this mean for our understanding of theology's development as a modern academic discipline in Britain, and more specifically in England? The aim of this book is to offer the first substantive attempt at an answer, through a study of the origins of theology as a modern discipline in the University of Oxford.

Even to this day, Oxford is unusual among British and European faculties. Despite changing its name to 'Theology and Religion' in 2012, as I write, its senior professors are still required to function as canons in the unusual Tudor union of college and Church of England cathedral that is Christ Church, leading worship and preaching regularly. Unlike even Cambridge, the Oxford faculty's life and work remains entwined with the work of the various theological halls of various Christian denominations (called 'Permanent Private Halls') that are constitutionally part of the University, and despite having supposedly succumbed long ago to the juggernaut of secularization,

---

53. L. Brockliss, ibid., 6:131.
54. One need only look at the architecture of most Ivy League campuses to observe the enduring ideal of medieval education. This was particularly true in the aftermath of the First World War, "which sent Germanic principles of university organization into temporary eclipse" (B. Harrison, "College Life, 1918–1939" in *History of the University,* 6:84): see also, E. Tamarkin, *Anglophilia: Deference, Devotion and Antebellum America* (Chicago: University of Chicago Press, 2008).

the vast majority of Oxford and Cambridge colleges retain their Anglican chapels and chaplains according to the stipulations of the Universities Tests Act 1871. The University sermons are still delivered in the official churches of the universities, the deans of dvinity survive, the higher degrees are awarded in the name of the Holy Trinity at Oxford, and all this to the irritation of the 'new atheists'.

There is almost no material, currently, which accounts for how this constitutional peculiarity endures, or what such peculiarity might suggest about the standard accounts of the supposed secularization of theology faculties and universities. Indeed, there are no historical surveys that describe how theology adjusted itself to the institutional reforms of the English universities in the late nineteenth and early twentieth centuries. One of the clearest of accounts of Oxford theology's modern origins probably remains Maurice Wiles' brief reflections in his inaugural lecture as Regius Professor of Divinity (succeeding Henry Chadwick) in 1971, entitled, "Jerusalem, Athens, and Oxford."[55] Surveying his field of early Christian doctrine, Wiles gives an engaging account of how approaches to 'orthodoxy' and the study of Christian theology had changed in Oxford since the time his distant predecessor, Renn Dickson Hampden, was appointed in 1836 amid controversy over his own orthodoxy.

The most substantive reflection on theology's changing position within the university remains Owen Chadwick's description of theology at Oxford and Cambridge in the second volume of *The Victorian Church* (1970), where he considers both institutions in the context of a chapter on secularization in Britain in the latter half of the nineteenth century.[56] The universities, Chadwick asserts, became

---

55. Maurice Wiles, "Jerusalem, Athens, and Oxford: An Inaugural Lecture as Regius Professor of Divinity in the University of Oxford" in *Working Papers in Doctrine* (London: SCM, 1976), 164-79.
56. Owen Chadwick, *The Victorian Church* (2 vols., London: A&C Black, 1966, 1970), 2:439-62.

"neutral in religion except for the historic connexions with the Church of England; and as places of academic enquiry, far more detached in their study of religion." This was most apparent in the faculties of theology that, Chadwick claims,

> inherited the duty of teaching the ordinands of the Church of England, and if they failed to perform that duty they would hardly find pupils. For this purpose they must teach religion [i.e., the practices of religion, rather than the study of religion] as well as theology. Yet if they were to gain the respect of their colleagues in the university they must become (or at least thought sometimes that they must become) drily academic, and seek to squeeze the last drop of religion out of their theology. And if they were to teach the growing number of nonconformists who came forward, they must not be denominational.[57]

In order to become "drily academic" and respectable to the secular disciplines, Chadwick suggests that theology became "scientific" and the "easiest way to make theology scientific was to make it historical." Chadwick claims this to be the reason behind church history and textual criticism becoming the primary activity at Cambridge under Westcott, Lightfoot, and Hort. In these few pages, Chadwick claims that the research interests of scholars and the subjects for examination were, as in Germany, shaped by the broadly secular interests of university reformers.

Little more information about English theology's development can be gleaned from the multi-volume histories of the universities. The magisterial eight-volume *History of the University of Oxford* carefully analyses the collegiate University's origins and development, with the two volumes allotted to the nineteenth century covering the dominance of Greats, the development of geology, medical education, modern history, law, English, modern languages, mathematics, the natural sciences, and music. Theology, however, is

57. *Ibid.,* 450–51.

notable chiefly by its absence, discerned only in several paragraphs in Peter Hinchliff's article on "Religious Issues, 1870-1914" in the seventh volume, and again in Frank Turner's article on "Religion" in the eighth.[58] Theology's development as an academic discipline has largely been considered marginal and its difficulties as an academic discipline are normally interpreted as part of the university's dismantling of its ecclesiastical structures in the second half of the nineteenth century and twentieth century.

Moreover, the sources employed in both articles in the *History of the University of Oxford* are limited to examination papers, the occasional pamphlet, and the University *Calendar*. This, at times, leads to broad generalizations: the thrust of Turner's analysis, for example, seems to turn on David Jenkins's contribution to a compendium on theology and the university, which, observed (with the outré liberalism characteristic of Anglican academia of the early 1960s) that "the present practice in the Theology faculty at Oxford is not constructive enough for believers and not open and relevant enough for unbelievers."[59] Employing another article by the Anglican theologian, Leslie Houlden, Turner infers that the theology faculty inexorably succumbed to that division between religion and theology that resulted in theology becoming "increasingly separated from personal devotional life, the priestly vocation and the corporate life of the church."[60]

The Faculty of Divinity in the University of Cambridge has been granted greater consideration in the official university history. The

58. Peter Hinchliff, "Religious Issues, 1870-1914" in *History of the University of Oxford*, 6:97–112; F.M. Turner, "Religion" in *History of the University*, 8:293-316.
59. David Jenkins, "Oxford: the Anglican tradition" in *Theology and the University*, ed. J. Coulson (Baltimore, MD: Helicon Press, 1964), 159; quoted in Turner, ibid., 308.
60. J.L. Houlden, *Connections: The Integration of Theology and Faith* (London: SCM Press, 1986), 21; quoted in Turner, ibid., 309. It ought to be noted that, within ten years of Houlden's book, the faculty had integrated vocational theological degrees (the BTh and the MTh) into its portfolio of degrees.

one volume that accounts for the history of Cambridge since 1870 by Christopher Brooke commits an entire chapter to theology, separating it from his survey of religious activity in the University. However, almost half of this chapter considers the important historical-critical and textual work of the Cambridge 'trio' of Westcott, Lightfoot, and Hort. The rest is dedicated to the establishment of the various theological colleges and the building of the Selwyn Divinity School, with references to leading theological figures in the early twentieth century such as J.F. Bethune-Baker and Charles Raven.[61]

The limited research into the institutional development of theology at Cambridge in the modern era is also evident in David Thompson's important book, *Cambridge Theology in the Nineteenth Century*. His study is a valuable *ad homines* survey of theology at Cambridge since the late eighteenth century, with Thompson advancing a 'Cambridge tradition' that he opines has been characterized by breadth and tolerance. By its focus upon the purely theological, rather than the institutional, however, little can be discerned about how Cambridge theology emerged as a distinct university discipline. Furthermore, Thompson's claim for a Cambridge 'tradition' of breadth and tolerance must rest to some degree upon a characterization of Oxford's theologians as narrow and intolerant of developments in philosophy and biblical studies. While there were certainly figures within Oxford's faculty who might have qualified for such a characterization, this judgement omits a number of highly influential theologians, both before and after the death of Edward Pusey, who demonstrated great originality – if not the same panache as Westcott, Lightfoot, and Hort – in their engagement with biblical criticism, modern philosophy, and church history. Even

---

61. C.N.L. Brooke, *A History of the University of Cambridge* (4 vols., Cambridge: Cambridge University Press, 1988-2004), 4:134-50.

Pusey, as we shall see, has his contemporary defenders: evidence, if nothing else, of the persistently diverse accounts of theology's purpose and methods still present in our universities today.

The Making of Oxford Theology

If it is accepted that the modern theologian's confusion over the place of theology in the modern university is to some degree rooted in a poverty of historical reflection, what might be gained from a closer examination of how theology developed as a discipline in a particular English context, namely the University of Oxford?

As has already been stated, it is necessary from the outset to recognize the indirect effect of revolution. Unlike in the continental universities, theology's position as a higher faculty at Oxford and Cambridge was never essentially threatened since the Church of England and its institutions (the universities included) never had to endure the sort of upheaval that was encountered in France and its vassals. On the contrary, the *ancien régime* idea of the university was strengthened by events across the English Channel such that both institutions sought, instead, to teach the religious principles that would avert the free-thinking radicalism that was perceived to have been so injurious to civil society and the church in France. Theology was consequently not rejected but rather bolstered as a foundational aspect of undergraduate education, with every student required to be examined in divinity to be able to graduate in the faculty of arts from the examination statutes at the beginning of the nineteenth century until as late as 1932 at Oxford. The Church of England's status as guarantor of this ethos was unquestioned for the first half of the nineteenth century.

Despite the religious turbulence and conflict provoked by wider changes in the relationship between the Church of England and society, and especially the Tractarian Movement at Oxford, this idea of theology as 'queen of the sciences' was only reinforced as High Churchmen and Tractarians sought to sustain the ecclesiastical ethos of the University. These men, as we shall see, also contended that the conversion of theology into a distinct discipline for undergraduates would be perilous; the content and manner of theology was not suited for young minds and, beyond the basic knowledge of Scripture and the Thirty-nine Articles that was expected of undergraduates in the divinity examination, theology should be preserved purely for graduates in the form of the Bachelor of Divinity (BD) and the Doctor of Divinity (DD) degrees.

This paradigm for theology is explored in the first chapter and how it altered as the threat of revolution ceded into the distance and a more utilitarian politics dominated public life. Central to the desires of the reformers, both in Oxford and Cambridge, was the expansion of undergraduate curricula beyond their diet of mathematics, classics and a basic examination in divinity. Alongside proposals for undergraduate courses in natural science, law, and modern history, there also emerged suggestions for a distinct theological school. Rather than wishing to rid the university of theology or to 'Germanize' its methodology (even the theological liberals were regularly critical of German methodologies), the desire was for ordinands to be trained alongside their peers at Oxford in the study of the Bible and the history of doctrine. The proposal was rejected by the High Church professoriate at Oxford, and instead theological education for ordinands began to be set, not in the university, but in extra-mural graduate institutions such as Cuddesdon Theological College, founded just outside Oxford in 1854. Consequently, despite the university still being an essentially Anglican institution, theology continued to fade as a distinct discipline even as the development of new undergraduate courses nurtured other studies. The compulsory divinity examination came to be seen as a questionable test in an age in which biblical criticism and the findings of the natural sciences were shaking wider society's confidence in the Christian worldview.

The second chapter surveys how this High Church and Tractarian response to theological liberalism continued to limit theology's development as a modern discipline in the university. When a theology school was finally instituted in 1869, it was understood both by its founders and the wider university as a means of consolidating Christian belief in a university that was about to loosen its bonds to the Church by Act of Parliament. As an overtly professional school, however, this reactionary institution was positioned uncomfortably in a university that was still resolutely committed to a liberal education for its undergraduates. With shrinking resources in the colleges, and with scholarships still largely reserved for classicists, theology was consequently an unpopular course with the colleges, suffered dismal results, and possessed weak appeal to potential ordinands. Graduates desirous of ordination could go, far more cheaply, to one of the theological colleges that had been founded by the very same figures who were now trying to spur a theological revival at Oxford.

Even Cambridge's theological tripos – their route to an undergraduate BA – was introduced too late (the first examinations were sat in 1873) to become a significant presence in the teaching provided by that university.[62] While Westcott, Lightfoot, and Hort had greater success in establishing the course, gaining better results for theologians than at Oxford, both theology courses were curious vestiges of Anglican dominance and played an ambiguous role both within the Church and the universities. Recognising that both universities were not the primary loci for professional ministerial training, theologians were soon trying to justify their place through

---

62. The name 'tripos' dates back to the seventeenth century, when candidates would read selected verses from a three-legged stool (a 'tripos') at graduation ceremonies.

a presentation of their schools as exemplary courses in liberal education, offering philosophical, linguistic, textual, and historical skills to undergraduates who might seek a more religious slant for their arts degree. Far from seeking to be *wissenschaftlich,* Oxford professors seemed concerned at a more basic level about convincing students and their parents that theology was an appealing course, a subject young Englishmen might like to read if they were unlikely to excel in studying classics.

Inevitably, however, part of persuading the wider university that theology was a satisfactory undergraduate discipline coincided with a growing appetite in British university life to compete with the German research universities. In the third chapter, we see how theologians after the death of Pusey became self-consciously "scientific" by the beginning of the twentieth century. In 1911, it was even proposed that the faculty of theology should become a department of comparative religion, setting aside completely its duties to the Church of England. As in the German faculties, however, the abiding influence of the national Church inhibited such attempts and the faculty's proposals to make theology an "undenominational" discipline were roundly rejected by Oxford's graduates, who flooded into Oxford to vote down the measure in the Sheldonian Theatre in the spring of 1913.

This is not to assert, however, that, with an inevitability implied by certain contemporary dogmaticians, English theology faculties felt duty-bound to imitate their German cousins. Indeed, the desire to turn away from confessional approaches to theology came not so much from secularist impulses so much as from the growing influence and presence of Nonconformist theologians at both Oxford and Cambridge in the late nineteenth and early twentieth centuries, particularly at the Congregationalist college in Oxford, Mansfield. Congregationalism, for historical reasons, had enjoyed stronger associations with continental theology and was evidently far less defensive of an inherited body of orthodox dogma, protected by a hierarchy. The impressive breadth of theological and philosophical knowledge and range of critical skills displayed by Nonconformists such as A.M. Fairbairn altered the tone and direction of Oxford theology merely by their presence. Despite Mansfield College students winning a very high number of first-class degrees and university prizes, however, the regulations still limited the higher Divinity degrees to Anglican clergymen, and Nonconformists were not allowed to be examiners in the theological school. This protective confessional framework for theology came under attack for what seemed like its manifestly unjust treatment of these leading Free Church theologians, and proposals for reform largely emerged from a desire to rectify this.

Rather than an 'undenominational' model of comparative religion, as was being explored in the new Victoria University in Manchester, or the strictly confessional faculties that defined the German theological system, what emerged at Oxford and Cambridge between 1913 and 1945 was a broadly ecumenical model that allowed for confessional pluralism within the faculty but which resisted its reduction to the purely 'scientific'. As a result of the Oxford faculty's historical bonds to the Church of England that could not be easily dismantled (most particularly in the fusion of the theological professorships with canonries at the college-cathedral that is Christ Church) and the large number of chaplain-fellows who dominated teaching in the faculty, it was a multi-denominational, rather than undenominational, faculty that emerged under the leadership of Arthur Cayley Headlam as Regius Professor of Divinity in the years following the First World War. It was this broadly ecumenical model of theology as a discipline of the humanities, secured in the inter-war period, that is explored in the fourth chapter. This ecumenical paradigm, undeniably shaped by the liberality of the Anglican ethos, served Oxford and Cambridge until the end of the twentieth century, when pressures for the study of other religions in an increasingly multi-faith society presented altogether different questions about theology's position in the university.

What will be shown in this book is that this distinctive development resulted in faculties of theology at both Oxford and Cambridge that were not wholeheartedly professional in their practice of theology (theology's anomalous position in the arts faculty ensured this), nor were they purely 'scientific' (their continued proximity to living religious communities, and in particular the Church of England, prevented this), nor even were they rigidly confessional, as the inclusion of Nonconformists had necessitated a limited denominational pluralism by the beginning of the twentieth century. This was an *ad hoc* development of theology as a university discipline, shaped by personal bonds of affection, the ecumenical enthusiasm of a string of Regius professors, the defiance of the 'orthodox' in the face of liberalism and 'unbelief', and the changing ambitions and interests of undergraduates as much as the changing methods of theology itself. It led to a model of theology in a leading English university that was distinct from those of Germany, Scandinavia, and the American departments of religion and the professional graduate divinity schools. Gently pluralist, bringing religious communities into conversation with other disciplines, this model resisted theology's simple assimilation into religious studies or its forced exile into seminaries.

Whether this model has proved 'successful' is, in a sense, another question entirely, largely counter-factual, and beyond the limits of this study. It is very hard to know, for instance, whether Christian life and thought in English public life would have been substantially different during the late nineteenth and early twentieth centuries had a theological honour school been introduced on a more Protestant model at Oxford in 1848 or a department of comparative religion established in 1912. Moreover, with such varying accounts of theology's character and purpose, it is very difficult to make any sort of judgment upon the success or otherwise of this settlement without inviting the criticism of different theological parties today.

There are clear limits to this particular study. This is not a work of historical theology and the primary material for analysis is unapologetically not those seminal moments in nineteenth-century religious history and theology that are already so well documented: the beginnings of the Tractarian Movement or John Henry Newman's conversion to Roman Catholicism, his monumentally influential *Idea of a University,* the nineteenth-century bestseller *Essays and Reviews,* the infamous debate between T.H. Huxley and Samuel Wilberforce, *Lux Mundi,* or the changing theological content of University sermons and the Bampton Lectures. While each of these events or publications are evidently not disconnected from theology's evolving practice at Oxford, this book has sought to bring to light the otherwise ignored events and material that constitute theology's modern institutional narrative: unearthed correspondence between many of the great theological figures from the Bodleian's Special Collections, Pusey House and Lambeth Palace Library; material from newspapers, pamphlets, and journals; examination papers; lecture lists and lecture notes; evidence before parliamentary committees on the condition of the universities; the minutes and reports of the Board of the Faculty from the University Archives; and the reminiscences of students and professors. Amongst other questions, the book asks how theology responded to: the effects of the Royal Commission of Enquiry (1850-52), the opening of the university and its government to non-Anglicans, the development of theology as a discrete undergraduate discipline, the growth of 'scientific theology' rather than the defence of a Catholic 'deposit of faith', the arrival of Nonconformist theological establishments, as well as wider social and religious changes prompted by scientific discovery, secularization, imperial growth, and global war.

What is offered here is a distinctive genealogy of theological practice in English intellectual life that might deepen our understanding of how theology is now practised both in the United Kingdom and internationally. A study of the University of Oxford between 1833 and 1945 clearly cannot, by itself, give a comprehensive account of English theology's modern institutional origins. Although reference is made throughout this historical survey to Durham, London, Cambridge, the Scottish universities, Germany, and the American divinity schools, this account will no doubt frustrate those who desire a more comparative approach. There, are for instance, all sorts of interesting comparisons to be made with the practice of theology in the new universities that were founded across the British Empire, in institutions that self-consciously imitated the English universities.

This study may also strike the contemporary reader as dominated by men, with women's voices and experiences being largely peripheral. This silence is not intentional but testament to a theological life that, for the period under consideration, was almost entirely dominated by Church of England clergymen. Those who read for the theology school or the higher degrees were either clerics or intending to be clergymen. For a large section of the period under survey here, there were not even any women's colleges, and the college fellowships consisted of celibate male clerics.[63] There still

63. The first women's colleges – Somerville and Lady Margaret Hall – opened in 1879. The first men's colleges to become coeducational – Wadham, Jesus, Hertford, and St Catherine's – did not do so until 1974.

remains important work to be accomplished in retrieving women's theological voices in nineteenth-century England.

Indeed, I hope this work functions as the beginning rather than the end of what might be a larger attempt to understand in greater depth the complex institutional contexts for theology's evolution as a modern university discipline in the West. Such was Oxford theology's role during the twentieth century as an internationally influential training-ground for theologians and for leading ecclesiastical figures globally, its institutional history alone merits closer attention. More than this, however, I hope this study might illustrate the importance of institutional histories, the challenges and complex environments, which have shaped theology as an activity of the human mind since the Enlightenment.

1

———

'Necessary Knowledge' or 'Inductive Science'? Theology at Oxford, 1833-60

Two Excursions to Germany

In the summer of 1839, Arthur Penrhyn Stanley, a probationary fellow of University College, accompanied the Balliol College tutor, Archibald Campbell Tait, on a visit to Bonn. Several decades later, Stanley would be the Dean of Westminster and Tait the Archbishop of Canterbury, but in 1839 they were two young scholars travelling to Germany in search of a better way to organize a university. Stanley had in the previous year won the university Chancellor's Latin Essay prize on "The Duties the University Owes the State," and this continental excursion was for both men an opportunity to develop their thinking about how Oxford might be reformed. In Bonn, the young Oxford men attended lectures, heard sermons, cross-examined students, inspected schools, and called upon celebrated Bonn professors such as Karl Immanuel Nitzsch, "sitting in his study, in a dirty old brown great-coat".[1]

Their research led to Stanley assisting Tait in the writing of a pamphlet on university reform ("hearing, criticising, and perhaps correcting, each sentence"[2]), entitled *Hints on the Formation of a Plan for the Safe and Effectual Revival of the Professorial System in Oxford.* It proposed a revival of the professorial system at Oxford. Having already registered "alarm" across the university that "this admirable part of our system be fast sinking", his experience of Germany led Tait to advocate a fourth year for undergraduates in which they would attend lectures and encounter "the progress of true science" in the labours of their professors.[3] Having observed the German university, Tait wished to induce a love of learning for its own sake in the English system, compulsory attendance at lectures, and such space within a four-year course that would allow students to explore their own interests and "the advancement of several branches of knowledge" through dissertations.[4]

Although Tait was anxious to stress the primacy of the liberal education provided by the faculty of arts, he believed the revival of the professorial class would also allow for a more rigorous professional education within the walls of the university. Even in theology, which benefited from a well-endowed, resident and relatively active professoriate, there was much that could still be done:

> ...it must be plain to every thinking man, that nothing really important can be done till all our Theological Professors are actively engaged

1. Rowland E. Prothero, *The Life and Correspondence of Arthur Penrhyn Stanley, D.D.* (2 vols., London: John Murray, 1893), i, 221.
2. R.E. Prothero, *Life and Correspondence,* 224.
3. Archibald Campbell Tait, *Hints on the Formation of a Plan for the Safe and Effectual Revival of the Professorial System in Oxford* (Oxford: J.H. Parker, 1839), 9, 13. See also, Robert Hussey, *An Examination of the New Form of the Statutes Tit. IV. Tit. V.: With Hints for Establishing a System of Professional Teaching.* (Oxford: J.H. Parker, 1839).
4. A.C. Tait, *ibid.,* 16.

in habitual instruction. The departments into which Theology divides itself are so multifarious, the necessity for thoroughly instructing the rising clergy in all the branches of their profession is of such paramount importance to the welfare of the nation at all times, and in these days of infidel activity is so generally acknowledged in our Church even by men who in ordinary times would have quietly acquiesced in stagnation – that, even though a Clerical Seminary were attached to every Cathedral in England, there would still remain ample room for the full operation of a great Theological Faculty in each of our Universities.[5]

Oxford compared poorly with Durham, Tait believed, whose theology professor had embarked upon "praiseworthy labours" to revive learning; similarly, the new diocesan theological colleges only highlighted Oxford's intransigence, and the neglect of its ample resources.

Tait's call for improved professional education for the clergy at Oxford (and, by implication, Cambridge) is worthy of attention because of, firstly, its comparison with German universities. Although very few scholars at Oxford even read German at this time, the influence and strength of Prussian theological faculties were notable and Tait's and Stanley's visit to Bonn was testament to an anxiety about England's comparative inadequacies. Secondly, Tait's pamphlet is the first of many pleas over the succeeding thirty years for improved professional education at Oxford, particularly in relation to the theological faculty. While committed to the primacy and foundational importance of the liberal education Oxford dispensed, the young Tait's frustration would be echoed in succeeding years in both clerical and secular circles. Thirdly, the visit was influential because both men would in due course sit on a royal commission of inquiry that presented recommendations for Oxford's reform in 1852. Considering the arguments over theology's role in the university that would inflame Oxford opinion over the coming decades, this visit

5. A.C. Tait, *ibid.,* 26.

to Germany in 1839 and its resulting pamphlet, *Hints* signalled a growing desire in 'liberal' Church circles for wholesale reform of the English university, and in particular the practice of theology.

Far more significant, arguably, for the future shape of theology at Oxford was the experience of another young scholar's visit to Germany fourteen years earlier. Edward Bouverie Pusey was a dazzlingly competent graduate of Christ Church and protégé of the Regius Professor of Divinity, Charles Lloyd (later bishop of Oxford). Pusey became a fellow of Oriel in 1823. It was a college that, under its provost Edward Copleston, had been "constructed to nurture and encourage genius within Oxford at the postgraduate level…with considerable catholicity, looking for prospective development rather than past achievement, and with a readiness to defend Anglicanism in fresh and challenging terms."[6] As Lloyd's student at Christ Church, Pusey had secured a double first having reputedly studied for sixteen hours a day and, in a bid to further his linguistic capabilities and critical faculties, Charles Lloyd encouraged Pusey to learn German and to visit the German universities so as to hear and read the new biblical criticism.[7] Accordingly, in 1825 Pusey travelled to Göttingen and Berlin and made a second visit, at Lloyd's prompting, in 1826.

Pusey did not waste the opportunities provided by both universities and learnt German, Chaldee, Syriac, Hebrew, and Arabic, studied with Schleiermacher, heard the lectures of Hegel, and formed friendships with Ewald and Tholuck. He wrote to his fellow lodger John Henry Newman of the high level of linguistic ability in the German education system (many learnt Hebrew from the age of fourteen, for example) and he returned ambitious for the rejuvenation

---

6. H.C.G. Matthew, "Edward Bouverie Pusey: From Scholar to Tractarian," *Journal of Theological Studies* 32 (1981):104.

7. A "double-first" refers to first-class results in both Moderations (second-year examinations) and the Final Honour School of *Literae Humaniores*.

of biblical study in England, keen even to produce singlehandedly a revised translation of the Old Testament.

Pusey seemed to have been no less impressed by the breadth and rigour of the German university system as Tait and Stanley. The fruits of his learning in Germany became evident in his book, *An Historical Enquiry into the Probable Causes of the Rationalist Character Lately Predominant in the Theology of Germany,* published in 1828. In the same year, Pusey's extraordinary linguistic capabilities and learning ensured that when the Regius Professor of Hebrew, Alexander Nicoll, died unexpectedly, the twenty-eight year old Pusey was chosen to replace him.[8] As Colin Matthew argued, the *Theology of Germany* is, by the standards of Pusey's later writing, a methodologically liberal document. Confident that Schleiermacher's method was a dawning of a new period for Lutheran Protestant theology, Pusey viewed in the latest theological work being done in Germany "rich promise, that the already commenced blending of belief and science, without which science becomes dead, and belief is exposed to degeneracy, will be perfected beyond even the degree to which it was realized in some of the noblest instruments of the earlier Reformation."[9]

As Matthew noted, Pusey's embrace of German historicist techniques in 1828 allows him to be viewed as a forerunner of later liberal Anglican historical writing.[10] The implications of Pusey's writings were quickly recognized by Hugh James Rose, who criticized *Theology of Germany* for its failure to register the importance of apostolic succession and the dangers of rationalism.

8. This was at the urging of Lloyd, who called upon the influence of his former pupil, Robert Peel.
9. E.B. Pusey, *Historical Enquiry into the Probable Causes of the Rationalist Character Lately Predominant in the Theology of Germany* (2 vols., London: C. & J. Rivington, 1828), 1:179, quoted in Matthew, ibid., 110.
10. Matthew likens Pusey's writing at this stage with Mark Pattison's contribution to the 1860 compendium, *Essays and Reviews,* which Pusey fiercely condemned upon its publication.

Although Pusey would write a defence in 1830, the parliamentary challenges to the position of the Church of England in national life in the years 1830-34 coincided with the young professor beginning to reject his earlier enthusiasm for German methodologies. Despite this methodology having been impressively employed by Pusey in completing Nicoll's cataloguing of the Bodleian's Arabic manuscripts, Pusey now saw it as part of a wider threat to the integrity of the faith. After he finished this project, Pusey sold his Arabic books and withdrew copies of *Theology of Germany,* later stipulating in his will that it should never be republished. His growing distaste for the historical-critical method was, as both Matthew and Timothy Larsen have indicated, borne out of a growing concern for the integrity of God's Word in the Bible; historical-critical methods for studying the Bible failed to recognize that "the Bible is God's Word, and through it God the Holy Ghost, Who spake it, speaks to the soul which closes not its soul against it."[11]

Unlike Newman, Pusey never wrote an autobiography that detailed the reasons for his change of opinions. Colin Matthew identified Rose's trenchant criticism of Pusey's book as the primary reason for his reversal of opinions. This criticism, Matthew suggested, made Pusey recognise that the integrity of dogma was deeply threatened by the historical-critical method, which saw no distinction between sacred and profane in its investigations. Understanding the potential destabilizing effects of his methodology, Pusey "buried" his earlier approaches and retreated into dogma. Timothy Larsen has moderated Matthew's assessment of Pusey by elucidating the Hebrew professor's extraordinary grasp of the Bible, even in his now largely forgotten (or derided) commentary on Daniel from 1864.[12] As Stanley noted in his experience of Pusey's lectures,

---

11. E.B. Pusey, *Daniel the Prophet* (London, 1864), xii, xxv; quoted in Matthew, ibid., 116; Timothy Larsen, "E.B. Pusey and Holy Scripture," *Journal of Theological Studies* 60 (2009): 490-526.

there was no other professor in the university so well acquainted with German scholarship; Pusey reminded him of Professor Nitzsch of Bonn, having "the same solemn and continuous flow, the same endeavor to exhaust the text in all its bearings, even the very same peculiarity of brief and systematic reference to other interpretations, versions, or parallel passages."[13]

Nonetheless, the reversal of Pusey's methodological instincts during the 1830s is mirrored in his subsequent determination to deliver Oxford from the godless professorial system of Germany, as we shall see. Although the young professor seemed poised in 1830 to spearhead the reform and development of Oxonian and English theology in the style of Göttingen and Berlin, his sharp rejection of German methodology and university life would characterise Oxford theology until his death in 1882.

The experiences of German theological life of Pusey on the one hand and Tait and Stanley on the other cannot, evidently, be viewed as the root of all disagreement about the nature and purpose of theology at Oxford during the rest of the century. Although the German university was perennially viewed as offering either promise or peril by 'liberals' and 'conservatives', the differing appreciations of these two excursions do symbolize how the influence of the German universities and their theological faculties was far from one of imitation and appropriation in the English context. Among Anglican liberals, there would be sharp criticisms of the German system and many viewed with suspicion as much as with awe the extraordinary output and energy of the German theological faculties.

As institutions of the Church of England, Oxford and Cambridge were altogether differently constituted from their continental counterparts. After revolution or invasion by revolutionary armies,

12. T. Larsen, ibid., 507ff.
13. Bodleian MS Eng. lett. d. 437 (ff.45-7).

many of the most significant European theological faculties, such as the Sorbonne, had been dismantled. Where new universities were being founded, theologians had to persuade the authorities that theology should be included, usually under the guise of professional training for the clergy. In these Church of England universities, however, theologians were more challenged by the less violent adjustments to the position of the Church of England in British public life as dissenters, Roman Catholics, and Jews were granted civil liberties previously denied them, and the concomitant desire for the universities to become more truly national – and not homogenously Anglican – institutions. Alongside these political alterations to the position of the Church of England and the universities, the position of theology in the university and how it engaged with other disciplines was also affected by intellectual challenges, arising from anxiety about how to read the Bible in relation to the higher criticism, and, ultimately, changing understandings of how God revealed himself to humans.

Pusey's rejection of his earlier writings was not purely the desire of a young zealot to close ranks with his fellow Oriel controversialists; it was borne of an acute passion that theology must speak of God, the Church must guard its deposit of revelation, and that *wissenschaftliche* biblical study – however impressive its results – was perilously relativist in its treatment of texts. The debates about the practice and purpose of theology in the English university, and especially Oxford, are as much rooted in questions of theological epistemology as concern for the position of the Church of England in public life. Nowhere is this tangle of political and theological concerns more visible than in the "whirlwind" that accompanied the election of Renn Dickson Hampden as Regius Professor of Divinity in succession to Edward Burton in 1836.[14]

The Hampden Crisis

The most significant date for Oxford's ecclesiastical life in the early nineteenth century has usually been given, largely because of J.H. Newman, as 14 July 1833.[15] This was the day that John Keble ascended the pulpit in the University Church of St Mary's to deliver his sermon, entitled 'National Apostasy', to His Majesty's Judges of Assize. This sermon has been seen as inaugurating the 'Oxford Movement' and its insistence upon the autonomy of the Church in matters 'apostolical'. Delivered in response to the proposed rearrangement of Irish dioceses by His Majesty's Government (rather than by the bishops of the Church of Ireland), the sermon brought High Church Tory resentment at Oxford into the national sphere.

While Keble's sermon was certainly significant, arguably far more important for theology's development at Oxford was the death in January 1836 of Edward Burton, the Regius Professor of Divinity. Who replaced him was in the hands of the Crown (in the person of the Prime Minister) and, such was their growing influence and stature in the university, Newman, Keble and Pusey were all candidates.[16] They had been recommended to the prime minister by the archbishop of Canterbury, William Howley. The prime minister, however, was the Whig Lord Melbourne and these Oriel men were all High Church Tories. After consultation with his sympathisers at

14. Thomas Arnold, 'The Oxford Malignants and Dr Hampden', *Edinburgh Review* 63 (1836): 226.
15. J.H. Newman, *Apologia Pro Vita Sua* (London: Oxford University Press, 1964), 100. Nockles has suggested that Newman's university sermon of 22 January 1832, "Personal Influence the Means of Propagating the Truth", is a better marker for the Oxford Movement's beginning. (J.Catto, ed., *Oriel College: A History* (Oxford: Oxford University Press, 1932), 328).
16. H.P. Liddon, *The Life of Edward Bouverie Pusey,* 3rd edn (London: Longmans, Green, and Co., 1893), 360-70. The suggested names from the archbishop did not purely consist of High Churchmen. The list also included Philip Shuttleworth (the liberal Master of New College), Charles Ogilvie, a chaplain to the archbishop and a former fellow of Balliol (a High Churchmen but not a Tractarian, later the first Regius Professor of Pastoral Theology), Thomas Short (a liberal, later bishop of St Asaph), John Miller (a conservative High Churchman from Worcester) and Charles Goddard (an Evangelical archdeacon of Lincoln).

Oriel, Melbourne disregarded the suggestions of Archbishop Howley and chose instead Renn Dickson Hampden, professor of Moral Philosophy since 1834, principal of St Mary's Hall since 1833, and for several years a fellow of Oriel. In 1832, Hampden had preached the Bampton Lectures, the most prestigious theological lecture-series in the University, entitled, *The Scholastic Philosophy Considered in its Relation to Christian Theology* (published in 1833). Of the Noetics, apart from perhaps Thomas Arnold, Hampden was considered to be the most theologically articulate.[17]

Hampden's appointment provoked a storm of protest from the outset, certain people having seen Melbourne's frank on the letter addressed to him in Oxford's post office. The Tractarians, in particular, were dismayed by Hampden's appointment, considering him heterodox and probably smarting from their failure to secure one of their own for this most senior of professorships. As the controversy reached its climax, Hampden tendered his resignation to the prime minister, who replied:

> In justice to ourselves and you, for the sake of the principles of toleration and free inquiry, we consider ourselves bound to persevere in your appointment to the Regius Professorship of Divinity, which has been approved by His Majesty.[18]

Why had Hampden's appointment proved so offensive to other theologians at Oxford? As one of the 'Noetic' group, Hampden wrote in the tradition of Joseph Butler, the eighteenth-century bishop who came to be associated with a revival of Anglican apologetics based on the 'reasonableness' of the Christian faith during the 1820s at Oriel.

17. The legacy of John Bampton in 1751 required eight divinity lectures to be delivered in the University Church of St Mary the Virgin annually; Renn Dickson Hampden, *The Scholastic Philosophy Considered in its Relation to Christian Theology* (Oxford: J.H. Parker, 1833).

18. Henrietta Hampden, *Some Memorials of Renn Dickson Hampden Bishop of Hereford* (London: Longmans, Green and Co., 1871), 56-57. Quoted in David B. Roberts, *The Church Militant: Interpreting a Satirical Cartoon* (Oxford: Magdalen College, 2013), 36.

The Noetics were not straightforwardly Whiggish or latitudinarian in opinion. Hampden, for instance had been editor of the High Church periodical, the *Christian Remembrancer* (1825-6), a position that he employed to publish criticisms of both Unitarianism and Calvinism.

What distinguished the Noetics at Oxford, and what offended Tractarians and Evangelicals alike was their theological methodology. Following Butler, the Noetics had asserted that the inductive study of the natural world was a means to identifying a divine creator and that this same method might be applied to the study of the scriptural revelation. As a result, they examined the 'facts' of the Bible with an acceptance that the ultimate cause of the phenomena described in scripture could not be – as in nature – straightforwardly identified. This approach naturally entailed a certain ambiguity beyond the clear scriptural facts that led to a grading of dogmatic truths, with those from the post-apostolic period regarded with greater scepticism as they could supposedly not be inductively proven.[19] This methodology was evident in Hampden's Bampton lectures, where he characterized the dogma of the scholastics (which covered any post-apostolic dogmatic writing, including the patristic authors) as marred by human imperfection and written for particular historical contexts for the purpose of securing 'orthodoxy'. This critical acceptance that doctrines had their own history and complex impulses led, in the minds of the Tractarians, to the perilous conclusion that creeds and formularies were "not so much apodictic conclusions as humanly construed definitions."[20]

19. For more on the Noetics of Oriel, see Peter Nockles' invaluable chapter in the most recent history of Oriel, "Oriel and Religion, 1800-1833" in J. Catto, ed., *Oriel College: A History* (Oxford: Oxford University Press, 2013), 291-328. A useful introduction is also Richard Brent's note, "The Oriel Noetics", in *The History of the University of Oxford* 6:72-76. See also Richard Brent, "Hampden, Renn Dickson (1793–1868)", *Oxford Dictionary of National Biography* (Oxford: Oxford University Press, 2004) and *Liberal Anglican Politics: Whiggery, Religion, and Reform* (Oxford: Oxford University Press, 1987).

For Tractarians, the authoritative reading of Scripture "did not lie with private individuals today, but rather people today should be guided by the collective interpretation of the early church fathers."[21] Dismissing the later 'speculations' of the fathers would surely, the Tractarians believed, lead to all manner of dogmatic dissolution.

Within the university, these methodological considerations also naturally affected attitudes towards the ecclesiological and institutional questions of the period. Hampden's less than enthusiastic appreciation of dogma as a vehicle of divine revelation led to his advocacy of abandoning subscription to the Thirty-nine Articles for those matriculating at the University of Oxford (as expressed in his 1834 pamphlet, *Observations on Religious Dissent*). The university was not, in Hampden's opinion, a Church institution so much as an institution that happened to be populated by Church members.[22] Hampden had quickly found himself under fire.[23] Henry Wilberforce, the youngest son of William Wilberforce, identified that Hampden's assault on subscription came from "purely theological" arguments. "He would remove subscription," he wrote in *The Foundations of Faith Assailed in Oxford*, "because he objects to all tests and creeds as conditions to communion, and sees no valid reason for any separation between ourselves, and those who 'unhappily' reject the doctrine of Our Lord's divinity and atonement."

20. R. Brent, "The Oriel Noetics", 74.
21. Timothy Larsen, *A People of One Book: The Bible and the Victorians* (Oxford: Oxford University Press, 2011), 14.
22. R.D. Hampden, *Observations on Religious Dissent* (Oxford: J.H. Parker, 1834); [H.W. Wilberforce], *The Foundations of Faith Assailed in Oxford* (London: Rivingtons, 1835), 14. This followed on from a bill in Parliament that sought to admit dissenters to the university. It was defeated in the House of Lords, but prompted a declaration at Oxford (signed by 1900 members of Convocation and over 1050 undergraduates) against any future attempt to challenge subscription.
23. For a detailed account of the divisions with Oriel, see Peter Nockles, "A House Divided: Oriel in the Era of the Oxford Movement, 1833-1860" in *Oriel College: A History,* 337ff.

Hampden's doctrinal comprehensiveness was deemed heterodox to Wilberforce, Newman, and Pusey. Paradoxically, they now became defenders of the Protestant Thirty-nine Articles, not out of love for the Articles themselves (Newman was deeply uneasy with their content) but as Peter Nockles has asserted

> [O]n the ground that religion was to be approached with submission of the understanding. While Protestant High-Churchmen regarded the tests as little more than fences of the establishment, the Tractarians bestowed a quasi-sacramental efficacy upon the act of subscription.[24]

The university was, for Wilberforce, "a sacred ark wherein the truth has been preserved" and its members must be "humble and teachable disciples, labouring to ascertain what has been the church's faith and practice."[25]

When Newman, Pusey, and Keble were passed over for the Regius chair, the charge of heterodoxy was again brought against Hampden. A committee met in the Corpus Christi College common room that consisted of High Churchmen, Protestant and Tractarian, as well as Oxford Evangelicals such as Charles P. Golightly (later a fierce critic of the Tractarians and 'Puseyites') and R.L. Cotton (about to become provost of Worcester College).[26] Pamphlets were quickly produced by Newman (*Elucidations of Dr Hampden's Theological Statements*) and Pusey (*Dr Hampden's Past and Present Statements compared*). They questioned the selection of Hampden as Regius professor and analysed his theological statements with regard to the Trinity, the divinity of Jesus, the atonement, original sin, grace, and faith. Pusey, in his pamphlet, recalled Hampden's reclassification of dogma, asking with no small degree of fury how Hampden distinguished between

---

24. P.B. Nockles, "'Lost Causes and...Impossible Loyalties': The Oxford Movement and the University" in *History of the University of Oxford*, 6:222.
25. [Wilberforce], *Foundations of the Faith Assailed*, 6.
26. *Oriel College: A History*, 340-343.

the life of Jesus Christ as a fact and not the consubstantiality of the Trinity.[27] In response to a well co-ordinated protest at Hampden's appointment, the Hebdomadal Board submitted a statute to Convocation that deprived the Regius Professor of Divinity of appointing the select preachers for the university and his right to sit on a board that judged the orthodoxy of Oxford sermons.[28]

While a triumph for Tractarians and High Churchmen, this success in Convocation was also the high point of clerical resistance to reforming pressures within, and from without, the university. It is important to note that, despite winning these limitations, Hampden was never formally censured for being a heretic; it was now possible to be a theological professor at Oxford without seeing one's role as primarily transmitting pure credal orthodoxy to new generations of students, much to the concern of Tractarians. Moreover, the coalition's success in limiting Hampden's influence can be overstated; it is important to remember that Hampden did not receive unstinting support from other 'liberal' figures in the university. Although Thomas Arnold launched a stinging attack upon the 'Oxford malignants' who were seeking to censure Hampden in the *Edinburgh Review,* to many moderates – such as his disciple Stanley – Arnold's article seemed excessive.[29] Hampden had also not received the support of the older generation of Noetics, with Shuttleworth noting that he "has alarmed many very moderate and liberal men in this

27. E.B. Pusey, *Dr Hampden's Past and Present Statements Compared* (Oxford: J.H. Parker, 1836), 6ff.

28. Convocation, according to the Laudian statutes of the University, consisted of all members of the University who were MAs, regent and non-regent (effectively, resident and non-resident). Unlike now, Convocation was able to appoint officers, enact and modify statutes, and examine and approve accounts. This statute was passed in Convocation on 5 May 1836 by 484 to 94 votes. For more on the Hampden controversy and Baden Powell's satirical cartoon of the whole episode, a print of which is kept in the archives of Magdalen College, see David B. Roberts, *ibid.*

29. R.E. Prothero, *The Life and Correspondence of Arthur Penrhyn Stanley* (2 vols., London: John Murray, 1897), 1:164.

place, not so much for himself as for the possible mischief he may do to the younger part of the University by his teaching."[30]

What was the legacy of the Hampden crisis in 1836 for the practice of theology at Oxford? It was certainly the 'zenith' of Tractarian influence in the wider university, as the coalition that Newman and Pusey had built with Evangelicals and other High Churchmen was now beginning to fracture. By the end of the decade, both Evangelicals and Protestant High Churchmen were highly critical and suspicious of the Tractarians as 'Romanizers', a suspicion only confirmed by the publication of Hurrell Froude's *Remains* and the steady number of Oxford figures converting to Roman Catholicism. That influence, however, was weakening. In 1840, the Hebdomadal Board sought to raise the position of the professoriate and broaden the undergraduate curriculum. Although the measure was quickly defeated in Convocation in 1840, it signified how the governance of the university was increasingly less susceptible to Tractarian influence.

Nonetheless, even if Tractarian strength was waning on the Hebdomadal Board, the Hampden crisis certainly demonstrated how theological methodology was a significant point of division in thinking about the role of the university and its relationship to the Church. If, as Pusey and Newman claimed, the credal statements of the early church were authoritative as inspired developments in thinking about God, then the Church – and, by extension, its universities of Oxford and Cambridge – were compelled both to revere and hand on that deposit of faith. Theology was, by virtue of its duty to guard the revelation, the 'queen of the sciences' and every other discipline, and the moral life of the university, ought to be shaped by its truths. Hampden, by his promotion of an inductive

---

30. British Library Add. MS 51597, fo 136, P.N. Shuttleworth to Lord Holland, 1 March 1836; quoted by Nockles, "The Oxford Movement and the University", 230, fn.196.

study of theology seemed to possess less commitment to the 'speculations' of men in later centuries, and so was less inclined to see the University as a guardian of the deposit of faith. As Stanley noted in an article for the *Edinburgh Review* in 1843, the Tractarians were seeking such a renewal of the university that would define education as

> ...the formation of moral character by habit, not the imparting of what is commonly called learning...Catholic theology and Moral Philosophy in accordance with Catholic doctrine, were to be the main foundations of the improved education of these newer days; science and literature were not, indeed, to be neglected, but to be cultivated as in subordination only to these great 'architectonic' sciences...[31]

The inductive method of Hampden, transferred from the natural sciences, threatened this concept of the university disciplines always being subordinated to the 'architectonic' sciences of Catholic theology and moral philosophy.[32] Hampden's theological approach may seem timid to the twenty-first century theologian (if not weak), but in 1836 it was offensive to the sensibilities of many Christians at Oxford, including many men who had been described as 'Noetic' and some who would later be called 'liberal'. In effect, however, the crisis and its aftermath brought into relief a more partisan approach to Oxford's theological life that was shaped by personal as much as theological enmities and resentments. Pusey became ever more ardent in his defence of the university as "priestly, seminarian in function, clerical in its educational core", grounded in an unwavering faith in God's immutable revelation.[33] On the other hand, a new generation of liberal, or 'Broad Churchmen' – several of whom had

31. [A.P. Stanley], "The late Dr. Arnold", *Edinburgh Review* 76 (1843): 375.
32. For more on the 'Catholic' reform of collegiate life in the 1830s and 1840s, see Peter Nockles, "An Academic Counter-Revolution: Newman and Tractarian Oxford's Idea of the University", *History of Universities* 10 (1991): 137-197.
33. Matthew, "Edward Bouverie Pusey", 121.

been pupils of Thomas Arnold at Rugby School – were beginning to broaden Hampden's sense of 'inductive' theology. Their aspirations for Oxford theology, however, would be limited by the events of 1836. The practice of theology was kept firmly under the control of the High Churchmen, principally at Christ Church, in subsequent decades. As Richard Brent notes, the crisis brought "to an end the process of Anglican renewal as a collaborative enterprise" in the University as the Noetics found themselves divided, liberals were separated from the High Churchmen, and Tractarians and Evangelicals found common cause in the defence of revealed theology.[34] Almost as an indictment of Oriel as a location for such life, Newman and Pusey rented a house on St Aldate's in the summer of 1837 which was nicknamed the *Coenobitium* or *Monasterio*. Those who lived there practised asceticism and read the church fathers; Mark Pattison and James Mozley (later rector of Lincoln College and the Regius Professor of Divinity respectively) would both live there.[35] Both, in due course, would repudiate their Tractarianism.

As divisions grew over the practice of theology at Oxford in the context of the religious ferment of the 1830s and early 1840s, what was it exactly that Pusey, Newman, and their associates were defending, and how and why did 'liberals', or 'Broad Churchmen' as they came to be known, hope to reform theology and the university?

Theology in the University Prior to Reform

When the first examination statutes were framed at the beginning of the nineteenth century, Convocation had ensured a compulsory examination in divinity in Schools as part of its desire for 'sound and godly learning'. Although it occupied a very minor position

---

34. R. Brent, "Hampden, Renn Dickson (1793–1868)".
35. J.B. Mozley to A. Mozley, *Letters of the Rev. J.B. Mozley* (London: Rivingtons, 1885), 78; quoted in *Oriel College,* 345.

– it was a pass examination and did not affect one's standing on the class list – no student could gain his *testamur* (the certificate that demonstrated he had satisfied the examiners) without showing knowledge of the 'Rudiments of Religion': according to the statute, "at every examination, on every occasion, the Elements of Religion, and the Doctrinal Articles...must form a part".[36] According to the *University Calendar* for 1813, the first document to give details of what was required in examination listed as the first requisite for admission to the degree of Bachelor of Arts:

> 1. The Rudiments of Religion, under which head is required a sufficient knowledge of the Gospels in the original Greek – of the 39 Articles of the Church of England, – and of the Evidences of Religion, natural and revealed.[37]

Even more so than classical study, the examination was considered by many as emblematic of the education that Oxford offered; an examiner from the 1820s would tell the Commissioners in 1850 that, "It has long been the glory of Oxford when her ablest and most accomplished Students stand up to be examined for the degree of BA, which is the turning point of life, *the first* book which is placed in their hands is the *Greek Testament.*"[38] However, like the classical exercises it accompanied, candidates were protected from any opportunity for radical speculation. One need only look at revolutionary Europe, the Tory High Churchmen averred, to see the terrifying results of rationalistic religion. Accordingly, undergraduates were only required to demonstrate knowledge of the Gospels in Greek, the outlines of biblical history, the Thirty-nine Articles, and the 'evidences' of Christian religion, being invariably

36. W.R. Ward, *Victorian Oxford* (London: Frank Cass & Co, 1964), 13.
37. *University Calendar,* 1813 (Oxford, 1813), 70.
38. *Report and Evidence upon the Recommendations of Her Majesty's Commissioners for Inquiring into the State of the University of Oxford* (Oxford: Oxford University Press, 1853), evidence, 489.

Joseph Butler's *Analogy of Religion* (first published in 1736). Although no divinity papers exist for this period (the examination was *viva voce*) the curriculum remained essentially unchanged from its inception until the 1880s, when questions on the Articles were removed. A paper from 1863 exemplifies the standard of the examination:

> 4. The chief instances of Abraham's faith, and references to him in the New Testament.
>
> 8. "That the Gentiles should be fellow-heirs and of the same body." Trace the stages through which, in the Old and New Testament, this truth was gradually revealed.
>
> 9. "Thou bearest record of thyself, thy record is not true." Give our Lord's answer: and distinguish the several kinds of evidence to which He appealed in proof of His Divine Mission.
>
> 12. Against what errors were the following Articles directed: (a) on the Person of Christ; (b) on Holy Scripture; (c) of Christian men's goods not common?
>
> 13. "The old Fathers did not look only for transitory promises." Explain, and show by our Lord's words, (1) that the Old Testament revelation was imperfect, (2) that its truths are eternal.[39]

As M.G. Brock has observed, the strictly limited level of criticism and understanding that was expected of candidates reinforced the tenet, rooted in the High Church reaction against continental theological speculation, that the "Christian faith, as the Established Church expounded it, was seen as a fixed system."[40] If revelation was essentially propositional and preserved in Scripture and the Church's historic formularies, there was no need to expect any kind of understanding of doctrinal or biblical history; it was sufficient – as far

---

39. *Second Public Examination: Honour School of Literae Humaniores* (Oxford: Oxford University Press, 1863).
40. M.G. Brock, " The Oxford of Peel and Gladstone", *History of the University,* 6:10.

as religious education was concerned – merely to repeat the received truths of the Thirty-nine Articles and the Bible, and show that one had understood Butler's triumph over the Deists in his *Analogy of Religion*. As Edward Copleston wrote in his reply to attacks against Oxford in the *Edinburgh Review:*

> The scheme of revelation we think is closed, and we expect no new light on earth to break in on us…We hold it our especial duty…to keep strict watch round that sacred citadel, to deliver out in measure and season the stores it contains, to make our countrymen look to it as a tower of strength, and to defend it against open and secret enemies.[41]

A core component of an undergraduate's career, yet evidently attainable by any schoolboy, the Rudiments of Religion became a rich source of mockery for students up until its abolition as a compulsory examination in 1932. A good early example is a pamphlet written by John Cockburn Thomson in 1858, *Almae Matres by Megathym Spleme, B.A., Oxon.,* which made extensive reference to the poor level of theological education at Oxford.[42] He remembered his own experience of a *viva:*

> In my own examination I was asked which of the minor prophets had the most chapters, and not remembering this – which had the fewest. I was asked what relationship there was between David, Joab, and Asahel, and whether Zeruiah was a man or a woman. In fact, the Old Testament is generally treated more like a peerage than a history; and I have even heard of a jocose examiner putting a very certain "pluck," whom he was engaged in tormenting, that very obsolete enigma – "Who was the Father of Zebedee's children?"…But the Bible may be well and ill read. If it is read only to know that there is only one chapter in Obadiah,

---

41. E. Copleston, *A Reply to the Calumnies of the Edinburgh Review against Oxford* (1810), quoted in Brock, ibid., 6:11.
42. John Cockburn Thomson, *Almae Matres by Megathym Spleme* (London: James Hogg & Sons, 1858). Thomson (1834-60) studied Sanskrit at Oxford and was a candidate for the librarianship of the India Office before he accidentally drowned when swimming off the Pembrokeshire coast.

that Asahel was Joab's brother, or that Huz and Buz (whom a modest curate of my acquaintance thinks it respectful in the reading-desk to call Hughes and Bews) were the grandsons of this man or that – I'm sure *I* don't know – you do not, in my humble opinion, read the Bible aright...[43]

As a purely factual examination, Thomson could wryly observe that "the eccentric young lady in Jonson's 'Alchemist,' who was mad on the subject of scriptural genealogies", was thus probably "the most fit person to have B.A. put after her name."[44]

Oxford's commitment to a common divinity education avoided the professional direction of theological learning that was evident in the Scottish and the newer English universities. Candidates for ministry in the Church of Scotland, for instance, were first required to complete a four-year arts course in one of the Scottish universities, where they would gain a foundation in philosophy, Latin and Greek. Then they would proceed to a divinity hall in their university for another three of four years, where they would systematically study Hebrew, theology, and ecclesiastical history.[45] Durham University had a Licentiate in Theology for both graduates and non-graduates since 1833 and King's College London had conferred its 'Associate in Theology' from 1847.[46]

There were attempts to improve the teaching of theology in Oxford. Apart from Newman's hope that college fellowships would return to their medieval vocation as spiritual brotherhoods of graduates engaged in the study of theology, with tutorials as the primary pastoral duty of the fellow in holy orders, Tractarians had

43. *Ibid.,* 241–42.
44. *Ibid.,* 243.
45. See J.C. Whytcock, *An Educated Clergy: Scottish Theological Education and Training in the Kirk and Secession, 1560–1850.* (Milton Keynes: Paternoster, 2007)
46. C.E. Whiting, *The University of Durham, 1832-1932* (London: The Sheldon Press, 1932), 259-262; S.W. Green, 'Sketch of the History of the Faculty' in *London Theological Studies* (London: University of London Press, 1911), xi.

supported a private offer to fund a new theological chair in liturgy in 1837 (only to be rebuffed by the Heads of Houses[47]), and supported the creation of two new theological chairs in 1840, eventually resulting in the Regius professorships in Ecclesiastical History and Pastoral Theology.[48] However, when the Whig, Edward Hawkins of Oriel, sought to improve the theological education of future clergy in 1842 through the introduction of a Voluntary Theological Examination, this was viewed by Tractarians as a step towards reducing the nature of theology from an overarching system for all academic study into a professional department of learning. In this opposition, however, the Tractarians were unsuccessful and the Voluntary Examination was offered once a year, and was open to all BAs.[49]

Between 1844 and 1863, however, only seven men passed the Voluntary.[50] Although no examination papers survive, William Jacobson, who was Regius Professor of Divinity between 1848 and 1865, detailed his course of twelve public lectures thus:

1. Introductory to the Study of Theology, and some points of Clerical Duty.
2, 3. On some of the aids at arriving at the sense of Holy Scripture.
4, 5. On Creeds; particularly on the three incorporated in our services.
6, 7. On the study of Church History.
8. On the Continental Reformation.
9. On the English Reformation.
10, 11. On the Book of Common Prayer.
12. On some of the practical Duties of a Clergyman in charge of a parish.[51]

---

47. I.e., the heads of the Oxford colleges.
48. For Newman on the tutorial as a pastoral office, see J. Catto, ed., *Oriel College: A History*, 338–39. Bodleian Law Library, *An Act to carry into effect…the fourth report of the Commissioners of ecclesiastical duties and revenues* (3 & 4 V., c.113, Pub.) (London, 1840).
49. W. Ince, *The Past and Present Duties of the Faculty of Theology* (Oxford: James Parker, 1878), 39.
50. *Ibid.* It has not been possible to determine how many students entered for the examination.
51. *Evidence,* 253.

As an examination which offered no distinction (there were no class lists for the Voluntary Examination), and which prolonged residence in the university (as students could not attend the divinity professors' lectures before graduation), there was little incentive for graduates to embark on the course, and, apart from their dislike of the course *per se*, Tractarians were disinclined to recommend the examination as it was overseen by R.D. Hampden, who remained the Regius Professor of Divinity until his equally controversial appointment by Lord Russell to the see of Hereford in 1847.[52]

Although the Archbishop of Canterbury supported the examination's institution, the episcopal bench never insisted that their candidates for holy orders take it; ordinands were merely required to gain a certificate that proved attendance at the lectures of the Regius Professor of Divinity and one other theological lecturer. This teaching, as Thomson records, was dismal: [53]

> ...those who have attended [the lectures] know what was their real value. The Regius Professor hurriedly mounts the pulpit in the small side-chapel of the cathedral, and reads a list of some four of five hundred works, which he recommends you, somewhat ironically, to study. The Margaret Professor, who is generally the other one attended, reads a series of terribly soporific discourses on the Creed, which add little or nothing to what Pearson has written. These lectures are commonly attended when the young aspirant is...totally engrossed by history, chemistry, or algebra; and even if he can give his whole attention to theology, it is only for a fortnight or three weeks, after which the lecturers begin the same course over again.[54]

52. *The New Examinations for Divinity Degrees* (Oxford, 1844), 13.
53. Cf. the speech of Hawkins on the theological statute in 1863 in the *Guardian*, 18 March 1863: 261.
54. J.C. Thomson, *Almae Matres*, 244. "Pearson" refers to the *Exposition of the Creed* (1659) by John Pearson (1613–86), Bishop of Chester from 1673. It was a staple text of theological study at Oxford, originating in a series of lectures extended over several years at St Clement's, Eastcheap. It was later combined with book five of Hooker's *Ecclesiastical Polity* to form a staple textbook, entitled *The Creed and the Church: A Handbook of Theology*, by Edgar Sanderson (Oxford: J. Parker, 1865).

This lack of systematic theological teaching was perhaps all the more striking when one realizes that the theological professors were perceived as being more diligent and active than most others in the university. Across Oxford, all the professorships had become largely redundant as valued instruments of education, with the primary duties of the university being undergraduate education in the classics. Only nine out of the twenty-five university professorships were supported by college endowments in 1840, and were consequently less attractive posts than many ecclesiastical offices or even college fellowships.[55] Christ Church, as a cathedral foundation, was unique in being able to incorporate professorships into its governing body and support them financially, since the canonries allowed the incumbents to be married. The divinity chairs enjoyed handsome stipends as a result and were naturally attractive destinations for preferment within the university and Church.

Despite this institutional support, one cannot claim that the divinity professors at Oxford occupied their offices in a manner any way comparable to their German counterparts, who published prodigiously and taught a range of specialized courses in biblical, historical, and theological subjects. Charles Lloyd, as the Regius Professor of Divinity between 1822 and 1829, was remembered as the "infuser of a new and more energetic spirit" in theological studies at Oxford; he was responsible for tutoring Robert Peel, Newman and Richard Hurrell Froude, amongst others, and encouraged that growing sensibility for the ancient origins of the Anglican liturgy among the younger Oxford scholars (and later Tractarians).[56] Yet, his own publications were slight, the most famous being the compendium, *Formularies of Faith Put Forth by Authority during the Reign of Henry VIII* (1825).

---

55. M.C. Curthoys, "The 'Unreformed Colleges'" in *History of the University*, 6:166.
56. *Gentleman's Magazine*, 1st ser., 99/1 (1829), 561.

Since the English universities were primarily committed to teaching rather than research for most of the nineteenth century, the relative lack of theological publications should not surprise us. Oxford theology was communicated largely through small-scale teaching, sermons (a large number of which were published either in pamphlets or in volumes) and the annual Bampton lectures. In the years succeeding Hampden's infamous series, the Bamptons were far more cautious, treading along the "well beaten tracks of Catholic Theology" where, Charles Ogilvie assured the readers of his own,

> will be found sure footing amidst the dangers and safety from the misleading temptations of a restless and speculative age, fond of novelty and eagerly aiming at discoveries even on the most sacred subjects.[57]

Similarly keen not to provoke further cross-party enmity in the Bamptons, Edward Hawkins in his 1840 series positioned himself carefully between Tractarian dogmatism and Hampden's latitudinarianism, reiterating the Anglican balance on Scripture and tradition.[58] Likewise, William Conybeare in his 1839 lectures, stressed that the lectures for the year, "however deficient in other respects, will sufficiently manifest, that to engage in personal and individual controversy, is of all things the most remote from the habits and intentions of the author."[59]

---

57. C. Ogilvie, *The Divine Glory Manifested in the Conduct and Discourses of our Lord: Eight Sermons preached before the University of Oxford* (Oxford: J.H. Parker, 1836), x.

58. E. Hawkins, *An Enquiry into the Connected Use of the Principal Means of Attaining Christian Truth* (Oxford: J.H. Parker, 1840); cf. *Oriel College: A History*, 346. Other post-Hampden Bamptons exhibit similar caution: see Thomas Vogan, *The Principal Objections against the Doctrine of the Trinity* (Oxford: J.H. Parker, 1837).

59. William Conybeare, *Analytical Examination of the Character, Value, and Just Application of the Writings of the Christian Fathers during the Ante-Nicene Period* (Oxford: J.H. Parker, 1839), vi-vii. His Anglican methodology, as with Hawkins, treated the tradition as "an important subsidiary aid in interpretation" of the Bible, carefully avoiding the less conservative methodologies of some Tractarians and some Noetics (ix).

'Suggestions' for Change

When and how did the High Church consensus over theology's position in the university come to be challenged at Oxford? On 3 October 1845, Newman resigned his fellowship at Oriel and six days later was received into the Roman Catholic Church by Dominic Barberi, an Italian Passionist missionary. It was a major blow to the Tractarian cause in the Church of England and in the university. Nockles has asserted that it discredited the Anglican defence of the university, "causing the [remaining] Tractarians in effect to jettison their previous academic vision for theological party ends"; a vision "that saw academic culture being fully integral with revealed religion at every point".[60] Mark Pattison, in his *Memoirs* written several decades later, famously wrote of the event:

> It is impossible to describe the enormous effect produced in the academical and clerical world, I may say throughout England, by one man's changing his religion. But it was not consternation; it was a lull – a sense that the past agitation of twelve years was extinguished by this simple act…[61]

Certainly, Newman's conversion was but the final stage in a series of measures (notably, R.H. Froude's *Remains* in 1838 and Tract 90 in 1841) that had alienated the Tractarians from mainstream High Church thought and life and provoked widespread controversy. The 'lull' of the Tractarian party in disarray and rudderless in the university certainly provided an opportunity for a new stream of scholars to emerge that, shaped likewise by a distinctive vision of learning and the church, hoped to induce the wholesale reconsideration of the university's purpose and theology's place within it.

60. Nockles, "An Academic Counter-Revolution", 180-1.
61. M. Pattison, *Memoirs* (London: Macmillan, 1885), 212-13.

This 'Young Oxford' group found its principal bond in the abiding memory of Thomas Arnold, who left Oriel College as a fellow in 1828 to become headmaster of Rugby School. A year before his death in 1841, Arnold had combined these duties with those of the Regius Professor of Modern History. His disciples, invariably from Rugby and Balliol (Stanley was exceptional as a fellow of University College, but had been an undergraduate at Balliol) represented that modern spirit which was "dynamic, bustling, practical, and 'professional'…so characteristic of the early Victorian era, with its demand for utility, efficiency, productivity and high priority given to the creation of wealth."[62] Since his time in Germany with Tait, Arthur Stanley had become a celebrated figure for his careful authoring of the best-selling *Life and Correspondence of Thomas Arnold* (1844), a book that became a template for Victorian biographical writing and Edwardian pillorying as hagiography. This group of young Oxford scholars included the Balliol company of Benjamin Jowett, A.C. Tait, Richard Congreve, Arthur Hugh Clough, and Bonamy Price, as well as former Tractarians such as Mark Pattison, H.H. Vaughan, and J.A. Froude.

After Newman's conversion and Lord Russell securing a parliamentary majority in 1847, liberals in the university identified an opportunity to reform the examination statutes, substantially alter the relationship between the university and the colleges, and open the university to non-Anglicans by loosening subscription. Before Jowett and Stanley departed for Paris in April 1848 to experience the excitement of revolutionary Paris, they had anonymously published a pamphlet entitled *Suggestions for an Improvement of the Examination Statute.* Considering "the present age, its increasing wants, and the

---

62. Nockles, 176. Stanley's beliefs were considered as possibly too liberal to be successfully elected as a Fellow of Balliol, and he was encouraged to apply elsewhere. (R. Darwall-Smith, *A History of University College Oxford* (Oxford: Oxford University Press, 2008), 356.

means of satisfying them, of the new methods of investigation which criticism has opened in so many different branches of knowledge," these two men could not help but query whether "the University answers the call...laying aside prejudice and fancy and the spirit of party and every other hindrance."[63]

Following swiftly upon a memorial signed by fifty-nine out of Oxford's sixty-three tutors that had demanded a revision of the examination statute, the proposals of Jowett and Stanley were ambitious. They suggested that the old final examination should come at the end of the second year, whereupon undergraduates could proceed to one of the new modern schools, of which there would be at least three. Apart from a school in philosophy, history, and philology, and another in mathematics and physical science, Jowett and Stanley also suggested the creation of a separate theology school.[64] The aim of their proposals was to restore the influence and activity of the professoriate and to provide alternative schools that could keep those students who were unable to excel in classics gainfully employed in more modern pursuits. With so many graduates destined for parochial life, theological honours seemed like an obvious and fruitful alternative to the classical.

Jowett and Stanley were propelled by the belief that the complete absence of theological teaching at a so-called 'seminary' of the English Church left the clergy scandalously unprepared for ministry in a rapidly changing world. They believed that the introduction of systematic theological education for future clergy could be part of

63. [B. Jowett and A.P Stanley], *Suggestions for an Improvement to the Examination Statute* (Oxford: Francis Macpherson, 1848), 5. An advertisement on the pamphlet is dated 13 March. The Memorial was presented to the Hebdomadal Board on 4 March. It was an open secret that Jowett and Stanley were the authors.

64. Although, it ought to be noted that the Memorial to the Hebdomadal Board had itself suggested a third examination which would consist of either theology, moral philosophy, history or mathematical and physical science. Jowett and Stanley, however, were the first liberals to suggest a distinct theological school for undergraduates in their final year.

the renewal of the Church of England in national life. Anticipating the resistance of the High Churchmen who continued to think of theology as an overarching framework for all university study, they stressed their belief that a separate theology school ought not to assume "too great a preponderance in the University system," and to avoid any such "division between the studies of clergymen and laymen [which] should spring up so early as to increase the mischievous isolation which exists (although in England happily less than elsewhere) between the two classes."[65] They identified four points, however, which compelled them to assert the need for certain undergraduates to commit themselves to theological study in their final year at Oxford:

> *1st.* That the theological instruction of the Clergy is very insufficiently supplied by the present system of the University.
> *2ndly.* That unless Theology be formed at this period into a distinct school, (through which none need pass unless they prefer it to one of the other two schools,) it will be impossible to require from those who pass through it a standard sufficiently high to be practically useful.
> *3rdly.* That so far as Theology is a necessary part of all liberal education, it will already have been required in the second Examination (as at present) from all candidates for the degree of B.A.
> *4thly.* That although doubtless the greater number of those who passed through in this school would be destined for Holy Orders, yet there is nothing to prevent the admission of others who are so disposed.[66]

Their fourth reason was, in part, why Jowett and Stanley organized a scheme of study which focussed "not on points of professional or clerical interest," but instead upon "the study of Holy Scripture, which of all the branches of Theology may be presumed to be one of most interest, at least in our age and country, to all classes". Crucially for our understanding of the distinctive pattern of English theological

65. *Suggestions,* 23–4.
66. *Suggestions,* 24.

education, the new school that was proposed by Jowett and Stanley in 1848 was to be set in the faculty of arts, and would not operate as a purely professional faculty like those in the German or Scottish universities.

Alongside the other two new schools, the two fellows drafted a syllabus for a theological degree, both for passmen and honours students:

A. *Minimum. For an ordinary Degree.*

1. Some portion of the Old Testament in Hebrew. (to be determined by the Examiners.)
2. Text and Criticism of the New Testament in Greek.
3. Passages to re-translate into the Greek of the New Testament, and difficult passages in the Original to be explained.
4. History of the Old and New Testament.
5. The History of the English Reformation, with knowledge of the XXXIX Articles.

B. *For Honours.*

1. Two out of three parts of the Old Testament, with specified portions in Hebrew, and the rest in the LXX [The Septuagint].
2. Text and criticism of the New Testament in Greek.
3. Passages to re-translate into Hebrew, and difficult passages in the Old and New Testaments to be explained.
4. History of the Old and New Testament.
5. History of the three first centuries (including, at the discretion of the candidate, the study of some writer of that period.)

This was not an especially ambitious or provocative curriculum, certainly by comparison with German faculties, and clearly avoided the expected charge from Tractarians and High Churchmen that liberals were seducing junior members into the kind of theological speculation that was thought to be the origins of 'unbelief' on the continent.

Jowett and Stanley were not shy in questioning the corseted character of Oxford theology, however. They queried whether theology in the university was not "at the mercy of any *a priori* speculator in history or theology" and whether the English were "not living 'behind our dykes' in fear of the German ocean?" Although they denied that they were seeking to turn Oxford into a German or Scottish university, they were no doubt aware – as even the most reactionary conservatives were – that English theological educational provision paled in comparison with those of the great German faculties, where the professorial system was robust. Even the principal opponent of reform, E.B. Pusey, had noted the 'completeness' of the German system during his time there. His record of the lecture-list at the University of Berlin for 1825 is astoundingly comprehensive by comparison with its Oxonian counterpart; twenty-three years prior to Stanley and Jowett writing their manifesto, Prussia could claim forty-five divinity professors spread across its seven universities. While indubitably committed to the principles of liberal education, these young Broad Churchmen at Oxford could only imagine how a languishing, yet richly endowed, professoriate at Oxford might be employed to improve clerical education for the nation.

Stanley was critical of those who were irrationally fearful of German theology. In a letter written in December 1845 to Julius Hare, one of England's leading interpreters of German theology, a mentor of Stanley, and archdeacon of Lewes, Stanley commented on Richard Trench's anti-German Hulsean Lectures at Cambridge:

> I wished to ask you whether you do not think it a pity that he should speak in them as he does of German theology with unmixed blame whenever he mentions it, as if only taking cognisance of its baser parts; when at the same time it is hardly possible to conceive how his lectures could have been written without it...I grieve over this partly because it goes against my sense of justice – but also because it seems to me fraught with practical mischief, if one who is likely to have influence I hope

here as well as at Cambridge should, while he knows the real debt which Theology and Christianity owes to Germany, throw his whole weight at the opposite scale, thus repel those who know the state of the case and encourage those who do not in their indiscriminate outcry against all that comes in thought to us from Germany.[67]

Stanley went on to lament "the peculiar prevalence here of a vague suspicion against anything German by all those who know nothing about it", citing Newman's *Essay on the Development of Christian Doctrine* and Pusey's debt to German modes of delivery in his lectures on the Psalms ("the whole atmosphere…whenever he speaks for himself and not from the Fathers is completely German, as anything can be…"). Both Jowett and Stanley in *Suggestions* were clear that German scholarship possessed great resources for challenging contemporary scepticism. While they confessed that there "may be enemies from whom it is right to fly", they were firm in their belief that "the tide of opinion cannot be escaped": many people were now dissatisfied with the apologetic "evidences of Paley and Lardner", which could no longer be "reasons for their belief, or the answers to their difficulties." They were now turning "to the Scriptures themselves as a simpler and more profitable study."[68] Yet it was precisely here – "the most hopeful mine in Theology" – that they asserted English theology was found most wanting. In a bold statement, twelve years before Jowett's infamous contribution on biblical interpretation to *Essays and Reviews*, the two men expressed their frustrated hope "that the meaning of Scripture, *like that of any other book*, might by this time have become fixed and raised above the fancies of sects or individuals."[69]

---

67. Pusey House Library, Stanley Papers: A.P. Stanley to J.C. Hare, 10 December 1845.
68. *Suggestions*, 6.
69. *Ibid.*, italics inserted.

This confidence that a deeper exploration of the biblical text held promise for theology was borne of the new historical methodology that had transformed classical study at Oxford, most notably in response to the works of August Boeckh, Karl Otfried Müller and Barthold Georg Niebuhr.[70] This new scholarship featured detailed commentaries of the original sources that approached the narratives of ancient Rome and Greece critically through a reading of social and economic history. In revisions to the examination statutes in 1830, students reading for *Literae Humaniores* were given a new definition of their reading as "not only the Greek and Latin tongues, but also the histories of Greece and Rome", as well as moral and political science "in so far as they may be drawn from writers of antiquity, still allowing them occasionally as may seem expedient to be illustrated by the writings of the moderns".[71]

The nature of textual study at Oxford was thus being subtly altered. Thomas Arnold had been an ardent enthusiast for the new methods and many of the Rugby men at Oxford became subscribers to Leonhard Schmitz's *Classical Museum* – a 'Journal of Philology, and of Ancient History and Literature' – which ran in seven volumes between 1843 and 1854. Stanley himself had been a contributor. It seemed only natural to this group that the new criticism should be applied to the Bible with the expectation of similarly rich rewards. Jowett himself had complained in correspondence of "the plasters we have been applying to theology" and planned to write a series of commentaries on the New Testament with Stanley, working together in "the same fashion that Liddell and Scott did in their

---

70. The first volume of Niebuhr's *History of Rome* was translated by two fellows of Trinity College, Cambridge, Connop Thirlwall and Julius C. Hare between 1828-1832, and the third by William Smith in 1842. See David Thompson, *Cambridge Theology in the Nineteenth Century* (Aldershot: Ashgate, 2008), chapter 4.

71. G.R.M. Ward and J. Heywood, *Oxford University Statutes Translated, Vol. II (1767-1850)*, 166. Quoted in O. Murray, "Ancient History" in *History of the University*, 6:530.

Lexicon."[72] They were certain that if the new methodology – the "scientific understanding" as opposed to the "devotional understanding" – were to be systematically applied to Oxford's theological study, then the reactionary fear of German thought would be dispelled; a new era of English theological scholarship would be inaugurated that was grounded in biblical study rather than the apologetic, anti–Deist, tomes of the eighteenth century.[73]

Nonetheless, the reliance of the Broad Churchmen upon German scholarship had already inflamed High Church theologians. Niebuhr, for instance, had interpreted Old Testament narratives alongside the myths of the Greeks, Romans, and Native Americans, and Friedrich August Wolf had called Homer's *Iliad* "the Bible of Greece."[74] Pusey identified this hermeneutic as perilous; he later expressed his certainty that "the scepticism of Homer [had] ushered in the scepticism on the Old Testament."[75]

This distrust of such methods was, Stanley and Jowett believed, damaging the position of theology in the universities. Jowett, writing to Stanley in August 1846, asserted that this fear of new methods was leading the clergy to become purely concerned with pastoral theology:

> If Biblical criticism spreads [the clergy] will be driven, as many of them have been by Puseyism, into the practical…Morality is, for the

---

72. Benjamin Jowett to R.R.W. Lingen, 21 August 1847; Benjamin Jowett to A.P. Stanley, August 1847 (Abbott and Campbell, *Jowett* i.160-1). Jowett, in a notebook entry of 1876 claimed that it was during Robert Scott's lectures on Niebuhr's critical study of Roman history that there 'first aroused in… [his] mind doubts about the gospels.' Quoted in G. Faber, *Jowett, a Portrait with a Background* (London: Faber, 1958), 134.

73. A.P. Stanley, *The Life and Correspondence of Thomas Arnold* (London: B. Fellowes, 1844), 164ff. See also P. Hinchliff, "Jowett's Liberal Protestantism" in *God and History* (Oxford: Clarendon Press, 1992).

74. Norman Vance, 'Niebuhr in England: History, Faith, and Order' in *British and German Historiography 1750-1950: Traditions, Perceptions, and Transfers,* ed. B. Stuchtey and P. Wende, (Oxford: Oxford University Press, 2000), 90.

75. E.B. Pusey, *Collegiate and Professorial Teaching and Discipline* (Oxford, 1854), 62.

sort of men you speak of, a great light; they must bury themselves in their parishes and learn humility and drink no more the dregs of Orthodoxy. If they could get rid of Theology altogether and learn the New Testament, especially the Gospels, by heart, it would be well.[76]

Their movement against what they perceived as the rigid orthodoxies of Oxford was met with a mixture of confusion and disdain by elements in the Church of England and the university. The High Church newspaper, the *Guardian,* thought that describing the new school as one of 'Theology' was

[A] strange misnomer, as it consists entirely of what is more commonly ranked under another kindred and very valuable head of sacred learning; that which comprises acquaintance with the original tongues of the Inspired Volume and Biblical Criticism, with some mixture of ecclesiastical history. To adopt such a scheme as this for a theological examination would imply a total disregard to doctrine, as such, and as capable of being systematized and taught dogmatically; and the omission of all such books as "Pearson on the Creed," in the present proposal, is remarkable and significant.[77]

Biblical study in place of the delivery of dogma – defined as conservative exposition of the creeds – seemed an oddity to the commentator, who suspected another motive at play:

We have no wish to underrate the value of an acquaintance with Hebrew and the Greek of the Seventy; but we will venture to say that there is hardly ever an examination for Deacon's orders in this country in which more "dogmatic theology" is not required than what is here proposed for the "honours" of the University examination; an argument, which, at all events, is good *ad homines* in the present case, for we are told, as an argument for the deep study of the Hebrew text, "in the most distinguished at least of the German Universities, every candidate for holy orders is required to know four books of the Old Testament in the original."

76. Abbott and Campbell, *Jowett,* 1:153.
77. *The Guardian,* 5 April, 1848.

The article implied that these "views of some of the most active and stirring among the tutors of the several colleges" were not aimed at simply improving knowledge of the Bible, but as a 'Germanization' of English theological teaching.

Within the university, influential figures – and by no means simply Tractarians – continued to insist that a separate theology school threatened the earlier ideal of theology as a common, general study which informed all the other disciplines and which was guaranteed by the undergraduate divinity examination. Robert Hussey, the first Regius Professor of Ecclesiastical History, was appointed by Peel in 1842 precisely because he was not involved in religious controversy. A High Church commentator, he nonetheless asserted that

> Theology is a subject which ought to be above such distinctions. It is *necessary* knowledge, and ought to be sought and valued by all for its own sake. If it is made the vehicle of Academical Honours, men will learn to esteem it for the sake of them, and to disregard it where it brings no such fruits; and moreover, they will be induced to study it in such a manner, and adopt such views of it, as will be supposed to suit the taste of Examiners from time to time. It will be a great change in our system of Examination, and a departure from the principles on which it is founded, if that which is required of all, because it is the duty of all to know it, be made one of the subjects of competition before the Public Examiners.[78]

Although Hussey believed that those taking the Voluntary Theological Examination – to become *Scholaris in Theologia,* according to the statute – ought to be allowed to attend the Divinity professors' lectures after their intermediate examination, he nonetheless found the suggestion of making theology the object of competition at the final examination unwholesome and a departure from the university's commitment to liberal education through the

78. R. Hussey, *Remarks on Some Proposed Changes in the Public Examinations,* (Oxford: J.H. Parker, 1848) 19-20.

classics. Theology was not to be pursued for academic glory or for the professional, practical training of the clergy, but "for its own sake" as an illumination of the mind by faith. To Hussey, defining theology as a voluntary study leading towards a position on the class list would necessarily undermine the "principles on which it is founded".

Although some of Jowett's and Stanley's proposals would contribute towards a new examination statute in early 1849, the persistence of High Church and Tractarian influence on the Hebdomadal Board in matters theological ensured that theology was not included as a distinct final honour school; it remained, in Hussey's words, simply "necessary knowledge" for all undergraduates. This avoidance of converting theology into a distinct undergraduate discipline qualifies, to some degree, Peter Nockles's claim that, after the theological crisis at Oxford from 1841-5, the Tractarian vision of the university was "in ruins". Certainly, the confessional university was beginning to be dismantled by the Oxford University Act 1854, and after 1845, the Tractarian 'counter-revolution' was, as Pattison observed, largely "extinguished". The failure of reformers to broaden the curriculum so as to transform theology for undergraduates witnesses, however, to the persisting influence of Tractarians, and principally Pusey, in the control and shaping of Oxford theology. Reticence towards altering the paradigm of, on the one hand, compulsory divinity for all undergraduates and, on the other, theology as a purely graduate discipline, left the discipline in a precarious position at Oxford and Cambridge. As new subjects for honours came to be introduced in the following decade, theology would be notable by its absence, save for its presence as a compulsory examination of knowledge of the Bible and the Articles.

The decision of both of the 'ancient' English universities to retain serious theological study as a purely graduate activity was accompanied by the foundation across England of diocesan theological colleges. In 1854, the Bishop of Oxford, Samuel Wilberforce, founded a theological college opposite his palace at Cuddesdon (a small village seven miles to the south-east of Oxford) where graduates might be offered theological education away from the "Germanization and secularization" of the university.[79] Commended by leading church figures in the university, these colleges would quickly become the primary *loci* of graduate theological education. Their foundation and development inevitably, however, limited the need and possibility of theology's development within the universities. This fracturing of the Church of England's provision for theological education between university and theological college would create further confusion and disagreement over the condition of theology in the university during the Royal Commission in 1850-52.

The Royal Commission and its Effect on Theology

After the establishment of three new examinations alongside classics in 1849, reform was still encountering problems in Convocation, with Tractarian supporters refusing to approve a grant from the University Press to pay for a new science museum (for the Natural Science course). They were unwilling to use profits from selling prayer-books to build new laboratories.[80] It was increasingly clear that for effective reform of the universities, external pressure would be required. According to Goldwin Smith, another prominent reformer of the period, the successful petition for the reform of

79. Keble to Sir J.T. Coleridge, 11 Dec 1855: "What sad accounts I hear of the Germanization and secularization of Oxford. I should think that it would be very soon necessary for people who wish their sons to have a fair chance for being Christians to send them to some other place; and for Bishops to resort ordinarily to the Theological Colleges..." Quoted in Owen Chadwick, *The Founding of Cuddesdon Theological College* (Oxford: Oxford University Press, 1954), 7.
80. W.R. Ward, "From the Tractarians to the Executive Commission, 1845-54" in *History of the University*, 6:315.

the university was planned in Arthur Stanley's rooms in University College:

> Mr. James Heywood, a Nonconformist Member of Parliament, was bringing forward an annual motion for inquiry into the Universities mainly with a view to the abolition of religious tests. His motion was regularly negatived. . . . A few of us, Mark Pattison and Jowett among the number, met in the rooms of Arthur Stanley at University College and addressed to Lord John Russell . . . a request that he would not allow the occasion of Heywood's motion again to pass without holding out hope of assistance to University reform.[81]

In "compliance with this request", in the spring of 1850, Lord Russell as prime minister announced that he was going to recommend to the Crown a royal commission of inquiry into the universities of Oxford and Cambridge and their colleges.[82]

Chaired by the Bishop of Norwich, Samuel Hinds (who had been tutored by Richard Whately, the Noetic principal of St Alban Hall, while an undergraduate at The Queen's College), the board of commissioners for Oxford appointed by Lord Russell consisted of knowledgeable liberals such as A.C. Tait, Baden Powell, and H.G. Liddell, and the Secretary and Assistant Secretary were Stanley and Goldwin Smith respectively. Despite the expected hostility to the work of the Commission from Tractarians, there nonetheless emerged a broad consensus about priorities across the university: governance, and in particular the work of the Hebdomadal Board, needed urgent revision; the professoriate needed to be strengthened;

---

81. Goldwin Smith, *Reminiscences* (New York: Macmillan, 1910), 101-2. Quoted in R.D. Smith, *A History of University College* (Oxford: Oxford University Press, 2008), 366. An earlier petition in 1847/48 had been to no avail.

82. *Parliamentary Debates* 23 April 1850, 3S cx. 747-55 (Russell). In British political life (and in Commonwealth realms), a royal commission is a formal inquiry into an aspect of public life. Commissioners wield power as determined by the terms of reference set out by H.M. Government. They are less common today than during the nineteenth century, partly because the conclusions of commissioners can sometimes be seriously incongruent with the aims of the Government.

and university education ought to be extended to larger sections of the middle-classes, including Nonconformists. When the *Report* of the Commission (known as the 'Blue Book') was published in May 1852, it was immediately recognized as authoritative.[83]

A central tenet of the 'Blue Book' was the twelfth recommendation "that during the latter part of the Academical Course, all students should be left free to devote themselves to some special branch or branches of study." It was not unreasonable to assume that, since almost half of graduates would take holy orders, theology too might now have its own school. This seemed to be in the minds of some commissioners during the inquiry. Henry Liddell, later the dean of Christ Church and at that time headmaster of Westminster School, corresponded in October 1851 with H.H. Vaughan, the Regius Professor of Modern History. Liddell had sketched four 'new' faculties that would organize education for undergraduates in their final year, with two schools in each. Theology was included as the first faculty, with a school in 'Biblical and Dogmatic' theology, and another in 'Historical' theology.[84] When the *Report* was published, the twelfth recommendation gave no explicit detail about the development of faculties, the commissioners being cautious not to threaten the university's commitment to liberal education. They would also have been aware, correctly, that explicit suggestions about theology would provoke a storm of opposition.

Although Colin Matthew associated Evangelicals with Tractarians on the subject of curricular reform during the Royal Commission, the *Evidence* received by the commissioners reveals that the case for introducing a stronger theological element to undergraduate education now found surprising sympathy from Evangelicals and the

---

83. Except for, perhaps, the Duke of Wellington, Chancellor of the University of Oxford in 1852, who famously died in bed having started reading it.
84. Bodl. MS. Eng. lett. d.435: H.G. Liddell to H.H. Vaughan, 14 October 1851.

more Protestant High Churchmen within the university.[85] Edward Litton, the vice principal of St. Edmund Hall, was representative of those who were anxious about ritualistic influences upon the new diocesan colleges: they "may be expected," he wrote "to exhibit a narrowness of feeling, a want of sympathy with the temper of the age".[86] He believed that the creation of these institutions – "one at a few miles' distance from the University itself" (i.e., Cuddesdon) – implied that "young men cannot at the University obtain that professional training, spiritual and intellectual, which they need to fit them for the duties of their future life." He feared that young men desirous of taking holy orders might now avoid the "threefold ordeal which the new Statute imposes and obtain their main object, admission to Orders, in an easier, less expensive way." With small staffs, the "preponderating influence of individuals" at the new colleges might be mischievously exercised, and clergy will be sent forth who, though "better instructed perhaps in Theology", are "less enlightened, less free from party spirit, and even less accomplished."[87]

Another royal commission, into the 'State and Condition of Cathedral and Collegiate Churches in England and Wales', was published in 1854. This similarly offered a range of critical responses to the new colleges from within the universities. Charles Heurtley, a High Church, although not Tractarian, member of the theological professoriate, disapproved of theological foundations in cathedral cities, along with William Jacobson, the more liberal Regius Professor of Divinity, who viewed them as an "hazardous experiment".[88]

85. H.C.G. Matthew, "Noetics, Tractarians, and the Reform of the University of Oxford", 211.
86. *Report and Evidence upon the Recommendations of Her Majesty's Commissioners for Inquiring into the State of the University of Oxford* (Oxford: Oxford University Press, 1853), 405-6.
87. *Report and Evidence*, 408. Cf. J. Bateman, *The Tractarian Tendency of Theological Colleges* (London, 1853); F.W.B. Bullock, *A History of Training for Ministry of the Church of England in England and Wales from 1800 to 1874* (St. Leonards-on-Sea: Budd & Gillatt, 1955), 95-6; Chadwick, *ibid.,* ch.1; and A. Atherstone, "The Founding of Cuddesdon: Liddon, Ritualism and the Forces of Reaction" in *Ambassadors of Christ,* ed. Mark Chapman (Aldershot: Ashgate, 2004).

Although there was some recognition of Wells Theological College as a success, there were still thirteen Heads of Houses at Oxford who were willing to express disapproval of these new foundations.[89]

These more Protestant figures still identified distinct advantages to strengthening theological education in the universities. Litton asserted that in its precincts ordinands are "brought into contact with men of various characters, pursuits, and destinations; undergo here a rehearsal of what they must expect in future life; the effect of which is supposed to be a largeness of mind and kindly tone of feeling not otherwise to be expected."[90]

The advantages of pursuing theology within the university rather than the seminary were not limited to the society that the colleges afforded. Both Charles Ogilvie – the first Regius Professor of Pastoral Theology (1842-75) – in the Royal Commission on cathedrals and Litton in the Oxford Commission believed that in a university there was, for theologians, a "great advantage in associating, as far as possible, the great departments of knowledge; cultivating them at the same place and at the same time."[91] Thus "they lend mutual aid to each other, the claims of each become recognised, and the one-sidedness of mind inseparable from devotion to a single pursuit is to some extent corrected."[92]

Litton argued, however, that the limited expectations of the divinity examination entailed that young men from Oxford "may, and notoriously do, enter upon the most important of all professions, with the most scanty preparation; – ignorant of Church History,

---

88. *The First Report of Her Majesty's Commissioners, appointed 10 November, 1852, to inquire into the State and Condition of the Cathedral and Collegiate Churches in England and Wales*, 785-6. Jacobson had been appointed by Lord John Russell as "moderately liberal, and not tory" (W.R. Ward, *Victorian Oxford*, 145). He was elevated to the see of Chester in 1865.

89. *Ibid.*, 798; F.W.B. Bullock, *A History of Training*, 92-3.

90. *Report and Evidence*, 410.

91. *State and Condition of the Cathedral and Collegiate Churches*, 795-7; *Evidence*, 407.

92. *Ibid.*

of the History of Doctrines, of the original language of the Old Testament, and as regards the practical part of their profession, utter novices." It "may be safely asserted," Litton told the Commissioners, "that no Church, but our own, satisfies herself with so inadequate an introduction to the ministerial office." In accordance with the twelfth recommendation of the Report, Litton argued that now was the time to introduce a distinct school of theology, with its own examiners. Allowing students to attend the divinity professors' lectures prior to the second examination, as afforded by the new theological statute, was insufficient; students are "so engrossed with the main object of passing the three examinations" that it is "in vain that the Tutor…announces lectures in the various departments of Theology." Unless action were taken, Litton suggested that general education would so consume the time and energy of the undergraduates that all opportunities for theological study would be vanquished, furnishing "with additional arguments the advocates of diocesan Colleges."[93]

Another more Evangelical promoter of theological education at Oxford was the former Professor of Poetry and archdeacon of Chichester, James Garbett. In a letter to the warden of Wadham College, Benjamin Symons, Garbett urged that a year be granted at the end of an undergraduate's course for theological study if he were seeking holy orders. If some kind of structure were to be offered, he believed that Oxford "might become what it has never yet been, the noblest theological school in the world":

> That grandest of sciences might be treated, as, from no fault of the professors but the system itself, it never yet has been treated among us, in all its length and depth, and we should no longer be mendicants to the Germans for our critical and historical learning. Moreover, students for holy orders might find in the Universities themselves that enlarged

93. *Report and Evidence*, 410-11.

and scientific training which they are now seeking in the narrow and, as man will suspect, the party field of Diocesan colleges.[94]

This surprising alliance between Broad Churchmen, High Churchmen, and Evangelicals in favour of a theology school within the university was testament to an anxiety about Tractarian influence over small theological colleges such as Cuddesdon. By the early 1850s, the Tractarian idea of theology in the university as an 'architectonic science' that framed the whole life of the university was evidently less credible and the consolidation of theological education in seminaries *extra muros* concerned many.

Despite these advocates of a systematic study of theology within Oxford, reformers also met a strong defence of the status quo.[95] Edward Hawkins was appointed as the first Dean Ireland's Professor of Exegesis in 1847, and was no great admirer of the Tractarians. Nonetheless, he was keen to defend his own creation, the Voluntary Theological Examination, arguing that it needed more time to become established as a course for graduates.[96] Similarly, Robert Hussey continued to uphold his opposition to a theological school.[97]

The most forceful rejection of a theological school, however, came from the Regius Professor of Hebrew in the months after the

---

94. J. Garbett, *University Reform: A Letter to the Reverend the Warden of Wadham College, Oxford by the Ven. J. Garbett M.A., Archdeacon of Chichester and Late Professor of Poetry* (London: T. Hatchard, 1853), 18-19.

95. A letter from leading liberals in the *Evidence*, including Mark Pattison, Richard Congreve, Bartholomew Price, Goldwin Smith and H.H. Vaughan, accepted all of the main proposals of the Commission (with some exceptions), suggesting that there was probably wider support for Litton's suggestion than is initially evinced.

96. *Evidence*, 359-60. Hawkins also cited the attendance figures for the lectures of the divinity professors which, despite the poor uptake of the Voluntary, were large: the Professor of Pastoral Theology claimed that in the previous ten years he had numbered 1135 attendants; the Regius Professor of Ecclesiastical History, 450 students.

97. *Ibid.,* 246. Although, it ought to be noted that Tractarians were not unique in their frustration with the all-encompassing demands of the examination system. Mark Pattison, for example, was particularly derogatory of the chasing after honours during the 1860s (H.S. Jones, *Intellect and Character in Victorian England* (Cambridge: Cambridge University Press, 2008), 91).

publication of the Report. In his 1854 pamphlet, *Collegiate and Professorial Teaching and Discipline,* it is possible to observe how Pusey still fervently upheld his convictions about the idea of a university:

> The problem and special work of an University, is not how to advance science, not how to make discoveries, not to form new schools of mental philosophy, nor invent new modes of analysis; not to produce works in Medicine, Jurisprudence, or even Theology; but to form minds religiously, morally, intellectually, which shall discharge aright whatever duties God, in His Providence, shall appoint to them.[98]

This understanding of a university's operation did not exclude the modern sciences, but certainly dictated its methods. For,

> God alone *is* in Himself, and is the Cause and Upholder of everything to which He has given being. Every faculty of the mind is some reflection of His; every truth has its being from Him; every law of nature has the impress of His hand. . . . All sciences may do good service, if those who cultivate them know their place, and carry them not beyond their sphere.[99]

Even if God was at the heart of all true language about the universe, this did not entail that theology ought to be a distinct discipline for undergraduates. In his evidence to the Commission, Pusey had argued that, if honours were to be introduced for theology, it would, "almost unavoidably introduce competition, and with competition, 'cramming' for distinction, into sacred study. It would tend to make distinction and 'the praise of men,' not theological knowledge, for its own sake . . . the object of that study."[100] This is why, Pusey concluded, no measure of distinction had been offered when the Voluntary Theological Examination was introduced in 1842.

98. E.B. Pusey, *Collegiate and Professorial Teaching and Discipline* (London, 1854), 215. Quoted in Nockles, 164.
99. *Ibid.,* 215.
100. *Evidence,* 102-3.

Furthermore, if theology became a route to graduation, it would instantly demand more theological lectures, tempting the divinity professors to educate in the fashion of their German counterparts. Yet, as Pusey told the commissioners, "'Active Academical life' has not been...the basis of our solid English theology". Rather, "'A great Theological school' can only be formed by solid study, deep thought, pious learning, calm meditation, holy life, devoted desire to serve God, from Whom it must obtain its wisdom, not by professorial lectures."[101] To Pusey, the academic apparatus that had emerged in Oxford since the introduction of written examinations, along with the promotion of an expanded professoriate, were incongruous with theology's object: God, who is known through reverence for his Word, worship, and holiness of life.

Pusey maintained that even as a professional school, the scheme would fall apart, as it required that the university act as a "preliminary tribunal for Candidates for Holy Orders":

> But in that they assign to the Professors the power of rejecting a student on doctrinal grounds, on their own judgment, apart from the question of his Theological attainments. Such a power is, in fact, essential to an examination in Theology, else the Examiners might have to accept Arians or Socinians, or, if they should assign honours, assign them to a Rationalist.[102]

For theologians in the university to cast themselves as arbiters of faith was nothing less than a "usurpation" of the duties of the Church. Rather,

> [The university's] office, with regard to Theology, is either general towards all its students whom it undertakes to educate, or particular, as to its own Theological degrees. It has a right to place where it will, its own standard for those who desire from it the testimonial of a

101. *Ibid.*
102. *Ibid.,* 104.

degree in Divinity. It has a right, as "a seminary of sound and religious learning," to require of *all*, to whom it gives any degree at all, that amount of knowledge of Holy Scripture and the faith, which it judges that an educated Christian ought to have. But it has no right to take into account the future profession of any candidate for a degree, or to interpose itself between the young student and the Bishop.[103]

By developing itself as a voluntary study in the third year, Pusey asserted that both the *general* educational value of theology was threatened, as well as the university's purely ancillary role to the Church of England.

For this reason and its close association with Hampden, Pusey had abstained from all involvement with the Voluntary Theological Examination, which he regarded as "overstepping the province of the University". It interfered with the responsibilities of bishops and tended "to place the selection of half the Clergy of England in a small Board, themselves, for the most part, appointed by the Prime Minister of the day."[104] As the university became another ecclesiastical target for modernization, Pusey sought to stress that the authority for licensing ministers lay in the sacramental authority of bishops, not in the vice chancellor's admission to the degree of BA.[105]

Pusey was not only suspicious of any reforms that might further damage the ecclesiastical character of the university. He regarded the suggestions of Litton, Jowett, Stanley, and others, which prized the "history of doctrines" and "a profound acquaintance with the history and criticism of Sacred Books", as something of a perversion:

It is to be hoped that under the word "the history of doctrines," the Commissioners do not mean what alone is meant under the term which

103. *Ibid.*
104. *Ibid.,* 106.
105. Pusey would no doubt have had in mind the German university where, after 1806, some felt ordination had become *ein Anhang der wissenschaftlichen Examina:* nothing but a mere supplement to university examinations in theology. See T.A.L. Howard, *Protestant Theology and the Making of the Modern German University*, 232-33.

they have translated, (Dogmengeschichte,) the gradual development of the fundamental truths of the Gospel, under the influence of powerful minds, or amid the pressure of heretical speculation. I am satisfied, for myself, that there is no such real history, because there is no such reality, the faith having been, once for all, fully made known to the inspired Apostles, and by them inserted in Holy Scripture, and committed to the Church.[106]

The theological learning as promoted by academic liberals was, to Pusey, nothing other than an invasion of the German tendency to view theological orthodoxy as the accident of historical developments.

Pusey made clear that such academic pursuits were not simply inappropriate for undergraduate minds but were, in the first instance, false. He denounced the Higher Criticism as "one battle-field, in which no result . . . has been gained. Rationalists have been enlisted against Rationalists. Theories have been set up ... only to be thrown down". And he firmly insisted to those preparing legislation that the only result of such ventures for the general student "could be a cramped, superficial, undigested and indigestible knowledge; well, if it were not inflating also, a real ignorance, which did not even know its own ignorance."[107]

Perhaps more so than any other aspect of academic reform, Pusey had made clear that the future of theology at Oxford ought to be the province of ecclesiastical authority; fierce resistance could be expected were university or parliamentary legislators to introduce a

---

106. *Evidence,* 106.
107. *Ibid.,* 108. Similar arguments were presented in a separate pamphlet, *A Summary of Objections against the Proposed Theological Statute* (Oxford: J. Parker, 1854) where Pusey asserted that for an undergraduate "to study the Creed, and its eternal truths, to cram up Scripture proofs of the Divinity of our Lord, His Eternal Generation, or His unchangeable Generation, or His unchangeable Priesthood, His continued intercession for us, or everlasting kingdom, or of co-eternal procession of God the Holy Ghost from the Father and the Son; to get up prophecies as to the Person or Offices of our Lord, or the universality of our redemption, in order to obtain a class . . . might make controversialists, but it would be a most grievous profanation of sacred truth, every step in which would be deadening to the soul." (9-10)

separate honour school for theology. Choosing their battles carefully, no doubt, the commissioners tactfully recognized Pusey's communication on a separate theological school as abounding "with valuable information and sound remarks" and promised that "whenever this grave question comes before the Board and the University, injustice will be done to it, if this Evidence is not carefully considered."[108]

Indeed, apart from his comments on theological education, Pusey wrote prolifically on what he perceived to be the needs of the University, his evidence accounting for over a third in substance of all that was published in the *Evidence* (from twenty-three contributions in all). Carefully argued, and always supported by ample evidence, it was a stumbling block to reforming impulses. Combined with Hussey's and Hawkins's remonstrance that the Voluntary Theological Examination had not yet been given sufficient time to prove its worth as a means of improving clerical education, the defence of theology as a general rather than a specific route of study was strong. Although the Oxford University Act of 1854 would result in the new honour schools of Law and Modern History, Natural Science, and Mathematics as alternatives to *Literae Humaniores*, there would be no new theological school: a decision aided by the accession of both Pusey and Hussey to the Hebdomadal Board in the elections of 25 October 1854.[109]

To reformers, the response seems to have been a mixture of dismay and frustration. Stanley had already expressed confusion at Pusey's branding of the reformers' proposals as an implicit Germanization of the University and its theological faculty. Remembering Pusey's lectures on Hebrew in 1846 and 1847, long after he had rejected

108. *Report,* 10.
109. I. Ellis, "Pusey and University Reform" in *Pusey Rediscovered,* ed. P. Butler (London: SPCK, 1983), 215.

the historical-critical methods that he had encountered in Protestant Germany, he recounted how the "whole atmosphere of the Professor's Lectures breathed the spirit of Germany to a degree, which I am convinced could have been found in no other Lecture-room in Oxford, Professor or Tutorial":

> There was of course much that was peculiar to the theologian – the long digressions, & the fanciful theories, drawn from the writers of the 4th & 5th centuries – There was still more that was peculiar to the man – the kindness, the sweetness, the unexpected devotion which no one who has ever witnessed it can ever forget. But all that related to the interpretation of the part of the Scriptures which he was lecturing – (in this instance it was the Book of Psalms) – was both in matter & manner almost entirely German. The table was piled high with German commentaries. They were often quoted freely, often of course with deprecation yet often with commendation. I heard there the names of more German writers than in the whole course of the instructions given in my whole stay in Oxford.[110]

Despite Stanley's portrait, in Pusey's mind, the grandeur of the Prussian theological and philosophical schools remained delusive and dangerous. By committing another generation of Oxford ordinands to those solid offerings of the past, "chiefly old books" such as Hooker, Bull, Butler, and Pearson, Pusey believed that the orthodoxy of Oxford theology had been secured.[111]

Ethos and Party

The Oxford University Act 1854 ensured that undergraduates did not have to subscribe to the Thirty-nine Articles in order to matriculate

110. MS Eng. lett. d. 437 (ff.45-7). Although in the Vaughan MSS, it seems as though this record may have been passed on from Liddell to Vaughan, who, in a letter of 18 December 1853 (ff.75-8) refers to Stanley's informing him about the dependence upon German scholarship in Pusey's lectures.
111. *Evidence*, 10, 29-38. "Novelty, not truth, has been again and again their object." (23) For earlier denunciations of the German system with regard to theological study by Pusey, see *Cathedral Institutions*, 31-38.

or graduate as a Bachelor of Arts. The educational opportunities of an Oxford or Cambridge degree were now available to non-Anglicans schoolboys even if it would not be until 1871 that non-Anglicans could supplicate for the MA and so enjoy the opportunities this degree offered for positions of influence and governance in both universities. Although the teaching and control of the universities remained in the hands of the Church of England, these institutions could less truthfully be described as 'seminaries'. Such a characterization became less and less meaningful as new courses for undergraduates were introduced which diversified undergraduate study and teaching from its primary focus on classics or mathematics. For example, a man who was now examined in the Final Honour School of Natural Science was only shaped by the ecclesiastical ethos insomuch as he was obliged to attend his college chapel regularly and pass the Rudiments of Religion examination – the latter containing, as we saw earlier, a less than edifying study of the Bible. While he might still be affected by an Anglican ethos, he could less accurately be described as anything like a 'seminarian'.

The claim of Pusey that the University of Oxford offered a treatment of theology that was "general towards all its students" in its desire to form Christian gentlemen was certainly true; he and others secured a paradigm of theological practice, as at Cambridge, that was explicitly non-professional and separate from what was considered the degradingly competitive environment of the honour school examinations. In the minds of Pusey and other High Church figures, theology was, instead, the preserve of the graduate who was more mature in years, capable of handling profound truths, and whose pattern of life was committed to holiness, rather than academic celebrity. Apart from the MA, those who supplicated for the degrees of Bachelor of Divinity (BD) and Doctor of Divinity (DD) at both universities would still be required to be in holy orders.

This paradigm for theology as a purely graduate activity looked increasingly anomalous, however, not least since Durham and King's College London had introduced theological courses.[112] In 1852, John Henry Newman presented a series of lectures in Dublin in anticipation of his assuming the office of Rector of the Irish Catholic University. Published as *Discourses on the Scope and Nature of University Education* (and later included in his *The Idea of a University*), they reflected Newman's developed thought on the nature of a university, as well as the place of theology within it. "Theology", he wrote, "is a real science, we cannot exclude it, and still call ourselves philosophers" and "Religious Truth is not only a portion, but a condition of general knowledge. To blot it out is nothing short, if I may so speak, of unravelling the web of University Education."[113] This, of course, was consonant with Tractarian understandings of the theology in the University during the 1830s. However, there is a recognition in Newman's writings that theology is itself a 'specialist' subject, and not simply a root for all other branches of knowledge: a "Science of God, or the truths we know about God put into system; just as we have a science of the stars, and call it astronomy, or of the crust of the earth, and call it geology."[114] Newman even asserted that, "Theology is one branch of knowledge, and Secular Sciences are other branches. Theology is the highest indeed, and widest, but it does not interfere with the real freedom of any secular science in its own particular department."[115]

---

112. C.E. Whiting, *The University of Durham, 1832-1932* (London: The Sheldon Press, 1932), 259-262; S.W. Green, "Sketch of the History of the Faculty" in *London Theological Studies* (London: University of London Press, 1911), xi.

113. J.H. Newman, *The Scope and Nature of University Education* (London: J.M. Dent, 1903), 43, 61. See G. Loughlin, "Theology in the University", *The Cambridge Companion to John Henry Newman,* ed. I. Ker and T. Merrigan(Cambridge: Cambridge University Press, 2009), 221-40.

114. *Ibid.,* 53.

115. Newman, *ibid.,* 152-53.

At Oxford, however, the divinity professors seemed to take little account of Newman's changing conception of theology and its relations to a university. Resistance to theology as a separate department of knowledge remained a shibboleth for Pusey and his followers, fifteen years after the Royal Commission. Complaints about the quality of theological education persisted, as is evinced in the publication of John Cockburn Thomas's *Almae Matres* in 1858 which, once again, called for the introduction of a separate honour school for theology ("At present there is no religious instruction at Oxford."[116]). Even the long-standing defender of theology as "necessary knowledge", Robert Hussey, was supposed to have changed his mind about theological honours before his death in 1856.[117] Despite a failed attempt of Francis Jeune, the master of Pembroke College, to alter the statute in 1860, theology at Oxford remained a purely graduate discipline pursued by few and an aspect of general learning as a factual test of biblical knowledge for undergraduates.[118]

Although undergraduate theology was unreformed, this did not prevent more ambitious scholars in the university from pursuing the critical study of the Bible that they had advocated for theological honours. Stanley's divinity lectures at University College were so popular that his pupils sought permission for friends from other colleges to attend them and, from 1844, Jowett and Stanley committed themselves to producing a series of New Testament

---

116. J.C. Thomson, *Almae Matres by Megathym Splene, B.A., Oxon.* (London: James Hogg & Sons, 1858), 241.
117. *Ibid.*, 243. H.C.G. Matthew, "Hussey, Robert (1801-1856)" in the *Dictionary of National Biography* (Oxford: Oxford University Press, 2004).
118. Changes to the theological statute, as detailed on a sheet in Bodl. G.A. Oxon b.25 (University Notices 1854-64); Pusey countered Jeune's proposals with *The New Theological Statute.* (Bodl. G.A. Oxon b. 30). The proposed changes to the statute were rejected in May 1860: *The Times,* 24 Feb. 1860 (p10); 2 March (p5); 11 May (p12); 25 May (p5); quoted in W.R. Ward, *Victorian Oxford,* 249.

commentaries using the textual approaches that they had learnt from Arnold.[119] In 1855, Stanley published commentaries on 1 and 2 Corinthians and Jowett, a two-volume commentary on 1 and 2 Thessalonians, Galatians and Romans. Peter Hinchliff describes the 'critical notes and dissertations' that accompanied the commentaries as "outspoken and radical comments on contemporary orthodoxy".[120] Jowett's essay on 'the doctrine of the atonement' was particularly provocative, as Andrew Atherstone has highlighted, for its denunciation of theories of vicarious sacrifice as "revolting" and "inconsistent with truth and morality".[121] Made worse by Jowett's recent appointment to the Regius professorship of Greek, viewing the doctrine of sacrificial atonement as nothing but a "human invention", Jowett aroused the ire of Tractarians and Evangelicals alike. Pusey in his sermon, *All Faith the Gift of God,* delivered in the University Church, insisted that those occupying "such ground as [Jowett's]…must go on to full unbelief, or they must return to definite faith."[122] Charles Golightly, a leading Evangelical in the university and scourge of the Tractarians, wrote to the Master of Balliol, Robert Scott, asking whether he was "doing right by God and man in upholding Mr Jowett in the position of a Tutor of Balliol College."[123]

119. George Bradley described Stanley's course as the "first germ of those inter-collegiate lectures which have revolutionised Oxford teaching…to be found in those close-packed chairs that crowded the still damp ground-floor rooms in the then New Buildings." (R.E. Prothero, *Life and Correspondence of Arthur Penrhyn Stanley,* (2 vols., London: John Murray, 1893), 1:355-56.

120. Peter Hinchliff, *Benjamin Jowett and the Christian Religion* (Oxford: Clarendon Press, 1987), 56.

121. Benjamin Jowett, *The Epistles of St. Paul to the Thessalonians, Galatians, Romans: with Critical Notes and Dissertations* (2 vols., London: John Murray, 1855), ii, 474; quoted in Andrew Atherstone, "Benjamin Jowett's Pauline Commentary: An Atonement Controversy", *Journal of Theological Studies* 54 (2003): 141.

122. E.B. Pusey, *All Faith the Gift of God. Real Faith Entire* (Oxford: J.H. Parker, 1855), 93.

123. Pusey House Library SCO 1/12/1, C. Golightly to R. Scott, 24 Jan. 1856, quoted in A. Atherstone, ibid., 148.

Jowett was invited by the vice chancellor to sign the Thirty-nine Articles, at the instigation of Golightly, and although Stanley urged Jowett, in reply, to question the Tractarians' compliance of those Articles relating to liturgy or the 'sacrifice of the mass' (Article XXXI), Jowett signed. His commitment to the Articles was questionable, but as Atherstone has shown, the commentary provoked a sequence of sermons and Bampton Lectures that were acutely concerned to dispel doubt over the doctrine of substitutionary atonement. In 1856 Charles Heurtley, the Lady Margaret Professor of Divinity, delivered his Bampton lectures on 'The Doctrine of the Atonement', the Evangelical Charles Baring preached on *Christ's Death a Propitiatory Sacrifice,* and the Bishop of Oxford on *Our Reception of the Truth of Christ's Message, a Part of Our Moral Probation.*[124] High Churchmen, Evangelicals and Tractarians alike moved strongly against Jowett's treatment of the doctrine.

For Jowett, however, the hostility that his commentary provoked paled in comparison with the reception of a collection of essays that he published with other Oxford liberals in 1860. Following on from J.S. Mill's *On Liberty* and Darwin's *Origin of the Species* in 1859, the publication *Essays and Reviews* has been described as "the story of the greatest religious crisis of the Victorian age."[125] Selling over 22,000 copies in its first year, more than *Origin of the Species* sold in its first twenty, the book included essays from: Frederick Temple (previously fellow of Balliol, then Headmaster of Rugby, who wrote on 'The Education of the World'); Henry Bristow Wilson (of St John's, writing on the national church); Baden Powell (the Professor of Geometry, writing 'On the Study of the Evidences of Christianity'); Mark Pattison (on 'Tendencies of Religious Thought

---

124. A. Atherstone, ibid., 149.
125. I. Ellis, *Seven against Christ: A study of 'Essays and Reviews'* (Leiden: E.J. Brill, 1980), ix.

in England, 1688-1750'); and, most famously, Jowett himself, who authored 'On the Interpretation of Scripture'.[126]

Jowett had asked Stanley in 1858 – the latter having just been appointed Regius Professor of Ecclesiastical History – whether he would like to contribute to the collection. There was some debate about whether the contributions, the "object" of which was "to say what we think freely within the limits of the Church of England", should be anonymous. Jowett did not hesitate in asserting that it should not be, "partly for the additional weight which the articles will have if the authors are known":[127]

> We do not wish to do anything rash or irritating to the public or the University, but we are determined not to submit to this abominable system of terrorism, which prevents the statement of the plainest facts, and makes true theology or theological education impossible. Pusey and his friends are perfectly aware of your opinions, and the Dean's, and [Frederick] Temple's and [Friedrich Max] Müller's, but they are determined to prevent your expressing them. I do not deny that in the present state of the world the expression of them is a matter of great nicety and care, but is it possible to do any good by a system of reticence?

To some degree, this provocative compendium of essays had been published out of frustration with "abominable system of terrorism" that was making "theological education impossible" at Oxford, both in terms of how theology was approached by senior scholars and how it was offered to the undergraduates. As an act of 'counter-terrorism', *Essays and Reviews* certainly provoked a reaction from the theological establishment: Archbishop Tait and twenty-four bishops issued a letter condemning the views contained in the essays; Frederic Harrison, in the radical *Westminster Review,* considered it neither religious nor rational; Pusey attempted to have Jowett censured in the

126. *Essays and Reviews.* (7th edn., London: Longmans, Green, 1861).
127. *Jowett,* 1:275: B. Jowett to A.P. Stanley, 15 August 1858.

university for teaching doctrines contrary to the Church of England (the vice chancellor's assessor rejected the case); and the Convocation of Canterbury formally condemned the book in 1864.[128]

More generally, the debate over how to read critically the Bible and dogma as a result of *Essays and Reviews*, along with Samuel Wilberforce's less than convincing engagement with T.H. Huxley over evolution in the University Museum in the same year, polarized attitudes to the Church in the university. As the young Cambridge biblical scholar B.F. Westcott wrote to A.P. Stanley:

> It is acknowledged by all that men of high intellectual culture have for some years shrunk from Orders...Now I fear this must be, and in fact is already the case, from the belief that all criticism, however reverent, is banished from questions of theology.[129]

Similarly, Joseph Barber Lightfoot, one of Westcott's colleagues at Cambridge, had stated in a lecture of 1855:

> the timidity, which shrinks from the application of modern science or criticism to the interpretation of the Holy Scriptures evinces a very unworthy view of its character. . . . It is against the wrong application of such principles . . . that we must protest. . . . From the full light of science and criticism we have nothing to fear.[130]

Theologians at Oxford, by contrast, showed only very limited signs of moving towards the "full light of criticism" of which Lightfoot spoke. Orthodoxy, for Pusey and many of his colleagues, was to be defended and guarded rather than analyzed and turned over by

---

128. For a comprehensive study of responses to the essays in the early 1860s, see V. Shea and W. Whitla, eds., *Essays and Reviews: The 1860 Text and its Reading.* (Charlottesville, VA.: University Press of Virginia, 2000). For A.P. Stanley's response to the book, see J. Witheridge, *Excellent Dr Stanley* (Wilby: Michael Russell Publishing, 2013), 216-17.

129. Protheroe, *Life and Correspondence of A.P. Stanley*, 40.

130. J.B. Lightfoot, 'Greek New Testament Lectures, Lent term 1855' in B.N. Kaye and G.R. Treloar, 'J.B. Lightfoot and New Testament Interpretation: An Unpublished Manuscript of 1855', *Durham University Journal*, 82: 2 (July 1990); quoted in D. Thompson, *ibid.*, 107.

critics in the manner of the Germans. The publication of *Essays and Reviews* would have only confirmed the convictions of those who believed that theological 'speculation' should be kept firmly out of the reach of undergraduates. As the book shook the theological and ecclesiastical establishment, Jowett withdrew from theological controversy to his duties at Balliol and Stanley was limited to teaching students biblical criticism of the Old Testament secretly under the guise of 'ecclesiastical history', a few doors away from the professor of Hebrew himself in Christ Church.[131]

The hopes for university theology that Stanley had harboured after his trip to Berlin in 1839 with A.C. Tait (by 1860, bishop of London) and which Jowett, Vaughan, Liddell and others had advanced at Oxford during these crucial years of reform, lay dead in the water. The influence of conservative High Churchmen and Tractarians in the key professorial chairs and on the Hebdomadal Board ensured that, unlike Cambridge during the same period, Oxford theology remained characterized by an anxious defence of Anglican orthodoxy rather than a patient and cautious engagement with the new criticism.

The duty of theologians in the university was, for those with influence at Oxford, less about expanding critical knowledge of the Bible and church history and more concerned with defending and sustaining the ecclesiastical ethos of the institution, in particular through the divinity examinations, university sermons, and a certain number of lectures for those graduates who sought to take orders. As theological colleges were founded across England for graduates (Pusey even donated £2500 to the foundation of Salisbury

---

131. *The Ecclesiastic* 1866:45, quoted in W.R. Ward, *Victorian Oxford*, 212. "Here he was always to be found standing at his desk, tossing off sheet after sheet, the whole floor covered with scraps of papers written or letters received, which, by habit that nothing could change, he generally tore up and scattered around him." (A.J.C. Hare, *Biographical Sketches* (London: George Allen, 1895), 65)

Theological College in 1861), so diminished the possibility that Oxford and Cambridge would become centres of professional theological education for the Church of England in a manner akin to the faculties of Germany or Scotland.

This evolution of theology in England was peculiar. Oxford and Cambridge were both ecclesiastical institutions. To be admitted to the degree of Master of Arts, and so to have the authority to teach and vote in the universities' governing assemblies, one needed to have subscribed to the Thirty-nine Articles. To be a candidate for the Divinity degrees or the vast majority of college fellowships, one needed to be in holy orders. It may seem paradoxical, then, that both institutions did not see fit to introduce systematic theological education, not least with so many of its graduates entering parish ministry. In the end, however, it was that ecclesiastical ethos of the university that shirked the professional education that was highly prized in continental Europe and in Scotland. For, as was made clear by Pusey, Hussey and others, Oxford did not exist to form clergymen through the dispensing of knowledge, but to form Christian gentlemen through a liberal education and the breeding of morals in the tutorial. Even liberals were not significantly different in this respect, recognizing that reading for a BA degree was not a professional training. They still prized *Literae Humaniores* (known as 'Greats') above the new modern schools.

This rejection of theology as a distinctive course of undergraduate education in institutions whose principle occupation was, instead, classics and mathematics, left English university theology in an altogether different position in public life from its continental and Scottish counterparts. Positively, there was no atheistic movement against theology's position in the university, as had been evident from such figures as Fichte during discussions around the foundation of the University of Berlin in 1809-10. The most serious threat that was perceived to theology in English universities was, depending on one's point of view, those who wished to include their critical approach to the Bible as a systematic element of undergraduate education or, on the other hand, those who opposed every form of theological education for undergraduates or reform of the Divinity degrees. Even University College London, which excluded all religious teaching and any form of religious subscription, did so in large part out of regard for not excluding any Christian 'sect' that would have found particular confessional commitments unacceptable. Rather, its founders claimed, "when the University abstains entirely from all interference in religious matters, the natural guardians of its pupils are fully and distinctly warned, that this most important part of education is left to their care and no excuse or palliation is furnished for their neglect."[132]

The persistent conviction of many in both of the 'ancient' English universities that theology was an 'architectonic science' (or 'necessary knowledge'), is testament to the particular development of the English universities in a society that did not experience political revolution or conquest. When Stanley and Jowett visited Paris in 1848 to encounter the raising of the *Tricolor,* they had wondered whether the Chartist demonstrations in England would develop into anything comparable.[133] Britain, of course, did not experience any comparable uprising in 1848 or throughout the nineteenth century, and its key national institutions – including its universities – avoided the radical upheavals that were experienced in France or in those territories conquered by Napoleonic forces. English theologians consequently never encountered the political upheaval of their

132. *University of London: Address from the Senate to the [Privy] Council in Support of the University for a Charter* (London: Richard Taylor, 1834), 5.
133. Bodl. MS. Eng. misc. e. 429: Journal of F.T. Palgrave's trip to Paris in spring 1848, entry for 20 April. Palgrave was accompanied by Benjamin Jowett, Arthur P. Stanley and Robert Burnet Morier, an undergraduate (who later became H.M. Ambassador to Russia).

French counterparts; in post–Napoleonic Europe, theologians were compelled to make very different arrangements with their societies, universities, and churches, and usually from positions of comparative weakness.

As Jowett made his last-ditch attempt to alter the practice of theology at Oxford with *Essays and Reviews*, it is important to note that, unlike Berlin, what evoked controversy was not how to secure the discipline of theology in the university; this was essentially unquestioned in universities that were still Church institutions. Rather, the question was how theology might best serve the Church of England and wider society. Both these questions were framed by the wider question of the purpose and role of the university, which was itself a religious consideration for many. Indeed, the first half of the nineteenth century saw these questions discussed almost exclusively by members of the Church, since they formed the governing élite in both the universities and in Parliament. After 1860, however, a new generation of university reformers emerged for whom the place of theology in the university, and the duties of the university to Church, were secondary considerations. The universities, it was increasingly felt, needed to serve more readily a society that had been changed significantly from the turn of the century by an enlarged middle-class, urbanisation and industrialization, and imperial expansion.

2

Theology as 'Breakwater' against the Tide of Secularism, 1860–1882

In a letter from September 1864, Jowett wrote solemnly

> I don't know whether one colours objects with one's own vision, but I sometimes think that the state of religion in England gets worse and worse. The very idea of the truth is becoming ridiculous and, more and more, religious teaching is losing its moral character. The two great parties which really could say 'Rise up and walk' in the last generation hardly have any moral purpose at all. The effervescence of their spirituality has passed away, and cunning, activity, and political tactics, have filled up the vacuum.[1]

Jowett was understandably pessimistic. Although Pusey had failed in his attempt to have Jowett censured for teaching doctrines contrary to the Church of England (the vice chancellor's assessor rejected the case), the Convocation of Canterbury had condemned *Essays and Reviews* in 1864. The energy and enthusiasm for biblical writing

---

1. *Jowett*, 1:368–69: unaddressed letter of B. Jowett, probably to A.P. Stanley.

and critical essays that Jowett had displayed in the previous decade dissipated; he never wrote a book or essay on theology again.

Arthur Stanley, whose appointment as Regius Professor of Ecclesiastical History in 1858 had so delighted Jowett, departed in 1864 for the deanery of Westminster not long after marrying Lady Augusta Bruce, a lady-in-waiting to Queen Victoria. While Arnold's disciples had been successful in initiating a process of reform in the wider university through the Royal Commission in 1850-52, they had still failed to reform Oxford theology in such a manner as to renew the Church of England with the more comprehensive and liberal spirit of their master.

If theology at Oxford seemed to be actively avoiding the questions of higher biblical criticism and the challenges of scientific enquiry, the university as a whole needed to address its unfinished business of reform. However, the new generation of academic liberals that was beginning to influence the future of the university was not propelled by theological questions or concern for the renewal of the Church of England so much as by a desire for freedom of enquiry in the interests of a secular and democratic state.[2] Whereas the Broad Church scholars of the previous decade had seen social progress and university reform emerging from the crucible of Christianity, this new contingent of liberals advocated a secular vision of a democratic commonwealth that united university and society.

To this end, reformers sought to widen the social constitution of the universities, broaden the curriculum yet further and, above all, remove the requirement of religious tests for the MA. Important alliances were formed with Nonconformists and likeminded Cambridge colleagues, facilitated by the advent of a railway connection between the two universities in 1863. From the lobbying

---

2. Christopher Harvie, *The Lights of Liberalism: University Liberals and the Challenge of Democracy, 1860-1886* (London: Allen Lane, 1976), 44ff.

in the mid-1860s that resulted in the Universities Tests Act 1871 (which removed the requirement of subscription to the Thirty-nine Articles for the MA at Oxford, Cambridge and Durham) until the work of the Selborne Commission from 1877 onwards, the universities of Oxford and Cambridge (and, to a lesser degree, Durham) sought to become truly national institutions and this entailed the dismantling of many of the ecclesiastical safeguards and positions that Pusey and his like-minded colleagues perceived as sacrosanct.

How did Oxford theologians understand their role and their discipline in the context of this reformed university? Whereas the previous generation had sufficient confidence that the Christian and clerical ethos permeated the life and studies of the university, reform raised questions about the sustainability of that ethos. There was a growing sense that strategies needed to be adopted to consolidate the Christian institutions of the university and especially the practice of theology. One of the central instruments of this consolidation was the introduction of an honour school of theology by the very men who had for so long ridiculed the idea. As we shall observe, however, this highly conservative programme of study for undergraduates generated few admirers from either within the university or in the wider Church. From being a seminary within the university, the theological school would be compelled by the end of decade to present itself – disingenuously perhaps – as a course of liberal education. This is an account of English theology struggling in a period of turbulent transition, and in the final years of E.B. Pusey's life, to nurture new institutions that would secure its position as a flourishing discipline in the modern university.

The Tide of Reform

Christopher Harvie has suggested that 1860 was the year in which the reform movement shifted decisively from Oxford to London literary society, after the Broad Churchmen had become politically immobilized by the reactions of the rest of the Church of England to *Essays and Reviews*.[3] Conservative anxiety with challenges to doctrinal orthodoxy was also illustrated in the same year by the infamous debate in April between T.H. Huxley and the Bishop of Oxford, Samuel Wilberforce. Wilberforce had once stood by F.D. Maurice when he was dismissed from King's College London on the charge of heterodoxy, but Huxley now left Wilberforce looking like an obscurantist; science in the university, Huxley successfully suggested, needed to be liberated from the ecclesiastical shackles of authority and dogma.[4] The more secular temper that was increasingly prevalent in Oxford is well illustrated in an undergraduate essay, written around 1857, by the young T.H. Green, who was to become one of the most influential thinkers of late Victorian Oxford. The essay title was 'The duties of the University to the state' and throughout the essay the word 'Church' appeared only twice.[5]

This is not to claim, however, that the university became a secular institution almost overnight. Harvie has usefully characterized the university after 1854 as a *polis* in which "all parties concerned – secular liberals, Broad-Churchmen, Tractarians, dedicated researchers, or popular tutors – had to find solutions within the system", engaging political strategies to achieve their goals.[6] Indeed, it is hard to characterize the various constituencies within the university as there were, invariably, so many disagreements among

3. C. Harvie, "Reform and Expansion, 1854-71" in *History of the University,* 6:709.
4. O. Chadwick, *The Victorian Church,* 2:11.
5. Balliol College Archives, T.H. Green MSS, essay-book 2 (n.d.), quoted in Harvie, ibid., 710.
6. C. Harvie, ibid., 702.

them. Mark Pattison, for instance, who could be considered a leading reformer, nonetheless encountered scepticism from other liberals like Goldwin Smith and Frederic Harrison; both were suspicious of academic specialization and of Pattison's proposals for the endowment of research.[7]

What united liberals in Oxford, Cambridge, and London was the abolition of tests, a campaign having begun in 1863 when Lord John Russell and John George Dodson MP presented a petition from 105 Oxford residents to Parliament. As the decade progressed, the calls for tests-abolition grew stronger and the defence of ecclesiastical Oxford looked far less sure. Pusey's toleration of ritualism in the wider Church had also alienated many of his natural supporters within and outside of the university and the coalition that had previously defended Church interests at Oxford was consequently weaker.

How did this lobbying for further reform of the universities affect the position of theologians? In some ways, the aftermath of *Essays and Reviews,* the silence of Jowett, and the departure of Stanley left the theological life of the university more firmly in the hands of those who had opposed the conclusions of *Essays and Reviews.* Pusey was led to publish a series of lectures on the prophet Daniel as his own reply to Jowett's contribution to *Essays and Reviews.*[8] This was a work which was sneered at by liberals at the time (and ever since) for its dating of the book of Daniel to the sixth, rather than the second, century. Nonetheless, as Timothy Larsen has shown, Pusey's magnum opus cannot be so easily dismissed as the work of an obscurantist. Pusey systematically worked through the arguments

7. H.S. Jones, *Intellect and Character in Victorian England: Mark Pattison and the Invention of the Don* (Cambridge: Cambridge University Press, 2007), 186; Goldwin Smith, *The Reorganization of the University of Oxford* (Oxford: J.H. Parker, 1868), 1-2.

8. E.B. Pusey, *Daniel the Prophet: Nine Lectures, Delivered in the Divinity School of the University of Oxford, with Copious Notes* (Oxford: J.H. Parker, 1864), vi.

for Daniel's second-century dating, countered false assumptions, questioned the *a priori* judgments of German critics, and used his extensive philological knowledge to provide evidence that negated the charge the book contained spiritual practices from other Eastern religions.[9]

Significantly, as Larsen has shown, the arguments he advanced in this significant publication were never challenged in the reviews that followed. Evangelical as well as Anglo-Catholic journals gave warm and admiring reviews. The liberal *Westminster Review* did not review it, perhaps unable to find a reviewer who could offer a serious reply to Pusey's argument. Even the Broad Churchman, J.J. Stewart Perowne, in his review in the *Contemporary Review,* admitted that Pusey had produced "by far the most complete work that has yet appeared, no continental writer having handled the subject with anything like the same fullness or breadth of treatment."[10] As a robust defence of a sixth-century dating of Daniel, its arguments were left largely unanswered during Pusey's lifetime; it was Pusey's successor at Oxford, Samuel Rolles Driver, who shifted the consensus around a second-century dating, and even then with admiration for Pusey's "extremely learned and thorough" monograph.[11]

Pusey was not afraid to employ the techniques of the biblical critics to reply to their revisions of the received opinions about the biblical texts, and *Daniel the Prophet* stands as an impressive testimony to his belief that English theology did not need to capitulate so readily to the conclusions of the radical German critics. He showed detailed knowledge of all the theories of the – mainly German –

9. Timothy Larsen, "E.B. Pusey and Holy Scripture", *Journal of Theological Studies* 60 (2009): 508-10
10. J.J. Stewart Perowne, "Dr Pusey on Daniel the Prophet", *Contemporary Review* 1 (1866): 96; quoted in Larsen, ibid., 514.
11. S.R. Driver, *The Book of Daniel, with Introduction and Notes* (Cambridge: Cambridge University Press, 1912), ciii-civ; quoted in Larsen, 518.

critics, and sometimes quoted them approvingly. Nonetheless, Pusey did not believe that the Bible could be treated purely as historical literature. He regularly used the apologetic device of showing how prophecies were fulfilled and, in his *Minor Prophets*, brought the fierce judgments of the prophets (and, thereby God) to bear upon the profligacy and injustices of Victorian England. This was not the sort of historical-critical commentary that one encountered emerging from the German universities and reflected Pusey's conviction that theology was, primarily, the revelation of God to his people; while biblical study in the university ought to be practised with the greatest care and detail, Pusey nonetheless asserted that biblical scholars should be seeking, with due reverence, to hear God's word rather than produce startling new historical and literary theories.

Accordingly, as movement towards the reform of the university approached, it was unsurprising that Pusey and others committed to his conception of theology were unsettled. If the university were to be opened to all, its teachers no longer required to be in holy orders or even to have subscribed to the Thirty-nine Articles, what hope could there be that Oxford theology would remain in the service of the Church and attentive to the God who had revealed himself in Jesus Christ?

The threat that reform posed to theology in the university would have been discerned by Pusey in the work of the parliamentary select committee that met in 1867 to work out the priorities for university reform. Chaired by the radical William Ewart, the committee questioned both Benjamin Jowett and E.B. Pusey in July of that year. Grant Duff asked Jowett, in particular, how theological education might be improved at Oxford, querying whether he agreed "that at Oxford there has been a feeling against teaching theology as a science, and that it has been rather discouraged rather than encouraged."[12] Jowett admitted, in something of an understatement, that, "It has been felt that there were great difficulties about it, owing to the great differences of opinion which have existed amongst us" but that

> I am definitely of the opinion that the University ought to be able to teach theology, and that the different parties in the University ought, so far, to compromise with each other, and live in harmony, as to be willing either to teach the same thing, or allow one another to teach different things.[13]

In reply to the next question from Chichester Fortescue, a Liberal MP, about whether there were currently "any theological lectures at Oxford ... which give a full critical treatment of the interpretation of the Scriptures", Jowett was less conciliatory:

> [Jowett:] I am not aware of any. There are lectures given on parts of the Scripture. There are the Exegetical Professor's lectures on the Epistles, and the Regius Professor of Hebrew's Lectures on the Old Testament, but I do not think that there is anything given which can be called a full critical treatment of the Scripture.
> [Fortescue:] Is there any critical treatment of the Scriptures?
> [Jowett:] No, I think not.[14]

Significantly, similar questions on the treatment of Scripture were not posed to Pusey, who spent considerable time eloquently denouncing the German university system.[15]

However, the prospect of tests abolition provoked Pusey and other conservative High Churchmen into decisive action to protect the interests of theology and the Church in the University. While the clerical party was still able to exert influence on the Hebdomadal

12. *Special Report from the Select Committee on the Oxford and Cambridge Universities Education Bill; together with the Proceedings of the Committee, Minutes of Evidence, and Appendix* (London, 1867), evidence, Q.2432.
13. *Ibid.,* Q.2433.
14. *Ibid.,* Q. 2434
15. *Ibid.,* QQ. 3324-3365. The committee was particularly keen to emphasize the quality and quantity of German theological scholarship over the limited publications of Oxford's scholars.

Council and Congregation, they decided to form a plan for the protection of ecclesiastical interests in the face of reform. Henry Liddon, a protégé of Pusey who had formerly been vice-principal of St. Edmund Hall and, earlier, of Cuddesdon Theological College, recorded in his diary of December 1867:

> ...went to Burgon's rooms where I met Woollcombe and Bright. We discussed the state of things in Oxford for 2 hours. Decided 1. To watch the examiners and try to bring about some change in the final philosophical school, 2. To try to set up a school of theology. Burgon will write a letter to the Vice-Chancellor.[16]

Several weeks later, Liddon wrote to William Bright, a fellow of University College and soon to be Regius Professor of Ecclesiastical History.[17] It testifies to the anxiety among the close colleagues of Pusey about the future of the theological life at Oxford. The group's concern for the final philosophical school (that is, Greats) no doubt emanated from the examiners' decision to remove Butler's *Analogy of Religion* as a compulsory element of the examination: a sign, in the mind of the High Churchmen, that the university was descending into 'unbelief' and heterodoxy. Liddon was worried about the reading list of the proposed theological school and was concerned that John William Burgon, the vicar of the University Church, might not realize the full implications of the reformers' intentions:

16. Pusey House Library MS Liddon Diaries, 20 Dec. 1867. Edward Woollcombe (1816-80) was a fellow of Balliol and an influential conservative figure in the university. He was despised by Jowett.

17. William Bright was elected Fellow in 1847 and, like Stanley, would later become Regius Professor of Ecclesiastical History (1868-1901). He was a High Churchman, but Stanley warmly congratulated him upon his appointment to the Regius professorship, to which Bright had replied: "I will never encourage – I will always discourage the temper of hard and unfair partisanship which would sacrifice truthfulness to the supposed interests of a cause. These are lessons which I learned from Arnold at Rugby, and from you at Oxford." (Prothero, *Life and Correspondence of Arthur Penrhyn Stanley,* 2:372-3). The foundation of the honour school was, however, an incredibly partisan process.

THE MAKING OF MODERN ENGLISH THEOLOGY

My dear Bright,
Your letter, as always, delights and instructs me. With you I think that there are 2 sides to the Theological School proposal. What will such a school be in 50, or 30 years hence? It is observable that Jowett in his Evidence before the Committee of the H[ouse] of C[ommons] & Pattison in his recent book, are both desirous of something of the sort. Not for nothing we may be sure. I doubt Burgon's being alive to their considerations. He takes it for granted that the Ex[aminatio]ns would be entirely in Pearson, Hooker & the like. It is quite possible that Ewald & Baur ought [sic] come to be text books...[18]

Liddon here refers to Mark Pattison's 'recent book'. This was his *Suggestions on Academical Organisation,* a blueprint for how the university could be committed to research in the manner of the German universities. It also included a section on how Oxford might reorganize its theological faculty. Pattison had recognized the "double position" of the faculty, bound as it would be to offer "scientific" theological studies alongside instruction for the clergy, for whom the "average level . . . which can be attained . . . is necessarily lower".[19]

Pattison did not elaborate further, noting that "the difficulty of touching on this matter at all can hardly be over-estimated", but suggestively ended his recommendations with a list of the thirty-eight different lectures on offer to students ("somewhat over 2000") in the University of Berlin's theological faculty for one semester.[20]

Four days after Liddon wrote to Bright with his worries about the direction of theology at Oxford, John Magrath – an influential liberal from The Queen's College – used the first university sermon of 1868 to make 'A Plea for the Study of Divinity'. Twenty years

18. Bodleian MS Eng. lett. d.300 (ff.62–63): H.P. Liddon to W. Bright, 15 January 1868.
19. M. Pattison, *Suggestions on Academical Organisation with Especial Reference to Oxford* (Edinburgh: Edmonton & Douglas, 1868), 176–78.
20. For more on Pattison's distinctive contribution to debates on university reform in the 1860s, see H.S. Jones, *Intellect and Character,* chapter 5.

after Jowett and Stanley had published their *Suggestions*, Magrath urged the introduction of a separate school of theology. A new generation of divines were needed, he averred, who could answer questions "as to the possibility of miracle and prophecy" which "have now passed from the cabinet of the *savant* and the little coteries of philosophers into the busy world of the artisan and the mechanic."[21] The current divinity examination, he suggested, "though of value, is not Theology", and that "an intellectual knowledge of, or opinion about, God, the world, the soul, is not the same as the apprehension of, and blind hypothetical assent to, dogmatic teaching on these subjects." The theologian was "he whose intellect has been carefully trained to exercise itself on the highest subjects, not he whose encyclopaedic memory is replete with undigested or ill-digested propositions."[22] Instead,

> The requirement of a scientific knowledge of Hebrew, Greek, and Latin, the cultivation of Exegetical Theology, would secure for candidates in this school the philological training as sound as that now given in the higher Arts courses, and the study of Comparative Theology and Historical Theology – the outcomings of the theological spirit in space and time – would supply the historical element in a complete education.[23]

By "Comparative Theology", Magrath gave as an example the "science" of the great Oxford philologist Friedrich Max Müller. Magrath cited his *Chips from a German Workshop,* recently published, which had sought to evince the benefits of comparative philology and religion to a wider public. Those who pursued this kind of "scientific" study, Max Müller had written, "must aim at truth, trusting that even

21. John Magrath, *A Plea for the Study of Divinity in the University of Oxford: A Sermon preached before the University of Oxford on the Second Sunday after the Epiphany, January 19, 1868* (London: Rivingtons, 1868), 6.
22. John Magrath, *ibid.,* 8.
23. John Magrath, *ibid.,* 10.

unpalatable truths, like unpalatable medicine, will reinvigorate the system into which they enter":

> To those, no doubt, who value the tenets of their religion as the miser values his pearls and precious stones, thinking their value lessened if pearls and stones of the same kind are found in other parts of the world, the Science of Religion will bring many a rude shock; but to the believer, truth, wherever it appears, is welcome, nor will any doctrine seem the less true or the less precious, because it was seen, not only by Moses or Christ, but likewise by Buddha or Laotse.[24]

Theological conservatives had displayed their resistance to the "shocks" of Max Müller's theological method by blocking the appointment of Max Müller to the Sanskrit chair in the university in 1864. Magrath was bold in suggesting that this early form of religious studies – that is, the examination of the data of religious experience rather than theological statements – might be incorporated into a theological school at Oxford. It was advanced nonetheless in the belief that "if this training is really to educate [future clergymen], it must be free", remembering that "in theological controversy, God's honour is best left in God's own hands":

> Truth and error on any intellectual subject imply thought; nay, imply free thought. Grant the student licence to think freely and you have exposed him to all the danger that is necessary. Give him adequate guidance, not constraint, and you have minimized the danger.[25]

Magrath's proposal for a theological school would have disturbed Pusey and those who were seeking to conserve ecclesiastical influence in the university; the agenda set out by both Pattison and Magrath, closely aligned to the pattern of theological study at German universities, went against the belief of those influential

---

24. Friedrich Max Müller, *Chips from a German Workshop* (London: Longmans, Green & Co., 1868), xxvii.
25. John Magrath, *ibid.*, 15.

theologians in the university who – as *Daniel the Prophet* and the *Minor Prophets* exemplified – asserted that true theology entailed obedience and reverence for a truth that was given (indeed, revealed) rather than 'discovered' by the research student or which helped provide a "complete education" through its philological, philosophical and linguistic offerings.

The suggestions of Magrath and Pattison were unrealizable, despite the momentum towards reform in Parliament. Those eager for reform still only occupied six out of the eighteen elected seats on the Hebdomadal Council, and any proposals for a new theological statute from leading liberal figures such as Pattison or Magrath could be vetoed by the ranks of clergy in Convocation. Instead, when John William Burgon published in February 1868 his *Plea for a Fifth Final School,* an open letter to the vice chancellor, members of the university would have understood this as indicative of what conservatives were intending to lay before Congregation and Convocation.

Burgon was not wholly inexperienced of the kind of 'scientific study' that Magrath and Pattison had been promoting. Like Pusey, he had been concerned for accurate historical detail in his own studies and, as a fellow of Oriel since 1846, had travelled across the Middle East and had examined manuscripts in St Catherine's monastery at Sinai. In 1863 he became vicar of the University Church and was part of a group of Churchmen – not homogenously Tractarian – who were repelled by Romanism and liberalism in equal measure. Nonetheless, the proposal for a fifth school was written to challenge "the tendency of recent legislation…to relax the once close connexion between the University and the Church". The "popular wave of infidelity" threatens to overwhelm us rather, in its onward course. What is to be done? Shall we not eagerly interpose a break-water, while yet we may? . . . Something must be done for Sacred Science if it is to retain any definite place in our system . . . [26]

Burgon did accept Magrath's contention that graduates were leaving "utterly *unfurnished*...absolutely *without sacred Learning*" and that the theological colleges could never "practically remedy the evil". Nonetheless, it was clear that his motivation was the approaching reform of the university and the abolition of tests. Churchmen needed to "interpose a break-water" to defend Sacred Science in the new system and a fifth final honour school was understood as instrumental in this respect.

It is important to recognize how significant this change of strategy was for both theology and theologians at Oxford. Since the university curriculum had been contested prior to the royal commission, theology had been defended by Tractarians and High Churchmen, as we have observed, as a purely graduate discipline. Otherwise, it was an 'architectonic science': an aspect of 'necessary knowledge' and general learning that, in the form of the divinity examination and the postgraduate Divinity degrees, was not given over to a scrambling after honours in the theological class list. As the ecclesiastical character of the university looked increasingly under threat in parliamentary committees at Westminster, this characterization of theology was discarded.

With those reforms, however, Burgon was clear that theology would need protection for "the sake of that Sacred Deposit of Divine Truth" that it was the duty of Oxford theologians to protect and pass onto to successive generations. He proposed that the three examiners in the honour school of theology should be nominated by the vice chancellor and the divinity professors "as a sufficient safe-guard for

26. J.W. Burgon, *Plea for a Fifth Final School* (Oxford: Parker & Co, 1868), 3.

their Orthodoxy".[27] This was to be an honour school that was carefully protected from what was perceived as less than orthodox forces within the university. With the High Church professors essentially in control of the examinations, Burgon and those supportive of his *Plea* were seeking to ensure that Baur and Ewald remained excluded from the reading lists. The collaboration that Jowett had spoken of between "different parties in the University" learning to "compromise with each other . . . as to be willing to teach the same thing, or to allow one another one another to teach different things" thus seemed unlikely to materialize as the Hebdomadal Council moved to prepare a new examination statute.[28]

The Foundation of the Honour School of Theology, 1868-69

Given the reasoning behind Burgon's "safe-guard", it was natural that the element most contended in the process of establishing the honour school was the method of appointing examiners. In every other honour school, the examiners were appointed by the vice-chancellor and the proctors of the university, and these names were approved by Convocation. The Theological Statute, as originally promulgated, had a nominating board of twelve members: the vice chancellor and proctors, six theological professors and three clerical members of Convocation. This proposal predictably incited hostility from liberal reformers who would almost certainly be outnumbered by conservative clergymen on such a board.[29] In its first hearing in Congregation on 13 June 1868 the liberals were victorious in voting down this method of selection, and the method of choosing examiners was deferred until the following academic year.

---

27. *Ibid.,* 5.
28. *Ibid.*
29. The system also advantaged those colleges, such as Christ Church, St John's and Magdalen, that had large clerical constituencies in Convocation and thus an unfair share of electors: see *The New Theological Statute* [Oppositions to] (Bodleian G.A. Oxon c.84 (470)).

Liberal opposition to the statute was incited to some degree by a pamphlet written by Pusey and published three days before the vote in June, in which he insisted that theology was "a subject quite apart, in that in it the question is not one of mere knowledge of facts, or of opinions, or of philosophies, or philosophical theories, but a revelation of God for the sake of man." Thus it was only logical that "to entrust the selection of Examiners in Christian Theology to persons non-Christian" would be a "monstrosity which no one…would think of." It would become "a machinery for propagating unbelief, and become a curse to our whole country."[30]

When a new statute was introduced that reduced the presence of divinity professors on the nominating board to three, with the suggestion that the board should include examiners from the previous year, it was still clear that radically changing the direction of theological education would remain difficult. Anxious that a student would now be rejected on doctrinal grounds, the Professor of Geometry, Henry J.S. Smith – a friend of Jowett at Balliol and a prominent reformer – stressed that the new degree should be

> worthy of the University; that is tainted neither by fanaticism nor irreligion; above all, that it is not removed from all possibility of control by those upon whom, mainly and above all others, rest the responsibility of the education given in this place.[31]

Student opinion was not dissimilar. The *Oxford Undergraduate's Journal* agreed with the need to improve theological education and also supported the sentiment that a man's position in the class list ought not to "vary with his soundness". This, the student journal suggested, "would be obviously too absurd; it would be to establish a kind of doxameter – a high and low water mark of orthodoxy –

---

30. E.B. Pusey, *The Board of Examiners for the Proposed Theological School* (dated 10 June 1868; Bodleian G.A. Oxon c.84 (470)), 3.
31. Henry J.S. Smith, *The Proposed School of Theology* (Oxford, 1868), 2-3.

with a very moveable scale in the shade of opinion of the examiner."[32] But where should limits be set? How audacious could Oxford's theological students be? The *Undergraduate's Journal* argued that while it was good to have "Divinity Professors allied with the changing representatives of more secular learning and authority", yet "it would be well that examiners should be chosen, who would themselves at least hold the Apostles' Creed, and that the books prescribed for study should not be the mere foam of Divinity – the books thrown up in the surgings of thought, as empty as they are evanescent."[33]

The new statute was passed by Congregation on 20 November 1868 and was due to be confirmed by Convocation in early 1869, but an extraordinary legal challenge from two prominent London barristers and Oxford graduates confirmed that the statute needed to be reintroduced; the Hebdomadal Council had acted illegally by dividing up the legislation that had been initially promulgated and the legislative process would have to start again, with the first examinations in Theology delayed until Trinity Term 1870 at the earliest.[34]

A new statute was introduced into Congregation on 4 May 1869, which provided for an examining board of the vice chancellor, the proctors, and the three divinity professors. A proviso was included that allowed the professors to veto the appointment of an unsuitable examiner if they were united in their disapproval. Henry Smith described the veto, if abused, as exercising "a chilling and deadly effect on the School."[35] The clerical grip might inhibit students from thinking originally and being given the opportunity to answer "the

32. *The Oxford Undergraduate's Journal*, 10 December 1868.
33. *Ibid.*
34. *The Theological Statute. Case submitted to Mr. George Mellish, Q.C., and Mr Charles Bowen, Q.C., with their Opinion* (privately printed, dated January 1869).
35. H.J.S. Smith, *The Proposed School of Theology* (1 June 1869; Bodleian G.A. Oxon c.85 (438)), 2.

very questions in which, perhaps, he takes the keenest interest, and in dealing with which he would be most likely to distinguish himself."[36]

Both Burgon and Pusey thought the possibility of an undergraduate heretic as "purely imaginary." Students "will *not* broach Heresy, who go in to be examined in Divinity. They have not done so in times past. Why should they begin to do so *now?*"[37] Pusey was more apocalyptic:

> It is the deep conviction of very many of us and of myself...that such a School must be either a great blessing or a great curse...My own conviction, impressed upon me from those early days of the study of that great heaving of German thought, has been that everything solid is subservient to faith, that shallowness is even a grievous injury to faith. Be a man's own opinions what they may, if he have anything solid, he must, so far, subserve truth, and, if truth, faith.[38]

As is evident, the different approaches to theological study and teaching in the writings of Smith and Pusey were not wholly dissimilar to those articulated between Hampden and the Tractarians in the crisis around the former's appointment as the Regius Professor of Divinity in 1836. There continued to be two divergent, and seemingly irreconcilable, approaches to theological epistemology. For Pusey, all theological study subserved faith and the source of Christian theology was *a priori*: a revelation from God to the faithful, conceived as a body of doctrinal truth, that was received rather than examined and analysed like a specimen of natural history. For Jowett, Smith, and other liberals, theological truth was not simply accepted but was the result of committed and critical study; faith had nothing to fear from the truths revealed by 'scientific' theology.

---

36. H.J.S. Smith, *ibid.,* 3.
37. J.W. Burgon, *To Professor Henry J.S. Smith (The Theological Statute)* (dated 18 May 1869; Bodleian G.A. Oxon c.85 (442)), 2.
38. E.B. Pusey, *The Proposed Statute for a Theological School* (12 May 1869: G.A. Oxon, c.85 (439)), 2-3.

The pattern of theological study and teaching that was thus secured by Pusey and Liddon was therefore far from what had been desired by liberals. Ten years after *Essays and Reviews,* the honour school seemed to be less a development in the direction of Oxford theology's reconciliation with the higher criticism and was, more, an instrument of reaction. This was an altogether different context for undergraduate theology from Cambridge, as we shall see, and nowhere are those differences more noticeable than in the content of the teaching and examination of the new honour school.

A 'Course of Reading for the Church's Service'

While the settlement that was determined in 1869 might have caused no small dissatisfaction for many in the University, it was nevertheless marketed with confidence to the Church Congress that convened in Nottingham two years later. During the afternoon of 12 October 1871, delegates were discussing 'Clerical education in connection with the Universities and theological colleges' and Robert Payne-Smith, a moderate Evangelical who had just vacated the Regius chair of Divinity to become dean of Canterbury, reported the developments at Oxford with enthusiasm.

Payne-Smith reflected upon how theology "had dwindled down" to that "homeopathic dose" in the *Rudiments of Faith and Religion,* the divinity examination: "If a man wanted more than this, his *alma mater,* instead of bread, offered him Geology or Chemistry." Now, he claimed theology at Oxford was placed upon "a fairer basis". Some people, he reported, had wished that the new examination would become "a school of Speculative Theology". With *Literae Humaniores* given over to greater post-Kantian reading, Payne-Smith reassured the assembled that Oxford theologians objected to "the direct learning of doubt" and "scientific scepticism" in their own school, recognizing that "even the most practised intellect may lose its right bearing if it venture out upon this sea, far from the old landmarks, which the experience of the past has set up."[39]

It was this concern, Payne-Smith claimed, which had been the cause of dispute over the selection of examiners. Nonetheless, he was pleased to claim that the final statute ensured that no "extreme and party men" would force their "opinions" upon the school's students, and secured Oxford theology from "that mighty wave of negative thought" which was evident in Greats. Truly, this was a "course of reading for the Church's service" while a first in the school requires "as much patient industry and as large natural powers as a first in the school of *Literae Humaniores*":

> If every year we can imbue young active minds with the love for these studies, and send them out into life with a competent knowledge at least of the foundation-lines of theology, we may hope, in due time, to see many of them become themselves master-builders, and the whole body of our clergy and laity feel their influence for good.[40]

"Advancing boldly during the last few years in the van of improvement", Payne-Smith's inference was that the clergy could confidently send their sons to Oxford if they wished to avoid "the Scylla of Rationalism and the Charybdis of Ritualism". Here, he implied, was a superior training in theology to that found in the 'partisan' theological colleges.

Payne-Smith's promotion of the new honour school seems to be aimed at reassuring those in the wider Church of England who were nervous about the secularization of the universities and the spread of agnosticism. Despite the continued commitment to liberal education in the university, he defined it clearly as a vocational school of the

---

39. *Authorized Report of the Church Congress, held at Nottingham October 10, 11, 12, & 13, 1871.* (London: W. Wells Gardner, 1871)
40. *Ibid.*

Church that scorned the modern Continental philosophy that was now being read in *Literae Humaniores*. After classical Moderations any student seeking 'moral excellence' could now find refuge, it was implied, in the theological school. Its curriculum was certainly conservative. At its foundation, there were six different components of examination: Holy Scripture (with New Testament Greek compulsory, and a knowledge of Hebrew and the Septuagint left optional); the Creeds and Articles; Ecclesiastical History and the Fathers; the Evidences of Religion; Liturgies; and, lastly, Criticism. "The first two," Payne-Smith said, were "indispensable for high honours"; for a first class, a student would have to select two further subjects. To gain a fourth class, the candidate had to pass an examination in St Paul's Epistles and in one other subject (but not Criticism), or in Hebrew. For a third, it was recommended that students could add a sound grasp of Pearson's *Exposition of the Creed*, Butler's *Analogy*, the Book of Common Prayer, and Book V of Hooker's *Ecclesiastical Polity* with three books of Eusebius, the last requirement, however, being optional.

Examination papers confirm Payne-Smith's presentation of the new theological school as a reading of the Bible and tradition that avoided philosophical speculation and the perils of historical criticism. The papers merely expanded upon the weak critical engagement with the biblical texts which was characteristic of papers in the *Rudiments of Faith and Religion*; questions demanded answers which were almost purely descriptive of biblical texts and were often apologetic in their intent; after all, theological learning was considered by the examiners as the reception of a body of a knowledge, rather than a certain kind of understanding. This is evident in the first available examination papers from 1873:

1. Give an account of the plagues of Egypt in their right order. How far did they correspond to phenomena of more or less common occurrence in that country? *(Old Testament I)*

7. The foreign and domestic policy of Hezekiah. *(Old Testament II)*

9. Describe the position of the chief places connected with our Lord's ministry, naming the miracles or other incidents which are associated with them. *(New Testament I)*[41]

Ecclesiastical history, which in the early years of the honour school did not extend beyond the Anglo-Saxon church, was no more demanding in the critical understanding expected from its students:

Describe the Council of Chalcedon. *(Ecclesiastical History I, question 4)*

What traditions of special interest as to the Apostolic Age are mentioned by Eusebius in these books? From what source do they come? *(Ecclesiastical History II, question 5)*

What do you know of the life and work, (1) of Archbishop Theodore, (2) of Alcuin, in connexion with the Anglo-Saxon Church? *(Haddan and Stubbs, 'Council and Documents', question 5)*

'Dogmatica' was limited to a reading of the church fathers, the Articles, and Pearson. Also descriptive, there was no awareness of historical context or the development of early Christian doctrine, unless

What fact in the religious life of the Jews after the Captivity tended to prepare them specially for the coming of the Messiah? *(Dogmatica, question 6)*

can be understood as presupposing such an awareness. The paper on apologetics expected students to have read Hooker (Book I of

---

41. *Second Public Examination: Honour School of Theology, Trinity Term 1873* (Oxford: Clarendon Press, 1873).

Ecclesiastical Polity) and Butler's Analogy, such that the examiners could ask such questions as

> Give a summary of the Chapter on the 'Appointment of a Mediator and Redeemer.' *(Apologetica, question 7)*

Beyond Butler, examiners seemed to believe that Tertullian's defences of the Christian faith were sufficient for the aspiring ordinand of 1873:

> [Describe] Tertullian's argument for the resurrection of the body, and for the eternal duration of a future state. *(Apologetica, question 12)*

For the student who took the paper in 'Liturgica', an understanding of the ancient Liturgies, the Sarum rite, and the various forms of the Book of Common Prayer, alongside Hooker's defence of certain liturgical practices were expected: a resolutely English curriculum that avoided all suggestions of ritualistic or Roman Catholic influence.

An historical consciousness was not even a feature of *Critica Sacra,* which was limited to the history of the Canon (according to Eusebius, the Muratorian Fragment, and Irenaeus) and – for the most adventurous – some basic questions on textual criticism:

> 1. The limits of conjectural emendation.
> 2. The critical value of a version. On what does it depend?
> 3. Ancient attempts at forming a harmony of the Gospels, and their influence on the text. *(Critica Sacra).*[42]

The format and content of the honour school was essentially as Pusey had intended: a combination of biblical, historical, and pastoral preparation for undergraduates intending to take holy orders. The

---

42. *Second Public Examination: Honour School of Theology, Michaelmas Term 1873* (Oxford: Clarendon Press, 1873).

manoeuvring over the selection of examiners had evidently been worthwhile. In 1875, the examiners were Thomas Espin, George Rawlinson, John Nutt, and Edmund Ffoulkes. Both Espin and Ffoulkes had left the university twenty years earlier, and were both non-resident clergymen of the kind that caused so much grief to reformers in Convocation. Nutt was sub-librarian at the Bodleian and was responsible for examining the language papers. Rawlinson, Professor of Ancient History, was similarly conservative; he had given the Bampton Lectures in 1859 on the 'Truth of the Scripture records'.[43] The primary object of English theology – as presented by the honour school in Oxford during the 1870s – was to engage with Holy Scripture in its original languages and to explore its exposition through assiduous reading of the church fathers. Although the examiners of the theological school were evidently reluctant to lead undergraduates 'astray', it is probably true to say that their questions faithfully mirrored the methodologies of the professoriate of this period, for whom the terms 'systematic' and 'speculative' were roughly synonymous.

The conservatism of the course is reflected in a lecture list from Michaelmas 1869: [44]

43. Peter Hinchliff, "Religious Issues, 1870-1914" in *History of the University,* 7:100.
44. "List of the Professors' Lectures for the Present Term" in *The Oxford Undergraduate's Journal,* 25 October 1869.

Subject of Professorship	Professor	Subject of course	Text	Books
Regius Professor	R. Payne-Smith, D.D.		Book of Genesis	Field's edit of the Septuagint
Margaret Professor	C.A. Heurtley, D.D.	The Creed.	Bishop Pearson.	St. Athanasius, de Incarnatione Verbi.
Hebrew	E.B. Pusey, D.D.	Psalms i.- l.	The Hebrew Text.	
Pastoral Theology	C.A. Ogilvie, D.D.	The Ministry of the Christian Church	The "Ordinal of the Church of England."	The "Clergyman's Instructor."
Ecclesiastical History	W. Bright, D.D.	History of the Early Church, from the close of the Second Century	Eusebius	
Exegesis of Holy Scripture	R. Scott, D.D.	The Epistle of St. James.		
Septuagint (Grinfield)	W. Kay, D.D.	On the Septuagint Version as a help to the Interpretation of the New Testament.	The Alexandrine Text of the LXX.	

Directed towards a basic understanding of the Bible with some practical elements of ministry included, lectures clearly avoided the modern theological writings that Pusey had so feared. The most recent work of English theology on the undergraduate reading list was Bishop Butler's *Analogy,* first published in 1737. By the late 1860s, the works of Butler were recognized by many prominent theologians at Oxford as dated, as containing arguments *ad homines* that failed to answer the questions of the nineteenth century. The most prominent questioning of the *Analogy* came from H.L. Mansel, until 1868 the Regius Professor of Ecclesiastical History. In his

Bampton Lectures entitled 'The Limits of Religious Thought' in 1858, Mansel had adopted a Kantian scheme, mediated through the writings of Sir William Hamilton, to assert the complete otherness of God and the limitations of the mind in ascertaining revelation.[45] The placing of Butler on the theology syllabus was a quite deliberate rejection of Mansel's approach and a rebuke to those, like Mark Pattison, who had been instrumental in its removal from the Greats syllabus in 1860.[46]

A set of lecture notes from Michaelmas 1869, the first term of the new theological school, reinforces the sense that in both content and method, many Oxford theologians were reluctant to engage with contemporary critical work. A young Reginald W. Macan, later master of University College and an advocate of theological modernism, attended Henry Liddon's lecture series on the First Epistle of St. Peter that term, and noted their content in some detail. He describes the conservative teaching of Liddon, who had asserted the Petrine authorship of the epistle, pointing out the "remarkable correspondences with Ep. to the Romans" and dating the epistle to the Neronian persecution in AD 64.[47] He stressed to his students the "historical objective fact of Christ's Resurrection", which was the "foundation" for all "subjective feeling". Most interestingly, Macan records Liddon's synthesis of the Genesis narratives with the geological findings of the previous decades:

> These instances by which the Ap[ostle] supports his argument are very remarkable, because in two of them the NT goes out of its way to

---

45. See especially S. Hennell, *Essay on the Sceptical Tendency of Butler's 'Analogy'* (London, 1859), which asserted that it was an argument *ad homines,* unfit for the philosophical challenges of the nineteenth century; quoted in Jane Garnett, "Bishop Butler and the *Zeitgeist*" in *Joseph Butler's Moral and Religious Thought: Tercentenary Essays,* ed. C. Cunliffe (Oxford: Clarendon Press, 1992), 71.

46. Mark Pattison, *Memoirs,* 324.

47. Bodl. MS. Eng. th. e. 42: R.W. Macan's lecture notes from Liddon's lectures on the First Epistle of St. Peter (1869), 15.

confirm the truth of parts of the history of the O.T. which have always been more inclined to be questioned; viz., the flood & the destruction of the cities of the plain. This passage is not decisive as to the universality of the flood: but looking to the Bk of Genesis we can scarcely doubt that a Universal Deluge is there meant. The Ark rested on Ararat (16,200 ft.) there are indeed higher mountains; but they wd. not be habitable at great elevation. The antiquity of the world may go back millions & millions of years before the creation of man; quite consistently with revelation. We are simply told that God created heaven & earth IN THE BEGINNING. The fossils that are now found, produced & quoted to confute the truth of the OT narrative of the Creation may perfectly well have belonged to some prehistoric age before the creation of man. Dr Buckland used to be a good authority on this question. The lecturer speaks with the greatest diffidence.[48]

To have quoted Buckland as a "good authority" for evidence of a universal deluge in 1869, thirty-three years after Buckland had rejected such conclusions himself, must have seemed very peculiar to the audience of undergraduates.[49] While Liddon, as Pusey's protégé, obviously represents the more conservative element of Oxford theology during this period, his condescending tone towards scientific developments must have encouraged the characterization of the teaching of the honour school as being isolated from other university disciplines.

A study guide written in 1880 by F.H. Wood, a tutor at St. John's, unambiguously stated that "the object of the Theological School is not to test the pious feelings of the examinees, or even the orthodoxy of their opinions".[50] Nonetheless, there was an unmistakeably

---

48. *Ibid.,* 168-9: lecture from 17 December 1869. Liddon's reference to Buckland is perhaps all the more surprising since the Tractarians had poured scorn on the responses of natural theology to modern scientific thought and, in particular, the writings of William Buckland since 1830. See N.A. Rupke, "Oxford's Scientific Awakening and the Role of Geology" in *History of the University,* 6:556-62.

49. Buckland had rejected his earlier belief in a universal deluge in *Geology and Mineralogy* (London: William Pickering, 1836).

50. F.H. Wood, *A Guide to the Study of Theology, adapted more especially to the Oxford Honour School.* (Oxford: James Thornton, 1880), 63.

'orthodox' direction and purpose to the young school, as is evident from Wood's advice to students to devote themselves especially to "*Biblia Sacra*" in the course of their studies:

> . . . it is obvious that the chief value of the study of Biblia Sacra, and of the New Testament especially, lies in its being the foundation to a very large extent both of the substance and form of expression of Christian dogma. Again, a very large part of Ecclesiastical History is the history of the gradual growth of doctrinal definitions, as they became necessary from time to time to controvert errors which denied or undermined one part of other of Catholic doctrine.[51]

For teachers of the newly created theological school, it was essential that the future clergy understood that – contrary to what was being taught to those students in the other modern honour schools – knowledge of God was not the by-product of a moral philosophy or subject to the methodologies of natural science. Rather, theological knowledge was carefully circumscribed as that revelation which was given in Scripture and preserved by the Church; by exposing the undergraduate to the triumph of orthodoxy in the first five centuries of Christianity, he too might "controvert errors" as they arose in his own generation.

Problems with the Honour School

The origins of the honour school, and the teaching and examination that it offered in its first years, did not naturally commend itself to the wider university. Gaining support from tutors in the colleges, in particular, was crucial to ensuring that able students were encouraged to read for the honour school. By the middle of its first decade, it was apparent that theologians would need to work harder to gain

51. Wood, *ibid.,* 8–9.

good candidates as poor results provoked concern among the school's teachers.

In 1875, J.W. Burgon published a pamphlet entitled 'A Plea for the Study of Divinity', which was concerned with the poor condition of theology at Oxford. Having been instrumental in the school's foundation, Burgon now wrote a critique of the university's efforts and a plea for renewed investment in theological learning.[52] His concern arose from the very disappointing results of the early years of the school, coupled with the approaching abandonment of clerical fellowships in the colleges. Of the 187 candidates who had graduated in the honour school of theology during its first five years, only twelve students had been placed in the First Class during that period, compared with 50, 64 and 61 in the Second, Third, and Fourth Class respectively. The "Divinity School rises somewhat slowly into the position which belongs to it by right ... It halts conspicuously in its progress", he wrote.[53]

Theology's travails as a new honour school were not unique; introducing any course to 'rival' *Literae Humaniores* was a struggle. An interesting comparison might be made with the undergraduate school of jurisprudence. Like theology, law at Oxford would never take the form of professional training as this was provided beyond the university, in the Inns of Court in London and from the Law Society. The university accordingly offered a course that was deliberately "comparative and philosophical" in nature.[54] The Honour School of Law and Modern History was introduced in 1850, and a separate School of Jurisprudence was introduced in 1872. Few who took the school in its early years as a joint school achieved distinction in later

---

52. J.W. Burgon, *A Plea for the Study of Divinity at Oxford* (Oxford: J.H. Parker, 1875), 2.
53. J.W. Burgon, *ibid.*, 3.
54. Barry Nicholas, "Jurisprudence" in *History of the University*, vii, 385ff. Cf. F.H. Lawson, *The Oxford Law School, 1850-1965* (Oxford: Clarendon Press, 1965).

life, and even less so after it become a school of jurisprudence.[55] The standard, Charles Firth later recalled, "was not set high, and was not designed to be high".[56] Like theology, those reading for law were obliged to study set texts in the form of Blackstone's *Commentaries on the Laws of England* and Justinian's *Institutes,* in part because there was a fear of professorial indoctrination, as was deemed to be the norm in Germany.[57]

Unlike the theology school, however, there was a very limited supply of teachers. Although the Regius chair of Civil Law was one of the oldest in the university, the Chichele chair in International Law was only established at All Souls' College in 1859 and the Corpus chair of Jurisprudence in 1869. The public teaching of law was offered by a small number of teachers, and was poorly supplied when compared with the abundance of clerical fellows in Oxford able to teach theology and the large theological professoriate.

Theology's poor results were thus more worrying. Both schools suffered from a lack of access to college scholarships (and, accordingly, scholars), which were almost all reserved for those preparing for *Literae Humaniores.* For Burgon, theology's problems went well beyond being denied college scholarships. He was certain that theology's difficulties were the direct result of recent reforms, which he believed were anti-clerical. He wrote to ensure that "Religious Education in this University shall not suffer *more* than recent legislation has rendered unavoidable".[58] He was particularly vexed by those Oxford colleges that had failed to fulfil the stipulation of the Tests Acts 1871 "to provide sufficient religious instruction for all members thereof *in statu pupillari* belonging to the Established

---

55. 'Jurisprudence', 387.
56. Charles Firth, *Modern History in Oxford, 1841-1918* (Oxford: Blackwell, 1920), 6.
57. Nicholas, "Jurisprudence", 387.
58. Burgon, *ibid.,* 3.

Church" and could name more than one college (in October 1874) in which there was no provision whatsoever for students preparing for the compulsory examination in the 'Rudiments of Faith and Religion'; no foundation was thus being given for those who might consider proceeding to the honour school of theology.

Burgon may have had in mind the diminishing provision for theology at Balliol College. Since becoming master in September 1870, in succession to Robert Scott, Benjamin Jowett had terminated the Catechetical Lectures that had been established in the college by the will of Richard Busby (who died in 1695). With the approval of the Charity Commissioners, monies from the fund were now used at Balliol for a theology prize. When Scott had heard of the reform, he had written to the Visitor of the college to complain that, "in the hands of the present Body, there is danger that it may turn out to be an inducement & stimulus to 'free handling' of Holy Scripture – the only thing that some people understand by Theology."[59]

Burgon would have empathized with Scott. Students in such colleges, Burgon asserted, "have nothing to build upon. . . . Not a few have come to me and freely avowed that though they entered Oxford with the intention of qualifying themselves for the Ministry, they found it impossible to persevere in that intention". A large number of students, he claimed, were thus being left "scandalously unprepared".[60] Such was the paucity of teaching fellows in theology that inter-collegiate lectures had been introduced, the first of their kind in the university, and Burgon was pessimistic about the chances of colleges investing in further provision for theologians.[61]

59. Balliol College Archives, MBP 23 (Letters to and from Visitors, 1854-1907): R. Scott to Bishop J. Jackson; quoted in John Jones, *Balliol College: A History* (Oxford: Oxford University Press, 2005), 213.
60. *Ibid.,* 13.
61. For information on the inter-collegiate lectures, see E.W. Watson's contribution to the *University of Oxford Commission* (Oxford, 1877), 96n. The unlikelihood of new fellowships was not just a result of anticlericalism, however; college investments were yielding poor returns in

Was Burgon correct in his assessment? He was certainly not alone in offering such criticism. This is revealed in the collection of replies that were attached to the copy of the pamphlet that Burgon, in due course, donated to the Bodleian. This collection is a valuable source for our understanding of how theologians perceived the progress or otherwise of their discipline during this period. There are replies to Burgon's pamphlet from such senior figures as Lord Salisbury (then at the India Office), a number of bishops, professors and tutors at Durham, Cambridge, and Oxford, and even a previous vicar of the University Church, a certain John Henry Newman.[62]

Many of the responses are short expressions of gratitude for Burgon's pamphlet. Many others replied, however, giving their own account of theology's travails. Evident in those responses is a shared frustration that university reform was broadly anti-clerical in character and damaging for theology's prospects as an undergraduate discipline. Oxford theologians, in particular, who might have been offended by Burgon's more caustic remarks, seem instead to have agreed with his criticisms.

Henry Liddon, who had been a key figure in the establishment of the School and was, like Burgon, a leading clerical conservative at Oxford, believed that if "it makes others –teachers and learners – as dissatisfied with themselves & anxious to do better, as it does me, it cannot fail to do a great deal of good".[63] Liddon believed, however, that little would be provided by the university in response to Burgon's plea for new professorial chairs, fearing that "we should

the last third of the nineteenth century, and expansion of both Oxford and Cambridge would not be possible until the creation of the University Grants Committee in 1919.

62. Bodleian, Oxford, MS Eng. th. d. 13: J.W. Burgon, *Schola Theologiae.* Many of the replies, such as those of Sir John Taylor Coleridge (f.35) and Salisbury (f.17), simply thanked Burgon for the pamphlet and detailed their intention to read the pamphlet forthwith, stressing that it was a subject of "extreme importance" (Salisbury) and that "there ought not to be two opinions about it" (Coleridge).

63. MS Eng. th. d. 13 (ff.11–12): H.P. Liddon to J.W. Burgon, 28 January 1875.

be told that each has already been provided for".[64] There was consensus, nonetheless, over Burgon's assertion that "our Colleges are no longer adequately manned" for the task of theology:[65] Charles Heurtley, the Lady Margaret Professor of Divinity, expressed astonishment at a recent examination for a clerical studentship (i.e. a fellowship at Christ Church) where no divinity paper had been set;[66] and James Mozley, the Regius Professor of Divinity, lamented that it "is just when theology resumes her place that she finds the old tutorial system fading, and discouragement in the colleges".[67]

Was this problem common to other theological departments in England? William Churton, a theological examiner, member of the Board of Theological Studies, and a divinity tutor at King's College, Cambridge, was in broad agreement with Burgon.[68] Like him, Churton denounced the "present system which makes Fellowships mere literary prizes enjoyed to a large extent by non-residents" and he believed a "large voluntary effort" was needed to secure fellowships in divinity in the coming years so that "appeals might be made to young men on obtaining Fellowships before their income is bespoken for other purposes", perhaps referring to his own college's tradition, reformed only very recently, that had allowed foundation scholars of Eton to become fellows of King's merely on account of residency.[69]

---

64. Liddon was wrong to be pessimistic; his request as the Dean Ireland's Professor of Exegesis for a new professorship for the interpretation of Holy Scripture in his submission to the University of Oxford Commission in November 1877, in part to correct the 'deficiencies on the score of biblical knowledge' in the Honour School, was accepted: *Minutes of Evidence taken by the Commissioner* (London, 1878),152-3, 290. John Wordsworth was elected as the first Oriel Professor for the Interpretation of Holy Scripture in 1883.

65. Burgon, ibid., 18.

66. MS Eng. th. d. 15 (f15): C. Heurtley to J.W. Burgon, 29 January 1875.

67. MS Eng. th. d. 15 (f113):J.B. Mozley to J.W. Burgon, undated.

68. Although Churton had been sceptical of the curriculum from the outset, suggesting that too much time was given over to historical study. For a report of discussions of the syndicate appointed to consider theological examinations, see *Cambridge University Reporter,* 1871-2, 41ff; quoted in Owen Chadwick, *Westcott and the University* (Cambridge, 1963),24-5.

The Regius Professor of Divinity at Cambridge seems to have been far less pessimistic about theology's prospects than his colleague at King's College. Brookes Foss Westcott, who had only returned to Cambridge in 1870, agreed that their age presented challenges, and that it "is impossible not to feel that the greatest danger of our Church in this her time of splendid opportunity springs from the influence of a number of clergy who have great years and little knowledge".[70] He was upbeat about current progress in his own university, however, stating that "at Cambridge we do not suffer from many of the difficulties which you describe". The results of the first year's "experiments" in the theological tripos, he believed, were "very satisfactory". The results of the tripos's first year certainly suggest a more stable, though by no means magnificent, record of achievement: two firsts, five seconds, and seven thirds. Six candidates left with an ordinary (pass) degree.[71]

There was also a far more positive response from Durham University. Adam Storey Farrar, Professor of Divinity and Ecclesiastical History, told Burgon in reply to his pamphlet that he was inclined to take

[A] more cheerful view, as a stranger, of the prospects of Theology in Oxford than you do, who view it only by noticing how far the standard reached falls short of your own high ideal. I think, from what little I have seen of the men trained in the Theol[ogical] School, that it is doing its work fairly. I think the general character of the work done at Ordinations by the Oxford passmen is improving. Also the tone of the

---

69. MS Eng. th. d. 15 (ff121-22): W.R. Churton to J.W. Burgon, 21 Feb 1875. Churton was appointed examiner in theology (initially for the Special Theological Examination) in 1867 (Cambridge University Archives Min. V. 101A: Minutes of the Board of Theological Studies, 52).
70. MS Eng. th. d. 15 (ff39-40): B.F. Westcott to J.W. Burgon, 1 February 1875.
71. *Cambridge University Reporter,* 1875-6. It is important to remember that at this stage, to leave Oxford or Cambridge with an ordinary or pass degree was not unusual, with honours far from being the expected course for undergraduates as today.

younger Fellows strikes me as intensely more reverent & believing than 10 or 11 years ago when I left the place.[72]

Even if the calibre of students passing through the theological school was poor, Farrar asserted that they were gaining a basic knowledge and grasp of the Bible, doctrine, and history, which would have otherwise escaped them prior to the school's creation, when their theological learning would been restricted to the paltry requirements of the examination in 'The Rudiments of Faith and Religion', and when ordinands would have known more of the *Iliad* than the Bible.

Examination of the replies seems to suggest that while there was broad support for Burgon's concerns about reduced resources for theology in the universities after the Tests Act, particularly from Oxford respondents, theologians were not altogether as pessimistic about their discipline's general prospects as Burgon, Liddon, or Churton. Farrar and Westcott, in particular, suggest that theologians at other universities were in fact hopeful for the opportunities for teaching and scholarship provided by the new theological courses that had been introduced simultaneously with the abandonment of religious tests; notwithstanding the impending threat to the remaining clerical fellowships, many saw the changes to the university as an opportunity rather than a danger for the Church of England and theology.

Reviving Theology

If anxiety about theology's condition was perhaps more acute at Oxford, how then did theologians like Burgon believe that standards might be raised? Although Burgon and many of his colleagues believed that theology's future looked dire as a result of reduced funding and a more secular culture within higher education, he, and

72. MS Eng. th. d.15 (ff138–39). A.S. Farrar to J.W. Burgon, 8 March 1875.

many of his respondents, also believed that there were identifiable priorities for theologians as they sought to raise their subject's position.

Part of the theological school's problems, Burgon believed, was that it was perceived as a "narrowing" course that took undergraduates away from a reading of the classics prematurely. Indeed, this was how the course had initially been conceived by the school's founders in 1868, Burgon included; the school had been created for the Church of England and its ordinands.[73] By 1875, however, Burgon had altered his definition of its purpose. Now, perhaps as a result of wider suspicion of a professional school for undergraduates, especially for clergy, he was keen to emphasize the school's position within the faculty of arts, stressing that its education was by no means purely professional and claiming that it was a more authentically liberal education than the increasingly popular alternative schools of Modern History or Natural Science. Theology, he asserted, continued the study of Greek and Latin after Moderations and even introduced Hebrew; keen to persuade those who were unconvinced that theology was a satisfactory course for undergraduates, the "prescribed course of study", Burgon asserted, "effectually ensures a prolonged acquaintance with those subjects which have ever been deemed the best instruments of liberal education".[74]

The 'restoration' of theology, he believed, would accompany such a deeper acquaintance with the Bible and tradition: "Theological Learning has declined," he wrote, "in this our Church of England . . . *as a Science*".[75] Little attention, he asserted, had been given in

---

73. For example, see Robert Payne-Smith's presentation to the Church Congress of 1871 that this was a "course of reading for the Church's service": *Authorized Report of the Church Congress* (London, 1871).
74. Burgon, *Plea*, 9.
75. *Ibid.*, 27. Italics are Burgon's.

the past generation to the textual criticism of the New Testament, the study of the Septuagint, the re-editing of the church fathers, and the study of liturgical history, and here now was an opportunity to begin such study and so strengthen the position of theology within the university. Burgon was careful to stress that he was not advocating the modelling of the theology at Oxford upon its German counterparts, where the

> 'advanced Criticism' so much vaunted, (chiefly I suspect by those who are only imperfectly acquainted with their Church Catechism,) stands towards the Scientific Knowledge of Divine Things somewhat in the same relation as deserters who have lost their way, and are floundering in the mire, towards the Army with serried ranks which is marching on to Glory without them.[76]

A renewed commitment to 'theological science' would not require undergraduates to employ the faithless methods of the continental sceptics that Burgon so feared ("Theology, instead of being a discovery, is always a revelation"[77]). Rather it was a call for the recognition that "Sacred Learning demands the highest intellectual gifts, as well as the largest literary attainments". If the honour school, and theology more generally within the university, were to regain the position that he believed the discipline merited, then all must attend to the study of the Bible:

> . . . I take upon myself to assert that until the dignity of Holy Scripture is more faithfully recognized, (by teachers and learners alike,) no real progress in Divinity will be made either here or elsewhere. The knowledge of the Bible is the best knowledge, after all: and assuredly without it there can be *no* Divinity. The Examiners in the School of Theology are respectfully invited to make proficiency in *this* Knowledge THE ONE ESSENTIAL THING in Candidates for honours; a real acquaintance with THE BIBLE the *sine qua non*, without which it shall

76. *Ibid.,* 36.
77. *Ibid.,* 37.

be simply impossible for those who come before them to achieve for themselves distinction of *any* sort in the School.[78]

This call to a more assiduous study of the biblical text as the means of raising standards mirrors an approach to theology that was by 1875 well established at Cambridge, with Lightfoot, Westcott, and Hort believing that careful attention to history and text was the best defence against German criticism and a wavering faith.[79] Burgon's call for a "scientific theology" that was rooted in study of the Bible was coupled with a frustration that religious enthusiasm seemed limited at that time to the 'structural decoration' of churches, Church music, "party feeling", and Church congresses and unions, while "sacred learning" was largely forgotten, and "slackness, [and] apathy" abounded.[80]

Interestingly, Burgon's pamphlets received unlikely support from one of the young liberal scholars and the leading advocates of biblical criticism, Thomas K. Cheyne, a fellow of Balliol. He responded warmly to the leaflet:

> I hope it is not presumptuous of me to thank you for your very interesting pamphlet on a subject in which, from different points of view, we both have so deep an interest. But I have long felt that there was one aspect of theology – viz., the philological & text-critical – [in] which persons of very different theological schools could help each other & the cause.[81]

78. *Ibid.,* 52. Liddon echoed this desire in his submission to the University Commissioners in 1877, and felt that a "too exclusive attention to the requirements of students in the theological school on the part of some of the professors" had meant theology as a discipline had suffered. "In their hands", he wrote, "the subject deserves an independent, and so to term it, disinterested treatment, which should make it attractive to older minds and to as large a circle as possible". (*Minutes,* 153)

79. Cf. Thompson, *Cambridge Theology in the Nineteenth Century,* 106-21.

80. Burgon, *Plea,* 14.

81. Bodl. MS Eng. th. d. 15, f. 63, T.K. Cheyne to J.W. Burgon, 3 February 1875.

Desiring editions of the various biblical codices and the Septuagint, and an improved knowledge of the Semitic languages, Cheyne commended Burgon's call for a more systematic study of text, and, rather sharply, ended the letter with the lament, "What a shame that the Oxford Professor of Hebrew [i.e. E.B. Pusey] cannot make up a Class for the Exact Criticism of Hosea!"

Such a sharply aimed attack at Pusey from Cheyne suggests that the younger generation of theologians at Oxford felt restrained by the model of scholarship promoted by the Regius Professor of Hebrew. Oxford needed to confront the question of whether it engaged in theology to defend what were considered *a priori* truths, or whether it was willing to allow the "Divine purpose" to be "ascertained . . . by unbiased *a posteriori* criticism", as was now largely accepted at Cambridge.[82]

While Cheyne, Burgon, and others were undoubtedly keen to provide an approach to the study of text and history that was now *de rigueur* at Cambridge, it was evidently still true that the vast majority of candidates for the honour school intended to take holy orders in the Church of England and, more likely than not, were also undergraduates who had not performed well in their first public examinations and were not likely to excel in Greats. As John Henry Newman commented in his reply to Burgon, it was very difficult to establish such a "scientific" school whilst still hoping to attract those students who were destined for ministry, and who were inclined to satisfy the practical requirements. "I shall be very glad", he wrote, "to hear that you succeed in forming a really learned theological school – but the difficulty is to do so, yet secure for οἱ πολλοί of your clergy such a general and superficial knowledge as is necessary for work in the world."[83]

82. J.F.A. Hort to J.B. Lightfoot, 1 May 1860 in A.F. Hort, *Life and Letters of J.F.A. Hort* (London: Macmillan, 1896), 115.

Graduates could, far more cheaply, find that "general and superficial knowledge" in one of the various diocesan theological colleges of the Church of England (or one of the theological halls of the Nonconformists) where graduates were not required to engage, for example, in textual criticism of the Codex Vaticanus. While certain figures were well intentioned in seeking to raise standards, they could not afford to be too specialist; the syllabus needed to reflect the requirements of the bishops for ordination (a good knowledge of the Bible, early Church history, Hooker, and the Book of Common Prayer). Accordingly, while providing a greater commitment to textual and historical criticism would naturally strengthen theology's position in the wider university, and commend itself more readily to the senior common rooms of the colleges, it was also likely to make it less attractive to prospective ordinands, who were disinclined to embark upon such a narrowly professional route to becoming a Bachelor of Arts and preferred to leave their theological studies until after graduation.

Raising the standard of theology at Oxford, therefore, was a task that was not simply about securing resources and fellowships. Convincing both students and the wider university that the theological school was a respectable course of liberal education required that the content of theology itself changed, and that the university undertake a more rigorous approach to study and teaching including critical textual and historical study. As Newman observed, it was unlikely that this could happen whilst still expecting students to gain the practical and pastoral skills that were seen to be "necessary for work in the world".[83] What also becomes apparent, however, is that such change as was required was not impeded just by structural problems, but by personalities (as noted in Cheyne's response). Correspondence from the Bodleian Special Collections and Pusey

83. Bodl. MS Eng. th. d. 136-7, J.H. Newman to J.W. Burgon, 6 March 1875.

House Library seem to confirm such an analysis, as we shall now observe.

Committee Wrangling

Despite a common concern for a more satisfactory, critical study of the Bible, the church fathers, and liturgy, and the renewal of theological learning within the Church of England, Burgon's manifesto did not result in a sudden rise in standards. Instead, results in the school worsened; in 1877, 1878, and 1880 the First Class was empty and by the end of its first decade, seventy-five percent of students who had achieved honours during the school's first decade had been placed in the Third or Fourth Class. However hard theologians worked to convince the rest of the university and prospective candidates that it was a worthwhile course in the faculty of arts, the theological school was still perceived as a professional course, intended for either those Greats men destined for the Church who could spare and afford an extra year to dedicate themselves to theological study (and, invariably, these were the same men who made up the First and Second Class), or those less able students unlikely to succeed in Greats, but who could be gainfully employed before ordination.

What is suggested in the final section of this chapter is that Oxford theology was also hindered by a basic inability of its leading figures to relate to the reformed structures of the university. Evidence for this assertion is drawn from an extraordinary board of studies that was established in early 1878 to consider how standards might be improved. The committee consisted of E.B. Pusey, William Bright (Regius Professor of Ecclesiastical History), Archibald Sayce (at this point, a deputy professor of comparative philology), Henry Liddon (Dean Ireland's Professor of Exegesis), and Charles Heurtley (Lady

Margaret Professor of Divinity), and was tasked with considering the curriculum and reading lists for the School.

Correspondence from the board, held in the Library of Pusey House and the Bodleian Special Collections in Oxford, reveals sharp disagreements over the purpose and composition of the school during the course of this committee's work. In particular, the sharply differing attitudes to the school and theology at Oxford are noticeable in the contentious discussion over alternative subjects in the Ecclesiastical History papers. William Bright had not unreasonably believed that students who were to become, almost to a man, Church of England clergymen, should be examined on their knowledge of the European and English Reformations. Pusey, however, strictly forbade any departure from the curriculum as then arranged, asserting that no alternatives should be permitted and students should not deviate from the compulsory study of early church history to AD 461. The inclusion or exclusion of the Reformation from the curriculum was not simply a minor syllabus dispute. As will be evident from the following correspondence, the debate over its inclusion evinces how different Oxford theologians understood the essence of the Church of England, theology's role in the university, and how the Christian tradition was to be communicated to the next generation of clergy.

For Bright, the study of the Reformation was an obvious means to students' understanding the distinctive character of the Church of England. In early February 1878, he had persisted in asserting the need for its inclusion and the special board voted against the will of Pusey to introduce the alternative. Bright wrote to Liddon – in the hope that he might mediate – that it was "very painful to find oneself bound to go counter to Dr Pusey's wishes". Yet

> He does not, I am sure, know…the sort of criticisms to which the School is subject…But, even were no such criticism inevitable…I

should be firmly convinced that it was our duty to recognize the events which determined the form of our existing Anglicanum, which made the Church of England to wear her special aspect as distinct from the mediaeval and Latin aspects, as an important and necessary branch of Ecclesiastical History to young English Churchmen.[84]

Pusey's principal objection, as communicated through Liddon as mediator between the two professors, was that the introduction of a further period in Ecclesiastical History "will play into the hands of Rome; not because they need do so, but, because if they are studied before the Primitive Period, there are plenty of materials in them for doing so."[85] The shape and role of ecclesiastical history was not merely a consideration of academic breadth for Pusey and Liddon. Rather, they were fearful that the introduction of an examination paper on the Reformation would bolster the position of the more Protestant members of the professoriate, such as Charles Heurtley or Robert Payne-Smith. Liddon wrote to Bright that,

> As you and I understand it, [the Reformation] is the purification (not without much accompanying damage) of the English Church, which yet it left intact as to all essentials; but it is also the act by which the Churches of the great part of "Reformed Xendom" ceased to exist, except in name and form. But Sayce, and Payne, and Heurtley and four-fifths of Oxford, understand something very different from this; and you seem without fuller explanation, to be taking part with their Protestant conception of the Reformation movement...[86]

Liddon offered a moderate expression of Pusey's fears to William Bright. Pusey, however, had written to Liddon only the day before, assuring his faithful friend that any look of weariness was not as a result of Hebdomadal Council meetings. Rather

---

84. Oxford, Pusey Ho., MS Liddon 27: Letter from W. Bright to H.P. Liddon, 9 Feb. 1878.
85. Oxford, Bodl., MS Eng. lett. d. 301 (ff.86-9): Letter from H.P. Liddon to W. Bright, 12 Feb. 1878.
86. Ibid.

> What does oppress me is Bright . . . Yesterday, the result of this plan of mine for the division of subjects promised to be that, as far as Oxford is concerned, all which other Tractarians (and among them myself) had tried to do for above 40 years for the Church of England would be reversed. One central intellectual employment had been to direct people's minds to early centuries: in them lies the strength and defence of the Church of England: in these we deepened our own faith and wished to deepen the faith of others ... Bright's plans for the study of Eccl[esiastical] Hist[ory] which the Board of Studies accepted yesterday will destroy among young men the study of antiquity.[87]

For Pusey, history ought to deepen "our own faith and...the faith of others," the study of antiquity having been central to the Tractarian agenda in the Church of England for the antecedent forty years. A reading in the mediaeval papacy, on the other hand, risked a "love for [that] which is grand and shows power, individual or collective." Professor Bright, Pusey claimed, "delights in what is strong and poetic" and Pusey told Liddon that he had recently "heard of a young man, who went straight from a lecture of Bright's, full of graphic pictures of S. Leo, to make his submission to the Roman Church."[88] For Pusey, the minor changes approved by the board resulted in "the work of my whole life" being "here undone." In a letter the following day, having heard of Bright's complaint to Liddon, Pusey was even more pessimistic, stating that "I then have no more to say about Theology ... the bitter fruit will be for you, alas, to gather ... I shall suggest nothing as to the School of Theology, and shall leave the question of Hebrew to [A.H.] Sayce."[89]

Pusey's departure from the board only further infuriated William Bright, who wrote in strong terms of this "letter of abdication", grieving Pusey's reception of his letter. It was, he stated, "very unlike the usual relations of Canons of Ch.Ch. to each other":

87. MS Liddon 27: Letter from E.B. Pusey to H.P. Liddon, 11 Feb. 1878 (italics mine).
88. Ibid.
89. MS Liddon 27: E.B. Pusey to H.P. Liddon, 12 Feb. 1878.

148

The plain conclusion forced upon me is that it would be best for him, could he see it, to resign the Chair, while it would be possible to do so on terms that would secure a Christian successor. But it is hopeless to speak of this. Meantime, we must simply do the best we can, ignoring as far as we can the obvious fact that he has got past the time at which he can work with others, as one of a body in which majorities must decide . . . it is not good for any man to be a Pope, and that it is not right that we, who are supposed to be associated with him as a colleague, should concede, even to him, a predominant authority.[90]

Even Edward King, the irenic Regius Professor of Pastoral Theology, was "of one mind" with Bright. "He thinks" Bright informed Liddon, "that to yield to the Doctor in this matter would be 'fatal' to the interests of the Theological School" and "wishes, as I do, to ignore as much as possible the Doctor threatening retirement, and put it down to his age."

Liddon pleaded with Bright to remember the age and dignity of Pusey:

We must, I think, feel daily that he cannot be with us for very long, and that when he is gone, we shall sorrow over anything that has caused him any pain that could have been spared him.[91]

Bright assured Liddon that he felt "very tenderly towards … [Pusey's] increasing infirmities, particularly his deafness amid a conversation on a subject which interests him deeply."[92] However, anticipation of the board's meeting that Friday in Pusey's rooms only exacerbated the situation, especially after Pusey told Heurtley that he had no intention of "holding himself aloof from … proceedings."[93] At the meeting,

---

90. MS Liddon 27: W. Bright to H.P. Liddon, 13 Feb. 1878.
91. Bodl., MS. Eng. lett. d.301 (ff.90–91): H.P. Liddon to W. Bright, 13 February 1878.
92. MS Liddon 27: W. Bright to H.P. Liddon, 13 February 1878
93. MS Liddon 27: W. Bright to H.P. Liddon, 14 February 1878. Pusey had told Liddon only the day before that "he will sit by [in his own house], taking no part." (Bodl., MS Eng. lett. d. 301 (f.90): H.P. Liddon to W. Bright, 13 February 1878)

nonetheless, Bright reported to Liddon (who had been absent) that Pusey had

> denounced our resolution about the alternative books twice over as "disastrous" and as a "deviation from the true duties of a Board of Studies," and expressed regret that he had ever proposed it, meaning, of course (for he does not mean anything else,) the School of Theology...[94]

While the argument continued, despite occasional relapses of gentility, Pusey retreated in despair. Later in the same month, he wrote to Liddon in apocalyptic language of what had befallen the school:

> Why will they have all the details of what I think pernicious to the young men and to the Church of England, settled before my eyes? It is enough to have survived all I care for in Oxford, except sound teaching for the good souls such as you and King or Wordsworth would give. Perhaps in years to come, when I am gone, if the bad effects which I apprehend come, some might have misgivings. But any how I simply get out of the way ... A father is not required to see the child, which was given him to nourish, bring up, strangled in his old age before his eyes.[95]

The "evil done", he wrote the next day, "comes from those who would secularize or rationalize the School of Theology".[96] For Pusey, the move to change the syllabus for Ecclesiastical History was perceived as partisan; in his mind, seeking to shift the emphasis in undergraduate study away from Antiquity was all part of that "evil" which sought to "secularize" theological learning at Oxford.

Correspondence from the board, on one level, indicates very personal difficulties, not least with what must have been a frustrating deafness for Pusey, his pain at the changes being made to the

---

94. Ibid.
95. MS Liddon 27: E.B. Pusey to H.P. Liddon, 18 Feb. 1878.
96. MS Liddon 27: E.B. Pusey to H.P. Liddon, 19 Feb. 1878.

university, and his inability to determine the curriculum. However, it also reveals that even the simplest of curricular changes could not be easily introduced in an atmosphere where some figures were concerned primarily for the improvement of academic standards and the introduction of more critical study while others remained fixated on the threat of "those who would secularize or rationalize" the school's work and defending the doctrine of the Church of England, as received. Nonetheless, despite his age and condition, Pusey's aggressive defence of the school is not altogether surprising; the school was, as he commented, comparable to his "child", it having been so instrumental in his and Liddon's plan to consolidate theology as a Christian discipline at Oxford.

What seems to be evident in the correspondence of 1878 is a growing awareness in the theological professoriate that the original character of the honour school was unhelpful for its position in the wider university and made the course unattractive for senior tutors, students, and parents. Such a characterization of the school, and theology more generally at Oxford, would not have been aided by the damage to Pusey's reputation following the ritualist controversies of the previous decade. "[Pusey] does not know," wrote Bright, "the sort of criticisms to which the School is subject", and ultimately a different model of teaching and study would be necessary if the school's position were to be secured within the University. Bright's complaint, too, of Pusey's "predominant authority" ("…it is not good for any man to be a Pope") also indicates that, in the end, the other professors had recognized that the theology's future was questionable so long as Pusey dictated its life.

An Alternative Model: Cambridge and the Theological Tripos

Oxford's political difficulties in responding to the changed circumstances of religion and clerical influence in the university are only confirmed when Oxford theology is compared with the work of scholars at Cambridge during the same period. At Cambridge, the introduction of the theological tripos was seen by its creators as less of a "break-tide" (as Burgon described the Oxford school at its introduction) than an opportunity.[97] Seven months before he had become Regius Professor of Divinity at Cambridge in November 1870, Westcott, aged 45, had been appointed to a university syndicate to consider theological examinations in the university, very possibly at the instigation of J.B. Lightfoot. In February 1871 the syndicate recommended, and successfully instituted, the demand that those seeking higher degrees in divinity provide a dissertation on biblical studies, ecclesiastical history, or dogmatic theology, and evince the sort of advanced study of language and history that was now seen as basic in other disciplines.[98] Defending the regulations in the Senate, Westcott had "supported the choice of such subjects as Ecclesiastical History and Biblical Criticism on the ground that faith depends upon the facts of religion, and therefore too much stress cannot be laid on the facts of criticism and history, especially in the present times."[99]

By May of the same year the theological syndicate also proposed the establishment of a theological tripos that would contain three papers on the Old Testament, two papers on the Greek New Testament, six papers on the history of the Church and its doctrines, and a twelfth paper of "selected works of modern theologians".[100] There was criticism of the amount of space allotted to history, including from Churton at King's, but it was clear that the course from the outset was intended to be 'scientific' in the manner that Cheyne and select others had desired at Oxford. Believing in the

97. Burgon, *Plea,* 13-14.
98. *Cambridge University Reporter,* 22 February 1871.
99. *Reporter,* 15 March 1871.
100. *Reporter,* 31 May 1871.

'catholicity of study', Westcott did not believe, as the ageing Pusey did, that the university should exist purely to convey a body of Christian dogma to the next generation. The first religious duty of the university was rather "to study man and his world, in science and history, and so to inspire the student with 'the sense of their sovereign wonder.'"[101]

Denying "the looming hiatus between a critical theology which was not religious, and a religious theology that was not critical', he thus sought to shape a tripos that, "on the same footing with the other Honour Triposes", sought to receive critical study and engagement with the rest of the University of Cambridge.[102] It was with good reason that Hort could write to John Ellerton in February 1872 that Westcott's enthusiasm was "resuscitating the theological faculty from its sleep of centuries".[103] This approach to theological work in the reformed university was evident in the examination papers of the two schools. In the first papers set for the theological tripos in January 1874, Cambridge students were asked such questions as "Describe briefly the structure of the Book of Genesis. What is meant by Jehovistic and Elohistic documents?" and "Illustrate from this Gospel [St. John] the theory that it is, in relation to the Synoptics (1) supplementary, (2) corrective of possible misconceptions. Does it ever indicate by implication a fact not stated in *its own* direct narrative?"[104] Even after Burgon's call for a more 'learned' study of Bible and tradition in 1875, by contrast, the honour school at Oxford still included such questions in its 1877 papers as 'How far can the age in which David lived be urged in excuse of the failings in his

101. *Reporter*, 1 November 1871; Chadwick, *Westcott*, 29, quoting B.F. Westcott, *On some Points in the Religious Office of the Universities* (Cambridge, 1873), 69.
102. *Reporter*, 25 October 1871.
103. A.F. Hort, ed., *The Life and Letters of Fenton John Anthony Hort* 2:167; quoted in Chadwick, *Westcott*, 21.
104. *The Cambridge University Reporter*, 1873-74: Old Testament, General paper, question 3; The Gospel according to St John and the First Epistle to the Corinthians, question 4.

character' (*Old Testament*) or 'Give an account of *either* the book of
Joshua, *or* the prophecy of Joel' (*Old and New Testament, 1877*).[105]
A question on the relationship between the Synoptic Gospels did
not appear until Trinity 1875, and the Mosaic authorship of the
Pentateuch was not questioned until 1879.

It seems clear that the theological tripos was initially more
hospitable to other disciplines and critical challenge than the honour
school at Oxford. There is no comparable evidence of serious
disagreement among Cambridge faculty members during the 1870s,
and from this fact it seems not unreasonable to assume that structure
for the tripos seems to have received wider support from Westcott's
colleagues than had the honour school among Pusey's colleagues
at Oxford. The collaborative leadership of Westcott, Lightfoot, and
Hort seems to have ensured a more visible unity within the faculty
and a commitment to the academic standards that were *de rigueur* in
other disciplines in the humanities; indeed, the triumvirate had been
working on a revised version of the New Testament since the spring
of 1853, with the gospels being published in 1871.[106] The 'Cambridge
model' certainly seemed to provide a context in which undergraduate
theologians performed better at examination. During its first decade
of examination (1875-85), 13.7 percent of Cambridge theological
students were placed in the First Class, in contrast to merely 4.8
percent of theology finalists at Oxford between 1870 and 1880. It
is not unreasonable to judge that these better results were in large
part because the younger Westcott and his colleagues had instituted
a course that was more successful than Oxford's at presenting itself
as a commendable programme in liberal education, attractive to both
students and tutors, and less haunted by the religious disputes of a
previous generation.

105. *Second Public Examination: Honour School of Theology* (Oxford: Clarendon Press, 1877).
106. Thompson, *Cambridge Theology in the Nineteenth Century,* 108.

Substantial evidence from results, examination papers, the correspondence between members of the board of studies at Oxford, and comparison with Cambridge's theological life, all seem to suggest that it was not merely the professional character of the honour school, nor its lack of resources in the reformed University, that hampered the life and work of Oxford theology during the first decade of its existence following the Universities Tests Act. Cambridge was not in a substantially different position from Oxford: theology was, in both universities, now a minority activity, and the reform of the university had certainly weakened the influence of theologians and the Church of England in both institutions. Likewise, the 'revival' of theological learning through the tripos and honour school, and reform of the higher degrees had, in both contexts, arguably occurred fifty years too late to make any radical difference to the growing marginalization of theology as a university discipline.

It seems, too, that it was Oxford's own leadership that was in large part responsible for the problems for its theological life in the decade following the Tests Act. Cambridge theologians, evidently, did not generally seek to struggle against the forces of secularism through the university's theological institutions as Pusey, Liddon, and other conservative figures had done at Oxford in the late 1860s and 1870s. Rather, the Cambridge faculty benefited from a collection of relatively young scholars enthusiastically embarking upon textual and critical study of the Bible while Oxford's senior positions were occupied by figures who still laboured under the belief that theology should act as a bulwark of Christian orthodoxy in a university that was otherwise surrendering to rationalism and 'unbelief'.

Conclusion: Theology after the Tests Act

This chapter has not sought to suggest that Oxford theology should simply be interpreted as Cambridge's obscurantist older sibling.

There was throughout the first decade of the honour school a group of scholars at Oxford, notably A.H. Sayce, Edwin Hatch, and T.K. Cheyne, who were engaging in the critical literary and historical study of the Bible and the Christian tradition – a so called 'scientific' theology – that had long been established in continental faculties and in some measure among theologians in Cambridge.

Substantial change and security for theological education within the wider university would only arrive with a new generation of professors, however, and a new 'Board of the Faculty of Theology' from October 1882 that, some decades removed from the political and religious turmoil of the 1840s, would be less exercised about the protection of the Church of England at Oxford and more concerned for the sort of 'scientific' learning that was advocated by Cheyne. In particular, the professors who would replace Liddon and Pusey upon the latter's death in 1882 – William Sanday and Samuel R. Driver respectively – sought a more dispassionate and neutral account of biblical and ecclesiastical history during successive decades such that the strident religious divisions of the preceding fifty years would soon be replaced by the more irenic routines and discourse of the modern research seminar, faculty-board work, and thesis supervision.[107]

Studying Oxford's theological life during this period of the university's secularization of its offices and degrees suggests that theologians would, after the Universities Tests Act 1871, be working in a context that was altogether more diverse and challenging. As ecclesiastical privilege was being steadily stripped from both universities, and an ethos of learning emerging that was no longer explicitly Anglican, theologians were eventually compelled to reconsider the very purpose of their discipline. As analysis of the honour school of theology during its first decade has suggested, it was clear that theologians at Oxford were developing an embryonic

107. The B.Litt. was introduced in 1895, and the D.Phil. in 1917.

sense of its need to satisfy various 'stakeholders' of its worth in the university after the Tests Act if it was to survive and flourish. Despite the proliferation of graduate theological colleges, the faculty would, for the coming century and beyond, always need to be valued by the wider Church of England, and especially the episcopal bench, which needed to be convinced that Oxford offered a credible course for the ordinands who would continue to constitute the large majority of candidates for the BA. Secondly – and it was not until the death of Pusey that this seems to have become crucially important – theologians needed to convince the wider university of theology's worth as a department of the humanities, offering a sound liberal education, a good number of firsts, and engagement at all levels with textual, historical and philosophical study of the kind that was expected from graduates and scholars in a leading university.[108] This transition from the seminary-faculty as shaped by Pusey would not pass without comment among theological conservatives. When the Board of the Faculty of Theology began its work in 1882, Henry Liddon would complain that, like Cambridge, Oxford was now overtaken by professors whose "first thought is, not the well-being of the Church of Christ, but the influence and reputation of the University".[109]

To satisfy one constituency inevitably resulted in disappointing another, and the theological faculties at Oxford and Cambridge would grapple with their complex responsibilities well beyond the circumstances of the 1870s; the honour school's curriculum was but one element in a process of readjustment for theologians over the

108. Cf. William Ince's inaugural address as Regius Professor of Divinity in 1878, *The Past and Present Duties of the Faculty of Theology* (Oxford: J. Parker, 1878) where, apart from delineating the Faculty's responsibilities to ordinands and the wider church, Ince insisted that the Faculty had a responsibility "towards the world of literature and culture, who are confronted with mighty theological problems raised by science and criticism" (41).

109. Bodl. MS Eng. lett. d. 302 (ff.8-9): H.P. Liddon to W. Bright, 12 Feb. 1882.

following century. The morally dubious exclusion of Nonconformists from the higher theological degrees and from being examiners in the honour school, in particular, would soon provoke further pressures for reform from within and outside university life, which in turn would evoke some altogether different reflections upon the object of a modern theology faculty. At the same time as theologians were struggling to interpret and employ new methodologies in biblical studies, the history of doctrine, and ecclesiastical history, their institutional context was changing considerably. Although Cambridge theologians can be deemed to have made significant steps in shaping theology for the reformed university, and indeed opportunities for reform would soon arise in Oxford after the death of Pusey, in the end both faculties would struggle to respond satisfactorily to their altered circumstances. Ultimately, the introduction of undergraduate courses in theology probably proved far less significant for the practice and vitality of theology in the university than the arrival, prior to the turn of the century, of Nonconformist theological institutions in both cities.

Left: Renn Dickson Hampden (1793-1868), by Henry William Pickersgill; oil on canvas, painted 1840s/1850s; by kind permission of the Governing Body, Christ Church, Oxford.

Right: Edward Bouverie Pusey (1800-1882), by George Richmond; black and white chalk, circa 1890; © National Portrait Gallery, London.

Top Left: Arthur Penrhyn Stanley (1815-1881), by Lowes Cato Dickinson; oil on canvas, painted 1840s/1850s; ©
National Portrait Gallery, London.

Top Right: Henry Parry Liddon (1829-1890), by George Richmond; oil on canvas, c. 1870; by kind permission of
the Warden and Fellows of Keble College, Oxford.

Bottom: Benjamin Jowett (1817-1893), probably by The Autotype Company; after Desire Francois Laugee
collotype, after 1871; © National Portrait Gallery, London.

Top Left: William Sanday (1843-1920), by Leonard Campbell Taylor; oil on canvas, 1908; by kind permission of the Governing Body, Christ Church, Oxford.

Top Right: Henry Scott Holland (1847-1917), by The Church Agency; published by Eglington & Co carbon print, published late 1880s-mid 1890s; © National Portrait Gallery, London.

Bottom: Arthur Cayley Headlam (1862-1947), by Unknown photographer; vintage bromide print, circa 1920s-1930s; © National Portrait Gallery, London.

3

———

Nonconformity and the *Lux Mundi* Faculty, 1882–1914

". . . the battle as to all outward things is lost . . ."[1]

At some point during the afternoon of Saturday, 16 September 1882, a telegram was delivered to Canon Heurtley at Christ Church which simply read, "All over very calmly 3.20pm please have bell tolled".[2] On the Monday the canons of Christ Church received the body of Edward Bouverie Pusey, brought to Oxford by road from Ascot Priory. His funeral on St Matthew's Day was described thus by Henry Liddon:

> The procession of clergy, five or six abrest, reached round three sides of the Great Quadrangle; the fourth, between Dr. Pusey's house and the Cathedral being kept clear. As the Coffin was brought out of the well-

---

1. E.B. Pusey to Henry Acland, quoted in H.P. Liddon, *Life of Edward Bouverie Pusey* (4 vols., London: Longmans, Green & Co., 1897), 4:358.
2. Pusey House Library, MSS Heurtley 2/1/1: Telegram of J. Brine to C. Heurtley, 16 September 1882.

known door in the south-west corner of the quadrangle, the Cathedral Choir came to meet it. By the sides of the Coffin there walked as pall-bearers those who represented the friendships and the labours of his life: the Archdeacon of Oxford and the three Canons who were also the Theological Professors (Dr. Heurtley, Dr. Bright and Dr. King), Mr. Gladstone, the Hon. C.L. Wood, the Earl of Glasgow, the Hon. and Rev. C.L. Courtenay, the Warden of Keble College, and Dr. Acland...At the west door of the Cathedral the procession was met by the Dean of Christ Church, the Bishop of Oxford, and Dr. Liddon, who read the opening sentences then said the concluding part of the Service, committing his 'dear body' to the grave beneath the floor of the central aisle 'in sure and certain hope of the resurrection to eternal life.[3]

The death of Pusey concluded fifty years of religious turbulence and controversy, and certainly marked the end of an epoch for Oxford theology. Pusey had been Regius Professor of Hebrew since 1828: fifty-four years in office, and sixty-three years since he had arrived at Christ Church as an undergraduate. The collegiate university that Pusey left behind was transformed from the 'seminary' of his youth. In his latter days, these changes had deeply disturbed him. He had written in 1879 to Henry Acland that

[F]or this place I trust that things are at their worst now. I have given up struggles which I once made; the battle as to all outward things is lost...There never was so much unbelief as now. I dread the compromisers much more than the antagonists...[4]

As Pusey wrote, the Commissioners appointed by the Oxford University Act 1877 were laicizing almost all of the college fellowships and headships. This marked the dissolution of the last significant bond of governance between Church and university, leaving clerical conservatives dismayed. When Pusey's protégé, Henry Liddon, sought to erect a library in memory of Pusey in 1882,

---

3. H.P. Liddon, *Life of E.B. Pusey,* 4:386-87.
4. E.B. Pusey to Henry Acland, quoted in Liddon, *ibid.,* 4:358.

he wrote to Friedrich Max Müller with a grim prognosis for the future of the Church in the University:

> ... the effect of recent legislation will be to confine the Clerical Element in Oxford to the Divinity Professors and the Chaplain-Fellows in the course of a very few years. As it is, no actual or intending clergyman would stand for a fellowship at some very distinguished colleges; he would know that he would have no chance of being elected. Probably it will take 25 years to work out these changes to their full results; but, by that time, the Church, already a very enfeebled and discredited force in the University, will be literally nowhere. . . . We Churchmen made poor use of . . . [the Colleges], and, probably deserved to lose them; but their loss is, in view of the future interests of Religion in this country, momentous. It means a threatened divide between faith and learning, more serious and mischievous than that which alas! already exists. And you know what this points to beyond.[5]

Before his death, the approaching "divide between faith and learning" left Pusey and Liddon anxious about the future of the Church and religion more generally in England. In 1878, Francis Paget described Liddon to his elder sister as "almost desperate and Dr. Pusey most sadly prophetic . . . it does seem as though the Church was practically set aside in Oxford by the changes which the Commission are making here [at Christ Church] and elsewhere."[6]

Frederick Temple, a contributor to *Essays and Reviews,* had noted the "extraordinary reticence" of the young men with regard to religious issues.[7] It was also true that more men with first-class degrees from Oxford were becoming schoolteachers in England's leading public schools and fewer were seeking fellowships and, thus, holy orders. Whereas 49.4 percent of those matriculating at Oxford

5. Bodleian Library MS Eng. c. 2806/1 (ff.87-88): Letter of H.P. Liddon to F. Max Müller, 21 December 1882.
6. S. Paget and J.M.C. Crum, *Francis Paget, Bishop of Oxford* (London: Macmillan, 1912), 52.
7. Ernest G. Sandford, ed., *Memoirs of Archbishop Temple, by Seven Friends* (2 vols., London: Macmillan, 1906), 1:303.

in 1848/49 would become clergymen, by 1878/79 that figure had dropped to 29.2 percent. With the most able graduates unable to compete for fellowships unless they accepted the possibility of ordination, the further reform of college posts had become a necessity. As Alan Haig has shown, the reforms of 1877-82 were responsive to, rather than instigative of, Oxford's laicisation.[8]

Increasingly, too, the philosophical sensibilities of Oxford and Cambridge were more influenced by John Stuart Mill and Auguste Comte than by Bishop Butler, the works of John Henry Newman, or the sermons of the divinity professors. Many of Oxford's tutors had witnessed the ecclesiastical and religious turmoil of the 1840s and 1850s in their youth and seen the turning of clerical attention from apologetics to the internal matters of the Church. This is not to suggest, however, that the university became overnight a bastion of rationalism. Although the colleges widely accepted that fellowships needed to be opened, this did not naturally mean an influx of lay fellows or the resignation of those in orders. Even if dons began to see themselves as professional academics rather than clergymen engaged in teaching prior to finding a suitable living, by 1890 nearly of a third of college fellows were still in holy orders; in 1912, nearly a fifth.[9]

What was visible by the turn of the century was a religious pluralism in Oxford and Cambridge that naturally unsettled those who had conceived of the university as an institution exclusively serving the Church of England. With an increasing number of Nonconformists present in the colleges of the university and, with permission given for Roman Catholics to attend Oxford and Cambridge from 1896, there was now, as Brock has written, an "unsectarian, undenominational culture" that was "simply a reflection

---

8. Alan Haig, "The Church, the Universities and Learning in Later Victorian England," *The Historical Journal,* 29.1 (1986): 197-98; see also A. Haig, *The Victorian Clergy* (London: Croom Helm, 1984), 51.
9. M. Brock, "A Plastic Structure" in *History of the University,* 7:56.

of those views held in the English professional class."[10] Along with the rising number of laymen who wielded influence in the university and the corresponding weakening of the Church party in matters of governance, the increasing numbers of Nonconformists in the colleges at Oxford and Cambridge transformed the religious life of both universities. The arrival in 1886 of the Congregationalist theological hall, Mansfield College and then the Unitarian Manchester College in 1889 likewise transformed Oxford's theological life.

This chapter seeks to understand how theologians began to interpret the role and purpose of their discipline and faculty in this changing environment. Liddon's lament that Oxford had been given over to 'unbelief' testifies to the end of an era in which the Church of England dominated the life of the university. It was also the twilight period for those who believed theology – largely administered to students through the divinity examination – was the framework for all intellectual investigation and teaching. Our second chapter saw how, as the university was reformed and non-Anglicans were allowed to supplicate for the BA and then the MA, certain theologians adopted a defensive position and sought to use undergraduate theological education as a means of consolidating Christian belief and Anglican influence: a perceived "break-tide" against a wave of secularism and unbelief. As we saw, the weakness of the honour school of theology during its first decade suggests that this role for the modern theological faculty was not proving effective by the time of Pusey's death in 1882.

How did the new generation of scholars who succeeded Pusey revise the Tractarian and High Church shibboleths about theology's place in the university? Their methodology was visible most

---

10. M. Brock, *ibid.,*57. Some Roman Catholics had ignored the ban before 1896. See Dom Alberic Stacpoole, OSB, "The Return of the Roman Catholics to Oxford", *New Blackfriars,* 67 (1986).

strikingly, of course, in the publication of *Lux Mundi* in 1889 – a collection of essays that sought to reconcile Anglican theology and the higher criticism (of the Old Testament, at least). More controversially, the 'orthodox' understanding of miracles was soon being challenged. The Dean of Divinity at Magdalen, J.M. Thompson, questioned the historicity of the Virgin Birth and the physical resurrection of Christ in his 1911 book, *Miracles in the New Testament*. This provoked an uproar in the ecclesiastical establishment and the withdrawal of his licence to minister by the Bishop of Winchester (the Visitor of Magdalen College, E.S. Talbot; he had been a contributor to *Lux Mundi*).[11] Likewise, the growing influence of scientific historical approach and early psychological thought was in evidence in a volume published in 1912 and edited by the New Testament scholar at Queen's, B.H. Streeter. *Foundations: A Statement of Christian Belief In Terms of Modern Thought,* was another compendium of Oxford essaysmen but, unlike *Lux Mundi*, it did not display the same deference to unexamined tradition, and argued throughout for liberty in the pursuit of theological study. It was, as William Sanday said in a lecture defending *Foundations,* entitled 'The Restatement of Christian Theology', a book which, on the one hand, expressed "the earnest desire not to lose touch with the Church of the past, and on the other hand the honest and persistent attempt to restate the old truths in the modern form that most nearly corresponds to them."[12] This 'restatement' of the faith was itself "a venture of faith":

11. For a good examination of this Oxford generation's changing understanding of miracles, see James C. Livingston, *Religious Thought in the Victorian Age: Challenges and Reconceptions* (Edinburgh: T&T Clark, 2006), 138-149.
12. Christ Church Archives, Soc. xxiii c.123: Sanday Lectures: 'The Restatement of Christian Theology', 17.

. . . a venture that will need some tenacity and perhaps some courage. I am well aware that we start upon it in a spirit simply of complacent optimism. If we believe that the universe is one, and if – in spite of what may be said to the contrary – we also believe that it is essentially reasonable, then we may also believe that it will in the end be seen to be reasonable, that will not break up into fundamental contradictions, but that our thoughts about it will also work together into ultimate harmony.[13]

Sanday himself struggled to make sense of miracles and their place in the Christian tradition, and his advocacy of a "non-miraculous Christianity" proved deeply unsettling for many; reconceiving his own thinking on miracles, Sanday would stress that the Churchman's "proper province is history" and he will not "have one measure for sacred history and another for profane. There will be no closed compartments."[14]

The spirit of liberty in these volumes can be recognized in Oxford's changing approach to the practice of theology in the university. In the period leading up to the First World War, Oxford theologians can be seen, even more so than their usually more audacious Cambridge counterparts, to be completely rethinking the institutional position of English theology in the university. This was in part the response of Anglican theologians to the academic success of Nonconformists (particularly from Mansfield College) and the injustice of the latter's exclusion from the Divinity degrees and from being examiners in the honour school. Finding an equitable solution nonetheless led to some dramatic proposals for Oxford's theological

---

13. Ibid., 20.
14. William Sanday and N.P. Williams, *Form and Content in the Christian Tradition* (London: Longmans, 1916), 104; quoted in Livingston, *ibid.*, 148. Sanday's developing thought with regard to miracles can be read in his article 'The Meaning of Miracle' in H.S. Holland, ed., *Miracles* (London: Longmans, 1911) and in his contribution to the Church Congress of 1912, "Historical Evidence for Miracles", *Report of the Church Congress, Middlesborough* (London, 1912).

life that were only prevented from being implemented by the veto of Convocation and the ruinous effects of war.

Contrary to some characterizations, it is suggested here that Oxford theology at the turn of the century was proactively trying to find imaginative ways of relating the denominational pluralism of Oxford to the university and its 'scientific' methodologies, while being attentive to the essence of theology as a discipline rooted in worshipping communities. This '*Lux Mundi* faculty' sought to present a bold framework for theological study in the twentieth century and in the process – *pace* Scott Holland's rather too ambitious pre-war proposals – can be seen to be leaving behind the partisanship that had marked university theological life during much of the nineteenth. There would be limits. The challenges that were brought against Scott Holland's statute in 1913 indicate that, despite the faculty being ambitious to accommodate the Nonconformist churches, any new theological statute would have to be firmly rooted in a Christian framework; the 'undenominational principle' would not be tolerated at Oxford or Cambridge, even if it was finding favour further north in Manchester.

The Selborne Commission

Long before 1913, however, theologians were struggling to respond to the statutory changes in Oxford colleges that were resulting in the widespread laicization of fellowships. For some, the principal problem lay in the dilution of Oxford's Church ethos. Liddon had decried the "critical and literary atmosphere" that had been nurtured in Oxford by the admission of Nonconformists and promoted by "academical Liberalism" in an anonymously published article in the *Church Quarterly* in 1881.[15] This change of ethos had made "belief in a canon of inspired Scripture . . . as difficult as belief in the claims of an historic Church". John Wordsworth, a tutor at Brasenose who became the Oriel Professor of the Interpretation of Holy Scripture in 1882 and was later bishop of Salisbury, also viewed the reforms as critical for the practice of theology in Oxford:

> The accredited ministers of a religion are the natural persons to explain its Scriptures, and to show the meaning and relevancy of the currents of religious thought and controversy, and the social movements which make up its history. A merely philological knowledge of the Bible, and a positivist view of Church history, is worse than useless.[16]

These *cris de coeur* were to some degree provoked by liberal proposals for theology at Oxford. James Bryce, a prominent reformer and lay fellow, had called for a "purely undenominational Theological Faculty" and even recommended the eventual secularization of the divinity professorships in a speech to Nonconformists earlier in 1880.[17] In the meantime, Bryce proposed the compromise of separating the Regius chairs in Ecclesiastical History and Hebrew from their canonries at Christ Church. When considering a person for the Ecclesiastical History chair, Bryce even suggested that it

> [O]ught to be, *if not a positive disqualification, at any rate a disadvantage, to a man who stands for a chair of that kind, to be a Clergyman of any religious body...* The subject of Ecclesiastical History is one of so much importance and so much difficulty, requiring a mind to absolutely fair and impartial, that *it would be more safely intrusted* [sic] *to a learned and judicious layman than to any Clergyman...*[18]

---

15. [H.P. Liddon], "Recent Fortunes of the Church in Oxford", *Church Quarterly Review* 21 (1881): 215.
16. John Wordsworth, *The Church and the Universities: A Letter to C.S. Roundell* (Oxford: Parker & Co., 1880), 19.
17. As reported in *The Nonconformist* and reprinted in *The Guardian*, 2 June 1880.
18. The Hebrew chair was not uncoupled from the canonry until 1960, and then with difficulty (*Oxford Magazine*, 12 Nov. 1959; 26 Nov.; 3 Dec.; 28 Jan. 1960). Bryce's suggestion was condemned by J.W. Burgon in *Disestablishment of Religion in Oxford, the Betrayal of a Sacred Trust; – Words of Warning to the University* (Oxford: Parker & Co., 1880), 20, 27.

Such changes were unthinkable to Oxford's more conservative theologians, for whom religious commitment was a prerequisite for becoming a teacher. "Woe to him", wrote J.W. Burgon, "who supposes that some familiarity with the learned languages and plenty of self-reliance will qualify him to become a teacher of Divinity!"[19] Echoing his earlier pronouncements on theology, Burgon insisted that theology, "in the first instance [is] not a discovery but a *Revelation*". Theology could not be reduced to literary techniques that could be mastered by any one. Burgon warned that the introduction of lay teachers would only "poison the very fountains at which you invite the youth of England to come and drink freely…You will inevitably in the end drive away from Oxford the future clergy of the Church of England."[20] Indeed, the reforms now left Liddon doubtful about the usefulness of the theological honour school:

> It has shared the unpopularity of the Church in "Liberal" common-rooms, and the most influential tutors throughout the University have explicitly or tacitly discouraged it. Very few men of the highest order of ability have read for this school; while examiners have been anxious, rightly as we hold, to make the high honours in it represent at least the same amount of work and ability that they do in the school of *Literae Humaniores* [Greats].

Advising that it was generally better for a man to read Greats first, as the mind needed to "make its first experiments in philology on some less precious subject than the text of either Testaments, and its first efforts at philosophical questions than those which arise out of Christian dogma and ethics", Liddon seemed exasperated – if not regretful – with the School as a means of securing Oxford's theological life for the Church.[21]

19. J.W. Burgon, *ibid.,* 20.
20. *Oxford and Cambridge Undergraduate's Journal,* 25 November 1880.

The theological colleges were, Liddon averred, now the Church of England's principal hope (despite the foundation of Keble College in 1868 as a college for Churchmen, incorporated into the University in 1870).[22] Liddon resigned the Dean Ireland's chair and committed himself to his duties at St. Paul's Cathedral and writing Pusey's biography. When he was later asked whether he would like to be co-opted onto the new Board of the Faculty of Theology, he politely declined.[23] Less politely, he expressed relief in a letter to William Bright that he had escaped the "learned mob" that would constitute the board, prophesying that the "future of the Theological Faculty and everything else worth keeping here seems to me to be a very dark one – if looked at from a Christian as distinct from an Academical point of view."[24]

The further secularization of the colleges had prompted new Church of England foundations that encouraged theological study from that Christian point of view. Wycliffe Hall was founded in 1877 as an Evangelical hall for ordinands (along with Ridley Hall at Cambridge in 1881), partly out of dissatisfaction with the University. As its first principal, Robert Girdlestone, wrote:

> It is not enough that they should be able to talk learnedly about the authenticity of Daniel, the date of Job, the deutero-Isaiah, the Elohist controversy, or the Synoptic Gospels. They must read God's Word from another point of view, if it is to be the means whereby they may convince men of sin, show them the way of pardon, and lead them in the path of righteousness.[25]

---

21. [H.P. Liddon], *ibid.,* 238.
22. [H.P. Liddon], *ibid.,* 243; for more on Keble's foundation, see M.C. Curthoys, "The Colleges in the New Era", *History of the University,* 7:117-18.
23. Liddon stated that, "having nothing to do with the work of formal instruction in Theology....[I] have come to know less and less of what is going on in this Department within the University, and so am little likely to serve [as] a useful member of the Board." (Oxford University Archives FA 4/19/1/1: Minutes of the Board of the Faculty of Theology, 24 May 1883 (p.23))
24. Bodleian Library MS Eng. lett. d.302: H.P. Liddon to W. Bright, 29 May 1884.

Graduates who attended Wycliffe would nonetheless attend the faculty lectures from "some of the leading theologians in England" and the Hall's proximity to the university kept ordinands "in contact with a number of laymen who are training for other professions", lessening "the danger of clericalism and narrowness".[26] St. Stephen's House was also founded in 1876 and Pusey House was opened in 1884 in memory of the Hebrew professor. The first was a hall for graduates preparing for the mission field, while Pusey House sought to exhibit "solid learning allied to Christian faith and piety" and, challenge those tutors "unfriendly to the claims of Divine revelation". In so doing, it hoped to become a "home of sacred learning and a rallying-point for Christian faith" in the university.[27] Although the university and the colleges were now viewed by conservatives, both Anglo-Catholic and Evangelical, as more concerned with academic success than piety, these institutions still signified that Oxford was still a desirable centre for theological study and education, even if that education was now offered on a more voluntary basis on the periphery of the university.

Moreover, the claim that reform had wrested theology away from the bosom of the Church of England was not without substance. The admission of Nonconformists had necessarily required the alteration of the divinity examination, what had been viewed as the cornerstone of theology as an "architectonic science". 'The Rudiments of Faith and Religion' ('Rudders') now offered "substituted matter" for those "who objected to an Examination in the Thirty-nine Articles", but

25. Robert B. Girdlestone, *Wycliffe Hall: Its Nature and Its Object* (privately printed, 1878 (Bodleian Library G.A. Oxon, 8° 208)), 1. See also, Andrew Atherstone, "The Founding of Wycliffe Hall, Oxford", *Anglican and Episcopal History*, 73 (2004): 78-102.

26. J.B. Lancelot, *Francis James Chavasse* (Oxford: Blackwell, 1929), 105-6.

27. H.P. Liddon, *Dr Pusey and the Pusey House: A Sermon by Dr H.P. Liddon* (Oxford: Friends of Pusey House, 1974). See also F.W.B. Bullock, *A History of Training for the Ministry of the Church of England in England and Wales from 1875 to 1974* (London: Home Words Printing and Publishing, 1976), 13ff.

its principal problem lay in its increasing irrelevance, both to the theologically literate as much as the irreligious. The *Oxford Magazine* described it in 1883 as a "survival, which by losing its proportion has lost its dignity and significance," which undergraduates did not take seriously as a pass examination and which sought the "irreducible minimum" from the student.[28]

Lionel Herbert sat the examination in 1893 and recorded the experience in his diary:

> Golf with Austin and W.E.C[leaver]. Divinity Schools at 2 p.m. Viva at 5.15 [Revd H.B. George] asked four questions, to which I answered "Don't know". Verdict – "Doesn't know much about Samuel, but perhaps enough, and Gospels good." Testamur [i.e., a pass] at 5.30pm. Record time?[29]

In Magdalen College, it was considered poor form if one passed 'Divvers' on the first attempt, and Christ Church students supposedly prepared for the examination by eating a bag of popcorn; if one continued preparing after finishing the contents of the bag, likewise, one was deemed to have been too keen.[30] By 1911, divinity *vivas* were being performed at the rate of eighty a day and, even by 1886, was described as a "mechanical reproduction of the Scripture skeleton [which] is a scandal, and retards so much as it does anything."[31] The Principal of Wycliffe Hall could thus comment with some justification in 1880 that "the possession of a University degree means

28. *Oxford Magazine*, 28 Nov. 1883.
29. *Memorials of Lionel Herbert* (London: Oxford University Press, 1926), 38.
30. *History of the University*, 7:783-84. See also J.C. Masterman, *On the Chariot Wheel* (London: Oxford University Press, 1975), 77.
31. Hebdomadal Council Papers 88 (1911), 245-46; *Oxford Magazine*, 8 March 1886. John Wordsworth had provided lectures in the subject, seeing it as "an opening for the religious instruction of some who would otherwise have no occasion to study sacred subjects at Oxford" (E.W. Watson, *Bishop John Wordsworth* (London: Longmans, Green & Co., 1815), 129). "In spite of the novelty of a Professor lecturing on a Pass subject, and of the excellence of his motives," Watson suggested that "the course cannot have been successful, for it was not repeated." (*Ibid.*)

absolutely nothing from a religious point of view. A Mahometan, a Hindoo, an absolute Atheist, may take his degree at Oxford."[32] Conservative dissatisfaction with religious education in the university was understandable, and the creation of 'extra-mural' institutions is testament to the increasingly voluntary character of religion at Oxford in the decades following the Universities Tests Act.

Alongside these new institutions, the theological faculty itself was experiencing significant change following the death of Pusey and the departure of Liddon. The new Board of the Faculty was introduced in 1882, along with other faculty boards in Law, Natural Science, and Arts (which was responsible for two thirds of honour-school teaching and examination). William Gladstone appointed Samuel Rolles Driver as Pusey's successor, a young Liberal-voting fellow of New College who, although a Greats tutor, had published a number of commentaries and an influential *Treatise on the Uses of the Tenses in Hebrew* in 1874. This was in preference to Archibald Sayce who, in his memoirs, recounted that "though Gladstone and I were personal friends, I was now regarded as one of the leaders of the "German" critical theology at Oxford, and I knew that he considered me to be 'unsafe'".[33]

Although Driver was considered a less controversial appointment than Sayce, preferring to keep to textual rather than historical-critical study of the Old Testament, he had nevertheless been an important member of the Old Testament Revision Company from 1875, which had set about preparing what would become the Revised Version of the Old Testament. Simultaneously, William Sanday was elected as Liddon's successor in the Dean Ireland chair of exegesis, held

32. R.B. Girdlestone, *The Training of the Clergy* (Oxford, 1880), 3.
33. A.H. Sayce, *Reminiscences,* 213. Indeed, Gladstone had told Liddon that "under no circumstances could I give [Sayce] an ecclesiastical appointment", such were his methods of biblical study. (*Ibid.*)

in conjunction with a fellowship at Exeter College.[34] Sanday had been principal of Hatfield Hall in Durham and, before returning to Oxford in 1883, had published *The Authorship and Historical Character of the Fourth Gospel* (1872) and *The Gospels in the Second Century* (1876). Like Driver, Sanday was not at this stage known for his ready exploitation of historical-critical methods and, before the First World War, it had been the widely held opinion in German circles that Sanday had been proposed for the post by the archbishop of Canterbury because he was considered a defender of orthodoxy.[35]

Despite being 'moderates' in the field of biblical study, Sanday advocated in his inaugural lecture "a more *constructive* method in Biblical theology" which took account of "the relation of German philosophy to German criticism" and which might be employed by an "army of trained collators", young graduates who would collect material for advanced textual criticism. Clearly signalling a very different methodological approach from Liddon's, the lecture was warmly greeted by the liberal-leaning *Oxford Magazine*.[36] Driver was similarly distant in tone from his predecessor when he gave his first university sermon on 21 October 1883 on "Evolution Compatible with Faith," attributing Genesis 2.7 to "the second of the two main documents, which have been interwoven with rare skill in our Pentateuch, and which can be traced side by side to the close of the Book of Joshua."[37] Although his successor G.A. Cooke would describe him as a "grammarian first, critic and commentator second", he nonetheless was thought to have demonstrated to those who thought that "historical criticism seemed to threaten the strongholds of religion...that, on the contrary, it is the trusty ally, the *angelus*

---

34. Sanday became Lady Margaret Professor of Divinity in 1895.
35. E.C. Hoskyns, *The Fourth Gospel* (2nd edn., London: Faber & Faber, 1947), 35.
36. *The Oxford Magazine,* 28 February 1883.
37. S.R. Driver, *Sermons on Subjects Connected with the Old Testament* (London: Methuen & Co., 1892), 1; quoted in Emerton, "Samuel Rolles Driver", 125.

interpres, of those who regard the Bible as the record of divine revelation."[38]

Momentum towards a more positive assessment of biblical criticism among Oxford theologians increased with the appointment of Thomas Cheyne to the Oriel chair following Wordsworth's departure for the see of Salisbury in 1884. As one of the pioneers of biblical criticism in the German mode at Oxford, he was probably the first British scholar to accept that the Priestly Code was probably post-Exilic. He had also advocated a second professorship of Hebrew to the Commissioners in 1877 whose remit was purely "philological", given that Pusey was "practically a member of the theological faculty; and the candidates for Holy Orders resort to his lectures, and take certificates of attendance of those lectures to the bishops before ordination."[39] Regarded as a Balliol College radical before Pusey's death, by 1886 Cheyne could write in the preface to the fourth edition of his *Prophecies of Isaiah* that he was grateful that "free and reverent investigation" was now "sincerely tolerated" and the "younger generation, trained in a more historical school than their elders...[are] friendly to critical investigations."[40]

Beyond the realm of biblical studies, Edwin Hatch as Reader in Ecclesiastical History caused no small controversy in 1880 when he applied purely historical methods in analysing the organization and growth of the early Christian churches ("the facts of ecclesiastical history, being recorded in the same language, and in similar documents, and under the same general conditions of authorship, belong to the same category as the facts of civil history"). With

---

38. G.A. Cooke, "Driver and Wellhausen", *The Harvard Theological Review* 9 (1916): 251.

39. *University of Oxford Commission,* evidence, QQ 3743, 3744. See also T.K. Cheyne, *Essays on the Endowment of Research* (London: Henry S. King, 1876)

40. T.K. Cheyne, *The Prophecies of Isaiah, Vol. I* (4th edn., London: Kegan, Paul, Trench & Co., 1886), ix-x. In early 1870 Cheyne had insisted that "*a priori* canons of a theological or philosophical nature" ought to be separated from philological questions. (*Book of Isaiah* (London: Macmillan, 1870), xvii)

Driver, Sanday, and Cheyne, Hatch quietly and methodically demonstrated that critical scholarship – 'scientific theology' – need not be viewed as naturally inimical to the interests of faith.[41] Sanday would later write that when he arrived in Oxford as the Dean Ireland's professor, "the doctrine I ventured to preach was: Don't let us be too ambitious; let us plan our work on a large scale, and be content to take the humbler departments first."[42] While their achievements were arguably less impressive than the Cambridge 'trio' of Westcott, Lightfoot, and Hort, these men nonetheless transformed the theological culture of Oxford. Compared to their infamous 'morning star', Benjamin Jowett, the critical work of these men had far stronger philological and grammatical grounding. In the less febrile religious atmosphere of Oxford in the 1880s, these men were also far less eager to overturn established orthodoxies and far keener to produce solid critical – largely textual – scholarship that would act as a foundation for further historical investigation and nuanced theological commentary.

These new members of the theological faculty at Oxford also seemed more collaborative in their research. Following the German practice, S.R. Driver ran a seminar in his rooms at Christ Church from 1884 to discuss the latest findings of biblical archaeology and criticism and Sanday's New Testament seminar met from 1895 to discuss the Synoptic Gospels and the hypothetical 'Q' document. The work of this latter group came to be published in 1911 as the seminal

41. E. Hatch, *The Organization of the Early Christian Churches* (8th edn., London, 1918), 2f. The lectures were translated into German by von Harnack, many of whose views Hatch shared. Hatch was also Jowett's godson and when he died prematurely in 1890, the faculty board gave thanks for his "keen interest in the promotion of the accurate and scientific Study of Theology" which had "enabled him to render most valuable counsel to the Board in its efforts to secure the right conduct and development of the School of Theology." (OUA FA 4/19/1/1: Minutes of the Board of the Faculty of Theology, 29 November 1889).
42. William Sanday, *The Life of Christ in Recent Research* (Oxford: Oxford University Press, 1907), 38. See M.D. Chapman, "The Socratic Subversion of Tradition: William Sanday and Theology, 1900-1920", *Journal of Theological Studies*, 45 (1994): 94-96.

Oxford Studies in the Synoptic Problem.[43] Those who attended included
John C. Hawkins, author of *Horae Synopticae,* W.C. Allen (author of
the Matthew volume for the *International Critical Commentary*), J.V.
Bartlet (instrumental in the foundation of the Church of South India),
B.H. Streeter (The Queen's College) and N.P. Williams, later Lady
Margaret Professor of Divinity. Sanday's more progressive approach
to academic study is witnessed too in that 'lady members' were
known to frequent the Synoptics seminar.[44]

The changing content and nature of academic research was also
reflected in the honour school, where students were being asked
questions that required more than simply a descriptive account of
Bible and tradition. Change was far from rapid in this respect,
however. A motion from Sanday to introduce a preliminary
examination in theology (at that time, undergraduates proceeded
to the theological final honour school only after second-year
examinations in classics, Moderations) was voted down in 1885 on
the grounds that "premature specialization" was inadvisable.[45] Despite
this, the nomination of Cheyne as an examiner in 1882 led to
candidates being invited to discuss whether the Fourth Gospel and
the Apocalypse were written by the same author. Later in the same
year, students were asked to consider the Pauline authorship of the
Pastoral Epistles.[46]

The measured pace at which Sanday, Driver, and Cheyne
introduced critical study to faculty life was deemed too slow by
some. In the tradition of her own family, Mary Ward, the niece

43. *The Oxford Magazine,* 21 May 1884; A.C. Headlam, *The Life and Teaching of Jesus Christ* (London: Macmillan, 1923), 5f.
44. Stephen Neill, *The Interpretation of the New Testament, 1861-1961* (London: Oxford University Press, 1964), 121, fn.1.
45. OUA, Minutes of the Board of the Faculty of Theology, 12 February 1885.
46. Second Public Examination: Honour School of Theology, Trinity Term 1882 (Apologetica II, question 1); Michaelmas Term 1882 (Apologetica II, question 4); cf. Peter Hinchliff, "Religious Issues, 1870-1914", *History of the University,* 7:100-101.

of Matthew Arnold and married to Humphrey Ward, a fellow of Brasenose College (and known as Mrs Humphry Ward) wrote an article entitled "The New Reformation: A Dialogue" in *The Nineteenth Century* in March 1889 that was scathing of Oxford's theological life. It was written as a conversation between two fictional characters: Merriman, an Oxford student who had abandoned ordination after experiencing theological education in Germany, and Ronalds, a cleric. In Germany, Merriman had discovered "that *historical* temper" which had failed to find in England. At last, he found out "that these men and women, these kings and bishops and saints, these chroniclers and officials, were flesh and blood; that they had ideas, passions, politics; that they lived, as we do, under governing prepossessions."[47]

Merriman now doubted that one could find "a scientific, that is to say unprejudiced, an unbiased study of theology, under present conditions" in England:

> All our theological faculties are subordinate to the Church; the professors are clergymen, the examiners in the theological schools must be in priest's orders...The results of our English system are precisely what you might expect – great industry, and great success in textual criticism, in all the branches of what the Germans call the *niedere Kritik* [lower criticism]; complete sterility, as far as the higher criticism – that is to say the effort to reconceive Christianity in the light of the accumulations of modern knowledge.

"All that could be expected" from an English theological faculty, wrote Ward, "was a certain amount of exegetical work and a more or less respectable crop of apologetic".[48]

---

47. M.A. Ward (Mrs Humphry), "The New Reformation: A Dialogue", *The Nineteenth Century*, 25 (1889): 454.
48. M.A. Ward, *ibid.*, 467-78.

William Sanday replied graciously to Ward's criticisms in the *Contemporary Review*, agreeing that there was a lack of a "constructive, unifying principle which should run through" a theological system, and the resistance of some to "assimilate and recombine the fruitful and progressive elements of the newer theology."[49] Nonetheless, he felt compelled to defend what progress had been achieved at Oxford:

> I did not know how the scientific impulse, proceeding largely from the study of Ancient History, was allying itself with the religious temper, which is a growing factor in the life of the University. But now I see no reason why we should not have a school of genuine English theology. We have the first and requisite men...We are doing our best (though not exactly in the way Mrs. Ward intends) to keep up an outlook over the whole field...But I would warn our well-wishers and those who look to the Universities to supply guidance to the nation in these matters, that they must be prepared for comparatively slow advances and for a good deal of that *niedere Kritik* which Mrs. Ward regards so compassionately.

"For my own part," wrote Sanday, "I have rather a partiality for the *niedere Kritik*."[50]

Cheyne also offered a reply in the *Contemporary Review* in which he spoke of a new model of English theology emerging:

> I see it in my dreams, but I also see it in course of formation. Not only in the longings and aspirations of all good men, but by the studies of Biblical scholars, it is being brought within the range of actuality.

49. William Sanday, "The Future of English Theology", *Contemporary Review* 56 (1889): 46-7. Sanday's critical approach towards to the Bible also changes. His lecture-series on 'The Origin and Character of the first two chapters of St. Luke', undated but probably from the second decade of the twentieth century (as he quotes Sir John Hawkins' *Horae Synopticae* (1909)), exhibits Sanday adopting form criticism, and quoting Weiss and Harnack, to make sense of the tradition behind Luke's infancy narratives. (Christ Church Archives, Soc. xxiii c.123: Sanday Lectures, 'The Origin and Character of the first two chapters of St Luke'). He believed that the first two chapters of Luke were the most archaic portions of the New Testament, the fruit of a well-established oral tradition.
50. William Sanday, "English Theology", 47.

Already a new kind of sect is springing up, which is of no import for present Church politics, but which will perhaps be a of no slight significance for the historian of the future...It is a sect which is not a sect; it is both inter-sectarian and supra-sectarian.[51]

Those committed to 'scientific theology' would no longer, he believed, be seen as part of a 'liberal' sect, but those from a variety of ecclesiastical backgrounds who in a "supra-sectarian" manner were committing themselves to careful research and theological renewal.

Likewise, Sanday wrote of his group of a

[D]ozen or more members – nearly all first-classmen or prize-winners of some kind, and large proportion of them first-classmen not in the narrower School of Theology, but in the wider arena of *Literae Humaniores* – [who] meet together over a table and are engaged in collecting, verifying, and tabulating data bearing, however remotely, on the history and theology of the New Testament.[52]

Both professors identified Nonconformists as an important factor in forming this "supra-sectarian" model of theology and reason to prove to Mary Ward that she "really knows very little what the Oxford teaching is like or what is being done there."[53] Without a doubt, it was the immigration of Nonconformists, more so than the appointment of new Anglican professors, that prompted the reconsideration of how theology was practised at both Oxford and Cambridge in the latter half of the nineteenth century.

Nonconformist Oxford

Nonconformist theologians in England had, by comparison with their Anglican peers at Oxford and Cambridge, been far less inhibited in their engagement with biblical criticism and Continental

51. T.K. Cheyne, "Reform in Old Testament Teaching", *Contemporary Review* 56 (1889): 232-33.
52. W. Sanday, *ibid.,* 52.
53. W. Sanday, *ibid.,* 43.

philosophy. Untrammelled by a clerical hierarchy and their institutions proudly free of religious tests, it was not surprising that these dissenting academies, translated to Oxford, would be altogether different institutions from those instruments of consolidation construed by Pusey and his colleagues a decade earlier in the University.

In 1882, a Nonconformists' Union had been founded with the permission of Jowett as vice chancellor, and with the support of leading academic liberals James Bryce and T.H. Green. On 12 May that year, the distinguished Congregationalist theologian, Andrew Martin Fairbairn, gave a lecture entitled "The Study of Theology and the Training for the Ministry". A member of the audience, it is recorded, communicated to the speaker that

> Some of the finest intellects that come to Oxford are being lost to Christianity for the want of another than the High Church Theology. That other Theology you men of the Free Churches alone can give; you can give it here only by the creation of a Theological School that will affect the Universities; and it is a duty you clearly owe to the nation and to our common religion to give it.[54]

By the end of 1882, Fairbairn had written to Robert W. Dale at Spring Hill College, Birmingham, about the possible establishment of a "Theological School or College" for Oxford graduates with a Chapel which would become a centre for Nonconformist ministry in the university.[55] This was at a time that the clerical party in Convocation had vetoed the election of Robert Horton, a Nonconformist, as an examiner in the divinity examination; how could a Nonconformist, it was argued, examine students on their

54. Elaine Kaye, *Mansfield College: Its Origin, History, and Significance* (Oxford: Oxford University Press, 1996), 54.
55. W. Selbie, *Life of Andrew Martin Fairbairn* (London: Hodder & Stoughton, 1914), 167f. Fairbairn claimed that it was Gladstone who was the first person to suggest the foundation of a Nonconformist college at Oxford, although the evidence is only oral. (W. Selbie, *ibid.,* 165–6).

knowledge of the Thirty-nine Articles? Many in the university had been appalled by the direction of the vote, with the *Magazine* commenting that the real question was

> [W]hether it is worse to have an examiner on this subject who is not an official representative of the Thirty-nine Articles, than to examine men in these articles as if they were believers in them, when it is notorious that the majority of those examined, however rudimentary their faith and religion may be, are certainly no more in accordance with the spirit of these old standards, we will not say than the ordinary dissenting preacher, but than the majority of the clergymen of the Church of England itself…the examination in question merely serves as a recurring occasion for the sorriest ribaldry, and its *vivas* supply in Oxford the place of a low comic theatre.[56]

Despite this lingering opposition to Nonconformity within the university, there was broader encouragement for a Nonconformist college after two articles were written by Fairbairn and James Bryce in the Nonconformist *British Quarterly* in April 1884. Bryce, in particular, was scathing of the remaining restrictions upon theology at Oxford. "The system of theological tests," wrote Bryce, has "made theology odious to many of the finer spirits, forced them into an attitude of hostility, surrounded every question with an atmosphere of political controversy."[57] Even the new divinity professors were "cramped by the conditions which the law imposes, and necessarily imposes, on the Established Church. The presence of critical and philosophical inquirers free from these restrictions will be a great benefit to religion."[58] For Bryce, the penetration of Oxford by the free-thinking Nonconformists would be advantageous to the whole

---

56. *The Oxford Magazine,* 5 December 1883.
57. J. Bryce and A.M. Fairbairn, "Nonconformity and the Universities: The Free Churches and a Theological Faculty", *British Quarterly,* April 1884, 899.
58. J. Bryce and A.M. Fairbairn, ibid.

university by the challenge they would present to the "cramped" Anglican theological establishment.

Progress was rapid. On 22 May 1884, Committee of Management of Spring Hill agreed for the college's removal to Oxford and from October 1886, Mansfield College – named after Spring Hill's founders – was operating out of rooms in 90, the High Street, with Fairbairn as its principal. A Mansfield student wrote the *Oxford Magazine,* claiming that the college was "best described as a Theological Faculty, not indeed incorporated in the University, but recognised by it, and having mutual relations therewith."[59] Fairbairn saw the college as having an important role in reshaping the theological life of the university. He asserted that in Oxford "two forces are supreme, the Anglican Church and Modern Agnosticism, and the one tends evermore to a higher sacerdotalism, while the other tends as inevitably to fastidious indifference or simpler negation." Fairbairn insisted "in this conflict our Churches are surely not so forgetful of truth and duty as to be willing to play the part of idle onlookers."[60]

One might think that Fairbairn's description of Oxford would have been provocative, if not offensive, to the Anglican establishment. However, relations between the younger divinity professors and the staff and students of the Congregationalist college were marked by generosity and cooperation. Indeed, whereas Cambridge Anglican theologians had almost no contact with the eminent Congregationalist P.T. Forsyth, there seems to have been a strong spirit of friendship at Oxford.[61] At the opening of the buildings of Mansfield in 1889, Edwin Hatch had told the assembled guests that

---

59. A letter from "An Oxford Graduate and Mansfield Student" to the *Oxford Magazine,* 28 November 1888.
60. From an appeal pamphlet entitled *Mansfield College* (n.d., probably 1888).
61. David Thompson, *Cambridge Theology in the Nineteenth Century,* 154.

Mansfield was "rendering…a service to the Church of England, and I believe the University, by helping it to fulfil its ideal":[62]

> The ideal of the Christian Church in its largest sense is the ideal which I find, not only in the New Testament, but also in the Old. It is the ideal of a vast community in which Judah shall not be swallowed up by Ephraim nor Ephraim Judah, but Judah and Ephraim shall live side by side, each working out its common purpose, but in which Judah no longer vexes Ephraim nor Ephraim Judah.

Hatch's obituary noted that he, in Mansfield, "saw a chance of a true and scientific school of Theology springing up in the University", and at his last lecture before his sudden, premature death, twenty men from Mansfield were present. As their college only had two tutors, it was perhaps not surprising that Mansfield students would go to faculty lectures. Nonetheless, Sanday, Driver, and Cheyne all engaged enthusiastically in teaching and examining Mansfield students, and participated in Mansfield's summer schools in 1892 and 1894.

The lectures given by tutors at Mansfield, however, ventured far beyond the biblical and historical focus of the honour school. Students in their first year at Mansfield, for instance, completed courses on Theism and the Philosophy of Religion. The latter lectures, delivered by Fairbairn, gave students some understanding of Spinoza, Bruno, Schopenhauer, Schleiermacher, Schelling, and Hegel, the works of whom would never be encountered by those preparing for the honour school, let alone Greats students.[63] The methods proved their value in the honour school, where between 1888 and 1913 forty-one university prizes were awarded to those Mansfield students who supplicated for Oxford degrees as 'Non-

---

62. S.C. Hatch, ed., *Memorials of Edwin Hatch*, xxxiii–xxxiv.
63. *Report of the Committee of Management of Mansfield College, Oxford, for the Session 1886-87* (Birmingham: Hudson & Son, 1887), 13.

Collegiate Students', with the result of eight Firsts and twelve Seconds in Theology and 10 Firsts and 22 Seconds in Semitic Languages.[64]

Mansfield exemplified what was regularly being described as 'scientific theology' across the university and by the divinity professors. There is no single definition for this term, but by this stage it seems to refer to theology studied from an historicist perspective, free from what was viewed as dogmatic 'prejudice', and also concerned to examine with care the data of religious experience, historically and in the present. To some degree it was a development of the 'inductive' method of the Noetics, but by the final decades of the nineteenth century 'scientific' theology – as a translation of *wissenschaftliche Theologie* – also bore the hallmarks of the historicist German methodology.

Mansfield's principal, A.M. Fairbairn, modelled this 'scientific theology' in his own writing and teaching. He had studied in Berlin under the influence of Hengstenberg and Dorner and was well read in philology. Crucially, as Peter Hinchliff wrote, Fairbairn also "understood Oxford and Anglicanism in a way that few Nonconformists, and even fewer Scots, could claim to do."[65] Reginald Macan, when master of University College, described him in 1917 as "the most accomplished and profound exponent of systematic theology in the University since Mozley."[66] Whereas Fairbairn was able to offer lectures on Kant and Hegel as "a mature theological scholar of wide knowledge and proved ability as a

---

64. *Report of the Committee of Management of Mansfield College, Oxford, for the Session 1912-13* (Oxford: Alden & Co, 1913), 12.
65. Peter Hinchliff, *God and History: Aspects of British Theology, 1789-1914* (Oxford: Clarendon Press, 1994), 189.
66. R.W. Macan, *Religious Changes in Oxford during the Last Fifty Years* (London: Oxford University Press, 1917), 14.

teacher", the same sort of admiration was not immediately attributed to the first principal of Manchester College, James Drummond.

When Manchester College, a Unitarian institution, relocated to Oxford in 1889 advertising itself as offering "Free Teaching and Free Learning in Theology, and Piety Free", it did not receive a warm welcome from the *Oxford Magazine.* It was pishly commented that it had always "hoped that piety was more or less free" and was keen to assure Dr. Drummond that "no charge is made in College Battels [bills to be paid by college members, usually for accommodation and board] for the Christian graces or moral excellences."[67] Implicitly critical of the Anglican faculties of Oxford and Cambridge, Drummond insisted that Manchester was "an open faculty of Theology" that did not make belief "primary". Among the sciences of the university, "Theology alone still fears to move in the ways of open knowledge, and, as thought dubious of her strength, shields herself with restrictive stipulations."[68] Those "stipulations" may have been a less than oblique reference to the clerical restrictions on the university's Divinity degrees and theological examinerships.

The Regius Professor of Divinity, William Ince, however, was of an earlier generation that was anxious about the Nonconformist presence in Oxford. He tried to prevent William Sanday from attending the opening of Manchester's buildings next door to Mansfield in 1893, concerned about their lack of "Catholic faith" as well as what the Ireland professor's presence at the college's opening ceremony might signify:

---

67. *The Oxford Magazine,* 23 October 1889. For more on Manchester (now Harris Manchester) College's history, see B. Smith, ed., *Truth, Liberty, Religion: Essays Celebrating Two Hundred Years of Manchester College* (Oxford: Manchester College, 1986).

68. J. Drummond, "Old Principles and New Hopes" in R.D. Darbishire, *Theology and Piety: Alike Free: from the point of view of Manchester New College, Oxford. A Contribution to its Effort, offered by an Old Student* (London: Kegan Paul, Trench, Trubner & Co. Ltd., 1890).

It seems to me that you see things from the point of view of a student and scholar – I who from long experience have a wide knowledge of. . . the historical relation of the University to the Church of England, especially the Bishops and Clergy connected with ordination preparation, am anxious for the sake of all to avoid any action which in my judgment would tend to the severance of the friendly relation subsisting between the University and the Church . . . You could not avoid what I am fully aware you would deem a misinterpretation being put upon your action. It would be widely felt . . . here is one of the Theological Professors…who is ready to encourage and fraternise with men who do not accept the Catholic Faith of Christendom. I much dread the possible effects of the existence of Manchester College in Oxford. I fear that it will attract to itself every form of scepticism and denial of the supernatural elements of Xianity [sic] and foster a negative and distinctive criticism both of the Bible and Theology.[69]

Ince's letter to Sanday exhibits Oxford theologians being presented with difficult questions by the presence of Nonconformists. The Unitarians, in particular, disturbed Ince as "men who do not accept the Catholic Faith of Christendom", a criticism that could not be attributed so easily to the Congregationalists of Mansfield. However, if students from Manchester were to attend faculty lectures and be examined in the honour school, how could the honour school be viewed any longer as an appropriate route to ordination in the Church of England by the episcopal bench? Did the faculty exist in the university for ordination preparation in the Church of England through the guarded study of Bible and theology (as understood by Ince) or was it for scientific theology for which, it was claimed, the student's confessional commitments were secondary, if not irrelevant?

---

69. MS Bodleian Eng. Misc. d.124 (1), f.15: William Ince to William Sanday, 13 Oct. 1893. Sanday, despite his initial assurances to Ince, attended the opening and dedication of the college's chapel, 18–19 October 1893.

Lux Mundi in Context

More concerning to the older generation of High Churchmen in the university was the publication of *Lux Mundi* in 1889. This celebrated testament of Oxford's limited acceptance of biblical criticism came not from the Nonconformists or from the relatively new generation of divinity professors, but from the men who had long been groomed to be the successors of Pusey and Liddon. Charles Gore had been appointed as the first principal of Pusey House and was consequently naturally associated with both men. From as early as 1876, however, Gore had come to believe that the critical study of the Bible was not incompatible with the Creeds. He had met with other young Oxford theologically minded scholars to commit themselves to a strong devotional life and to reconciling the claims of science and biblical criticism with their Catholic faith. This 'Holy Party', as it was known, consisted of the religious philosopher J.R. Illingworth, the young Balliol man Henry Scott Holland, Francis Paget, and Edward Talbot, and the fruit of their conversations led to the 1889 publication of this collection of essays with the subtitle, 'A series of studies in the religion of the Incarnation'.

This seminal text, which was naturally compared to the publication of *Essays and Reviews* almost thirty years earlier, was an explication of moral philosophy that was rooted in the personality of Christ, and bearing the hallmark of the Idealist ethic learnt at the feet of the influential Oxford tutor T.H. Green. The *Magazine* described it as bearing "the unmistakeable impress of the 'Greats' school, the permanent influence of Aristotle, the temporary of Green."[70] Its themes varied from Francis Paget writing on 'Sacraments', Henry Scott Holland on 'Faith', Walter Lock on 'The Church' to Robert Moberly on 'The Incarnation as the Basis of Dogma' and E.S. Talbot

---

70. *Oxford Magazine,* 12 Feb. 1890.

on 'The Preparation in History for Christ'.[71] The most controversial contribution, as with *Essays and Reviews,* considered how the Bible ought to be read: an essay by Charles Gore on 'The Holy Spirit and Inspiration', interpreted revelation as an evolutionary process and accepted that there were parts of the Old Testament that were not strictly historical. Christ's invocation of the Old Testament texts did not, Gore argued, depend on their factual accuracy. Gore's kenotic Christology allowed for the Son – having renounced divine omniscience – to reason according to the beliefs of his own time and did not mean that every word of his relating, for example, the book of Jonah, entailed their historical truth.

Although Gore's arguments seem dated to readers today (Gore was notably reluctant to apply historical-critical methods to the New Testament), his essay nonetheless clearly marked a break from the approach to biblical study evinced in Pusey's *Lectures on Daniel* or in Liddon's own lectures on the New Testament corpus. Liddon was greatly disturbed by the publication and wrote to William Bright:

> I cannot tell you how miserable the whole thing has made me. It has destroyed very much of the confidence of my younger friends here. They avoid the subject, even dear [unreadable] and Burrows do not speak of it. I see Paget every week, – but there has not been any allusion however remote to Lux Mundi; & even J.O. Johnston, who is I suppose over-awed by the Keble influences, is for the first time, distant, & – so far as so kindly a creature can be, – antagonistic. . . . It all shows how widespread and powerful Gore's influence has been: what might it not have done for us, if instead of playing into the hands of unbelief, it had been consistently greeted on the side of positive truth!

71. For more on the theology of this group, not all attached to Oxford, see Peter Hinchliff, "The Essays in *Lux Mundi*" in *God and History,* 99-121, and Geoffrey Rowell, "Historical Retrospect: *Lux Mundi* 1889" in *The Religion of the Incarnation: Anglican Essays in Commemoration of Lux Mundi,* ed. Robert Morgan(Bristol: Bristol Classical Press, 1989), 205-16.

Liddon identified Driver as responsible for the more controversial of Gore's passages on the Old Testament. In a letter to Lord Halifax not long before he died, Liddon wrote of the "Pusey House difficulty", recounting a meeting with Charles Gore:

> I could not but see that he is more than ever under Dr. Driver's influence on all questions connected with the Old Testament, though he was, as he always is, anxious to do and say anything he could to lessen his divergence from the old and Catholic estimate of Holy Scripture, which he has actually altered for the better two of the more painful passages that bear on the Person of our Divine Lord.[72]

Of Sanday, Liddon wrote excoriatingly, "He has no idea of the Catholic Rule of Faith and is bent on literary originality, and all that sort of thing."[73] Both Driver and Sanday defended *Lux Mundi* and correspondence between Driver and Gore after the publication of *Lux Mundi* does suggest a fruitful relationship between the two men; Pusey's successor expressed his commiserations that the volume had been met with dismay in some quarters and even asked for advice on a new essay of his own.[74] Despairingly, Liddon had written that "These young Critics sometimes appear to one to have taken leave of their moral sense about as completely as M. Renan."[75] Unable to understand the change of methodology among the younger generation, he told Scott Holland in a letter that Oxford was

---

72. J.O. Johnston, *Life and Letters of H.P. Liddon* (London: Longmans, Green & Co, 1904), 382. The Oxford 'trio' of Sanday, Cheyne and Driver had also influenced other essayists. Before Cheyne had become a professor, Scott Holland had written to him in appreciation of his work, commenting that it "is most refreshing to feel that we hold in Oxford the capacity to open out the new knowledge that the years have brought in, which scholarly skills, and devoted patience" and that his book on Isaiah "takes its place, at once,; my men are set to study it...from the first." (Bodleian MS Eng. lett. e.28 (f.25v): Henry Scott Holland to T.K. Cheyne, n.d., probably early 1882 due to Scott Holland's reference to Cheyne's book on Isaiah and gratitude that Cheyne would be "with us one term longer" – probably referring to Cheyne's Hebrew teaching at Christ Church *in lieu* of Pusey.
73. Bodleian Library MS. Eng. lett. d.302 (f.175): H.P. Liddon to W. Bright, 14 March 1890.
74. G.L. Prestige, *The Life of Charles Gore: A Great Englishman* (London: Heinemann, 1905), 118.
75. Bodleian MS Eng. lett. d.302 (ff.167): H.P. Liddon to W. Bright, 15 Feb. 1890.

"undergoing a silent but very serious change – through its eagerness to meet modern difficulties and its facile adoption of new intellectual methods."[76]

However shocked the volume had left Liddon, his reading of the Bible was now far from what considered normative by the mainstream of scholarship. The young biblical scholar Arthur Headlam wrote a defence of the compendium in the *Church Quarterly* that asserted the essayists represented the views of "the vast majority of the younger men who think about the subject, of far more laymen and clergy than you think, who are loyal to the Church and to Christianity."[77] Having been sent Headlam's review by William Bright, Liddon could only assert in response that

> Mr Headlam complains of our falling back on a priori arguments, – meaning Our Lord's Authority. I suppose he has never asked himself very clearly why he received the O.T. at all? . . . I receive them in the block on our Lord's Authority; just as I receive the N.T. on that of His Church, which is, in a certain true sense, His organ in Christian History. But if His Authority is set aside, as it practically is by Gore & Driver, I have nothing to fall back upon – no adequate reason for thinking that . . . the O.T. books can have any place in the Self-Unveiling of the Divine Mind to man. Does Mr Headlam think that Prof. Driver's account of the compilation of the Chronicles . . . is compatible with any belief whatever that a book so compiled reveals the Mind of the GOD of Truth?[78]

There was no opportunity for Liddon to temper his opinion. Having gone very grey, he died the following September unreconciled to the "young Critics" at Oxford.

The publication and reception of *Essays and Reviews* had resulted in the effective silencing of Jowett and other theological liberals within the university; rather than provoking the theological

---

76. S. Paget, *Henry Scott Holland* (London: John Murray, 1921), 112.
77. *Church Quarterly,* 10 Feb. 1890.
78. Bodleian MS Eng. lett. d.302 (ff.166-67): H.P. Liddon to W. Bright, 15 Feb. 1890.

THEOLOGY AT OXFORD, 1882-1914

establishment, however, *Lux Mundi* now represented it. In 1885, four of the contributors to the volume (Gore, Lock, Aubrey Moore, and Scott Holland) had been elected to the Board of the Faculty of Theology. Symptomatic of the new generation, in 1891 the first meeting of the Society of Historical Theology was convened with Professor Cheyne as its first speaker. Present were Sanday and the principals of Manchester and Mansfield, along with many others. Committing itself to an historical, "scientific" theological method, this multi-denominational group met to hear and discuss papers ranging from aspects of medieval Christian theology to 'Abd-al-Kadir and his Order in Islam'. Max Müller, who had had practically no involvement with the theological faculty since his arrival in Oxford, became the Society's president in 1893 and Adolf von Harnack was made an honorary member in 1897. Many of its members would also become contributors to the *Journal of Theological Studies,* which began publishing articles and reviews along the same lines in 1899. Perhaps the greatest testament to the Oxford theology's integration into modern scholarly world was the inclusion of Driver, Sanday and Fairbairn in the Charter of Incorporation of that centre of English *Wissenschaft,* the British Academy, in 1902.[79]

The combination of this acceptance of biblical criticism within the Anglican theological establishment at Oxford and the growing influence of Nonconformists from both Mansfield and Manchester was evidently combining to create a different environment for theological study and education than had been known under Pusey's aegis. As Cheyne had envisaged, there was emerging a "supra-sectarian" commitment to historical-critical engagement with the biblical text that – across denominations – was less concerned about *a priori* claims of faith. This change was described by Owen Chadwick

79. Ernest Nicholson, ed., *A Century of Theological and Religious Studies in Britain* (Oxford: Oxford University Press, 2002), 11.

as taking hold, at least among the Anglican professors, in order "to gain the respect of their colleagues in the university"; they had to "become (or at least thought sometimes that they must become) drily academic, and seek to squeeze the last drop of religion out of their theology."[80] For Chadwick, in order to accommodate themselves to the secularized universities, the faculties of Oxford and Cambridge were themselves secularized.

There is some truth to Chadwick's claim. The faculty at Oxford could evidently no longer be considered straightforwardly as an *amanuensis* of the Church of England, by virtue of both the increasingly multi-denominational character of the university and the lack of feeling among professors that they did not exist to defend "the deposit of revelation" that was guarded by the Church of England. Confessional and apologetic theology of the kind that Pusey had vigorously defended until his death had now moved to the fringes of faculty life, in the form of the theological colleges and from the pulpits.

Nonetheless, there is no evidence that Oxford theologians were self-consciously seeking to satisfy the expectations of their academic colleagues by their adoption of these research methods. Evident in Sanday's response to Mary Ward, these methods were employed not to impress colleagues in other faculties so much as to speak freshly and truthfully about the nature of God and his action in history, to create a "school of genuine English theology."[81] As he later commented, as an historical religion "Christianity is so much bound up with history that the first duty of the student is to ascertain, as nearly as may be, what were the historical facts" even though "the historical method must not be employed as a covert means of getting rid of the supernatural."[82] For Sanday, at least, there seems to have been no clear

---

80. Owen Chadwick, *The Victorian Church*, ii, 451-52.
81. W. Sanday, "The Future of English Theology", 53.

dichotomy between the mission and education of the Church and the 'scientific' methodology that Oxford theologians were eagerly employing. As Fairbairn also insisted at the opening of Mansfield,

> [T]heology had to be studied both as a living science and the science of life. As a living science, it was in the process of growth, for a science that did not discover did not live. As the science of life, it had to be regarded in its correlation with life as reflected in the spirit of the Church, and as expressing that spirit.[83]

As a "science of life", the teaching of the faculty was sufficiently attractive that the students of Wycliffe Hall, Mansfield and Manchester all sought to benefit from it rather than organize their own confessionally 'pure' and 'religious' provision. The multi-denominational context for this teaching may have encouraged a less overtly religious mode of study and education, but as this chapter shows, the continued 'secularization' of the university did not result in the dissipation of either religious or theological energy at Oxford. Clearly no longer the institutional embodiment of the Church party in the university, the challenge at the turn of the century was how the statutes that bound the faculty to the Church of England as a result of the settlements of 1869 and 1871 might be successfully changed to give a more accurate account of the reality of Oxford's more plural theological life.

Disestablishing the Faculty?

Writing about the honour school in an open letter to William Ince in 1898, the formidable principal of Mansfield, A.M. Fairbairn, asserted that theology occupied the highest position in the university not because it was the handmaid of the Church, but because

82. W. Sanday, "The Historical Method in Theology" (a paper read to the Church Congress in Nottingham in 1897), *The Expository Times* 9 (1897): 4.
83. *The Oxford Times*, 23 Oct. 1886.

It has all the elements that make for educative efficiency; philology, philosophy, history, criticism, are inseparable from its academic study; and it has to exercise these as regards the most impressive and permanent beliefs, the most important events, the most potent personalities, and the most quickening literature in the world.[84]

If "educative efficiency" was now the essential mark of theological study, rather than service to the Church of England, this was still far from apparent in the faculty's statutory arrangements. One still needed to be in holy orders of the Church of England to supplicate for a Divinity degree (the BD or DD) and to be an examiner in the honour school. While these arrangements had ensured orthodoxy during a decade of religious controversy, they now seemed embarrassingly anachronistic in what was now a national university.

The university itself had not been insensitive to the claims and rights of Nonconformists with regard to the Faculty of Theology. In 1894, when the faculty board had tried to reform the Divinity degrees by improving the quality of exercises required to supplicate for the degree, the executive Hebdomadal Council of the University requested that, before any changes were made, the board "should consider and advise on the expediency of removing the [clerical] restrictions" upon the degrees.[85] At that stage, the board had resisted change, considering it "doubtful and contentious matter."[86]

Six years after Fairbairn's public letter, however, movements within the Faculty suggested that demands for equity could not be ignored any longer. In a memorial sent to the Hebdomadal Council, and prepared by W.C. Allen, a fellow of Exeter College, fifty-five members of Congregation sought a statute removing limitations

84. A.M. Fairbairn, *Letter to the Regius Professor of Divinity on the School of Theology* (Oxford: Horace Hart, 1898),2.
85. Oxford University Archives FA 4/19/1/1: Minutes of the Board of the Faculty of Theology, 8 June 1894; 15 October 1894.
86. *Ibid.,* 26 October 1894.

upon those examining in the honour school of theology. This petition was not simply another dissenting cry from the Nonconformist fringe of the university. Signed by such influential members of the Church of England as T.K. Cheyne and B.H. Streeter, the memorial believed that removing restrictions would "emphasize the value of the School as an Honour School for the educational discipline of candidates, and as a preparation for more advanced research work . . . a method of education in the development of human life and thought."[87]

The Memorial became a source of considerable interest for those beyond the University. A clerical correspondent to the *Times* asserted that theology was currently presented to the undergraduate

> not, like other departments of learning, as a country to be explored, but as a preserve, carefully fenced round, in which all roads will lead to certain foregone conclusions. We may deplore some of the results of free research at German Universities, but truth must in the end be advanced by freedom, even at the risk of temporary confusion and unsettlement.[88]

Evidently, while support for change emerged primarily from a desire to end the exclusion of Nonconformists from the theological life of the university, enthusiasm for change also found support among those with methodological grievances with theology in the 'ancient' universities; they perceived theology as a scientific discipline, a study in human life and development, that warranted no religious safeguards. The faculty's research and teaching, they believed, ought to find its authority in the material and quality of study itself.

---

87. Oxford University Archives FA 4/19/2/1: Theology Reports, 4. Cf. W.C. Allen, *The Clergy and the Honour School of Theology* (Oxford: Parker and Son, 1904), 4f.

88. *The Times,* 17 May 1904, 8: letter from W. Bartlett, Vicar of Sutton. See also Lewis Campbell's comments on the theological faculties in his *On the Nationalization of the Old English Universities,* London: Chapman and Hall, 1901, 263-64. Campbell was the biographer of Benjamin Jowett and a fierce critic of the Established Church's control of theological education in the Universities.

This approach to university theology was already taking shape at Manchester, where in December 1903, the University Court had sanctioned the creation of a faculty of theology: ". . . the first occasion in this country on which theology, unfettered by tests, has been accepted as an integral part of the University organization and has been treated like any other subject."[89] A.S. Peake, one of the faculty's first professors, was himself a product of the honour school of theology, having been taught by Driver, Sanday, and Cheyne. He also maintained strong links with A.M. Fairbairn at Mansfield and J. Estlin Carpenter at Manchester College. There was no clear precedent in the British university system for denominational equity, but Oxford's maintenance of tests no doubt appeared increasingly anomalous.

The growing emphasis upon the school as a route in liberal education, rather than a professional training, must have had all the more potency in 1904: a year after the first women had appeared on the Class List of the theological school. Ethel Georgina Romanes, the daughter of the religious activist and writer Ethel Romanes, was placed in the First Class in Trinity Term 1903 as a student at Lady Margaret Hall; F.D. Hannam, also of Lady Margaret Hall, was placed in the Fourth. The number of female students reading for the honour school over the next decade would be slight, with only eight being placed on the Class List prior to the First World War. Their presence, however, must have reinforced the impression in Oxford that the degree was no longer simply a professional qualification for prospective Anglican ordinands.

However, this growing desire to reclassify theology as an "educative discipline" rather than *regina scientiarum* dismayed several

---

89. A.S. Peake, ed., *Inaugural Lectures delivered by Members of the Faculty of Theology during its First Session, 1904-05*, (Manchester: Manchester University Press, 1920), 20; quoted in E.J. Sharpe, *Comparative Religion: A History*, (London: Duckworth, 1975), 131.

readers in the *Church Times* and some senior members of the faculty. The *Church Times* editorial sought to stress "the official and *statutory* Church of England character of the School" on 29 January 1904.[90] Walter Lock, Warden of Keble College and a member of the faculty board, also rejected theology being treated merely as "a method of education in the development of human life and thought". Rather, theology must always be located in a "living society, which has assumed some Revelation as true, and which has created its theology to interpret adequately the secrets of its own religious consciousness and its own history."[91] To erect the "undenominational principle", as at Manchester, and reduce theology to just another department of the humanities, seemed to be a gross mistreatment of the character and methods of theology itself, according to Lock.

Lock's comments persuaded two thirds of the board to uphold the restrictions, even if it did not prevent legislation nonetheless being introduced to Congregation by the Hebdomadal Council on 3 May 1904. The statute that removed restrictions was approved *nemine contradicente* by Congregation. In Convocation, however, which had the right of veto, there was an overwhelming backlash against the proposals. Almost a thousand MAs converged on Oxford, roused to action by articles in the Church newspapers, to vote down the measure. Such was the anger of the crowds in the Sheldonian Theatre that Charles Bigg, the Regius Professor of Ecclesiastical History who supported the changes, was shouted down with cries of "Judas" and "Antichrist".[92]

The failure of Congregation to remove religious restrictions in 1904 showed a faculty that was still divided over its purpose and methods. At the turn of the century, many still clearly believed that

90. *Church Times,* 29 Jan. 1904, leading article.
91. W. Lock, *To the Members of the Board of the Faculty of Theology* (privately printed, 1904).
92. V.H.H. Green, *Religion at Oxford and Cambridge* (London: SCM Press, 1964), 332.

the faculty was the handmaiden of the Church while others asserted that for scholarship to be restrained by any sort out authority, other than the standards of scientific research, was mistaken. Despite a few notable exceptions, however, the faculty at the beginning of the twentieth century was still wedded in statute and spirit to the Church of England: legally committed to a model of theology that was characterized as human response to that divine revelation, and guarded by lecturers and examiners who were in holy orders.

Henry Scott Holland and the 'Holy Party'

On 13 November 1910, William Ince died in his rooms at Christ Church and was buried at the east end of the Cathedral three days later. Elected in 1878, he had published almost nothing during his tenure and had taught with little imagination, and, by comparison with Sanday or Fairbairn, could not be described as a modern scholar. While the Board could posthumously praise him, rather limply, as the man "who probably did more than anyone else to organize lectures for the Theological School at its first foundation," he was also the man who had protected the Church of England's historic place within the University, and had been reluctant to accept the existence of Nonconformist theologians in Oxford.[93] As early as 1889, Cheyne could write to Sanday that his appointment as Regius Professor had been "a blow to theological study, as indirectly stopping the way and keeping out more helpful teachers."[94]

At the end of 1910, Asquith offered the Regius chair to one of the canons of St Paul's Cathedral, Henry Scott Holland. Scott Holland was not an obvious choice, having had little academic responsibility since leaving the University for London in 1884. Prior to that, his teaching responsibilities at Christ Church had, in accordance with

93. OUA FA 4/19/1/2: Minutes of the Board, 8 December 1910.
94. Bodl. MS. Eng. misc. d. 122 (f11): Letter of T.K. Cheyne to W. Sanday, 12 Oct 1889.

his own education, been primarily classical with theological interests. The only 'scientific' piece of theological work that Scott Holland had produced had been an article on Justin Martyr printed for the *Dictionary of Christian Biography*.[95] His principal publications were sermons, for which he was justifiably celebrated, and after twenty-six years in the pulpit in St Paul's the return to Oxford was a cause of anxiety for him. He wrote to E.S. Talbot, co-contributor to *Lux Mundi* and then bishop of the new diocese of Southwark, that "for thirty years I have ceased to have the power to read or study. We must have a scientific theologian honourably representing learning. I could not do it. I should feel myself a scandal."[96] Despite this, and on the advice of Charles Gore (translated to Oxford as bishop from Birmingham in 1911), Scott Holland accepted the professorship and returned to Christ Church.

Although Scott Holland could not be considered a professional academic in the same sense as many of his colleagues (such as Driver or Sanday), his appointment resulted in a faculty board with a professorial leadership that was committed to historical-critical methods in biblical studies, open to the Idealism prevalent in Oxford philosophy at the time, and with a growing interest in the possibilities of psychology for religious self-understanding. It was also a board that now largely recognized the authority of its subject being derived from the material of religious and historical experience, rather than the Church of England. With many members of the faculty and Scott Holland, in particular, being associated with the revival of moral philosophy under the tutelage of T.H. Green, there was also a renewed emphasis upon the personal and moral in response to the person of Christ.

---

95. B. Reardon, ed., *Henry Scott Holland: A Selection from his Writings* (London: SPCK, 1962), 11.
96. S. Paget, *Henry Scott Holland: Memoir and Letters* (London: John Murray, 1921), 236.

Scott Holland was keen to affirm this new model of theological learning. His approach to theological work can be discerned in a sermon entitled 'Authority and Faith', published in 1892. He spoke of "this secret of Jesus – this rock of peace" that is not easily discernible through the "order and framework" of traditional ecclesiastical authority and the Bible.[97] This latter authority, he wrote,

> is not the authority that we need to support so immense, so awful a demand upon our belief. This authority never gets itself free from the wretched entanglement of discussion – discussion critical, historical, literary, scientific.

Rather, the search for something "less hesitating, less dubious, less fluctuating" leads us to search for an authority "that elevates and purifies and educates and expands the spirit of those who submit." It is, rather, that ability to recognize "the voice of their higher self – the voice of that paramount self which they have never realized, perhaps, and could not hope of themselves to attain, but yet which is their veritable reality in the sight of God."

For Scott Holland, while religion may have abandoned a rigid dogmatism, it would not rediscover itself in the technicalities of biblical criticism: an authority that can be as equally removed from the lives of individuals as the ecclesiastical diktat. Rather,

> Authority, then, in all the forms in which it ennobles them over whom it is exerted, can never be wholly external or mechanical. It must come from within as well as from without; the authoritative force must include within its identity some element of the personal self over which it puts out its claim, so that the surrendered self, instead of becoming servile and lowered by its surrender, is lifted and expanded to a higher form of existence.[98]

97. H. S. Holland, "Dogma" in *Pleas and Claims for Christ* (London: Longmans, Green & Co., 1892).
98. *Ibid.*

It was this concern for the individual, lived, religious existence that marked Scott Holland's own sense that theology in a university should not be confined to purely scientific techniques, that which might be termed "external or mechanical."

Within seven months of his appointment, Scott Holland was beginning to think about how these considerations of authority, religion and the practice of theology might be applied at Oxford. In the summer of 1911, following his return to Oxford, he met with the 'Holy Party' in the vicarage at Longworth (a village to the south-west of Oxford), the residence of the incumbent Richard Illingworth. Following this meeting, on 21 June 1911 Henry Scott Holland wrote to William Sanday, by then Lady Margaret Professor of Divinity and a fellow canon at Christ Church. He told him that they had "had a talk at Longworth over the theological prospect, and . . . arrived at this rather revolutionary policy, for which Gore at one end and Walter Moberly at the other were especially keen."[99] Obviously aware of the pressure within the university to allow non-clerical theologians – both members of the Church of England and Nonconformists – to supplicate for the Divinity degrees and become examiners in the honour school, they

> desired ardently that the initiating move should come from our side, and should anticipate any proposals from without. They were very anxious that the whole position should be taken in hand and we really were singularly clear about it, although of course it does seem rather audacious. They suggested a memorandum signed by all the Theological Professors, and I am have tried to draw out, this morning, the kind of thing I would suppose it would mean.[100]

99. Bodl. MS. Eng. Misc. d. 126 (127): Letter from Henry Scott Holland to W. Sanday, 21 June 1911.
100. *Ibid.*

This draft memorandum, to be signed by the professoriate and sent to the vice chancellor of the university, was indeed "audacious". In a break with all previous faculty self-description, those who signed it were "convinced that the University ought not to select and approve, by sanction of its own, any form at all of dogmatic teaching on matters of religious faith and experience. On such matters it is not qualified to speak with authority, and it has quite rightly repudiated long ago any such claim."[101] Indeed, Scott Holland and his Longworth friends believed, in a manner similar to the faculty of theology at Manchester, that "it has ceased to be morally or equitably possible, to favour any one religious body by special and privileged position in the University." Rather,

> We consider that the religious phenomena of humanity should be studied in a University, not from within any dogmatic position, but simply as a body of fact and experience which can be defined, classified, examined, compared, and discussed according to the intellectual standards of historical and philosophical criticism. We believe that this allows for a perfectly intelligible and justifiable basis on which a proper academic treatment of such facts can proceed, working within the limitations prescribed by the very conditions of the study. (No treatment that is purely intellectual can cover the whole of the religious experience that it handles).[102]

In accordance with Scott Holland's previous writings on matters of religious authority, theology was neither the repetition of dogma nor the technicalities of biblical criticism, but properly the analysis of the "religious phenomena of humanity" and their outworking in the facts of historical and personal experience. Removed from the confines of denominational tests, it was only sensible that the degrees of the faculty should have all their restrictions removed.

101. Bodl. MS. Eng. Misc. d. 126 (128-30): Draft Memorandum on the Faculty of Theology, prepared by Henry Scott Holland, and attached to his letter to W. Sanday, 21 June 1911.
102. *Ibid.*

Scott Holland's draft memorandum did not limit its liberalizing tendencies to discussion of the Divinity degrees, however. The Longworth group proceeded to discuss the professorships of the university. Almost all of the professorships were, at this point, paid for – to some degree – with money from the Cathedral canonries. These were now called into question in the draft memorandum. They asserted that the Regius Professor of Divinity, the Lady Margaret Professor, and the Regius Professor of Moral and Pastoral Theology might be considered exempt from alterations to restrictions, being "dogmatic by their very condition, i.e. they express and expound a definite theological conception of human values". They believed, however, that the other professorships (the Regius chairs in Hebrew and Ecclesiastical History), ought to be disassociated from the Cathedral canonries and endowed afresh. "We advocate such a reform", they wrote, "because, in our opinion, it would immensely strengthen our theological position to be released from a very doubtful state of apparent privilege which confuses spiritual issues and compels ignominious compromises." Those who signed the memorandum would be unapologetic in their belief that theology, confessionally conceived, was redundant in the university: "we could only support such a reform if it were made perfectly clear that the entire field of religious experience, non-Christian as well as Christian, came within the domain of the new Faculty."[103]

In his letter to William Sanday, Scott Holland stressed that, "We felt strongly about the last point, and would include other religions than the Christian under the term Theology."[104] This startling redefinition of the theological enterprise at Oxford was rooted in the group's consideration of the subject as a scientific analysis of religious

---

103. *Ibid.*
104. Bodl. MS. Eng. Misc. d. 126 (127): Letter from Henry Scott Holland to W. Sanday, 21 June 1911.

experience ("which can be defined, classified, examined, compared, and discussed according to the intellectual standards of historical and philosophical criticism"). Viewing the locus of theology's study and teaching in the experiential rather than the credal formulations of biblical orthodoxy, the parameters were so loosened by Scott Holland and his colleagues that it seemed only appropriate that other religions might be studied alongside Christian theology, as was now the case at Manchester; there, each undergraduate was compelled to take at least one paper in Comparative Religion for the BA.[105]

This radical reformulation of the theological task at Oxford in the summer of 1911 was a significant departure from the faculty's previous self-understanding, and if it had been implemented, would have resulted in an extraordinary institution. Walter Lock, Scott Holland informed Sanday, was in support of the principle. Lock was, of course, the same individual who had rejected proposed reforms in 1904 in the belief that theology must always be carried out in a "living society, which has assumed some Revelation as true". There was no such guarantee within Scott Holland's memorandum, as the Regius professor's detractors noticed with concern when it was presented in Congregation. Gore's support for the memorandum is also significant and reflects his social radicalism and its accompanying disregard for those institutions of the Establishment that encouraged what the memorandum calls "ignominious compromises". It is very likely that the bishop's support for a faculty that included non-Christian, as well as Christian theology, originates in the commitment to liberty of conscience that led Gore to support the disestablishment of the Church in Wales (to the dismay of many) in 1912.[106]

---

105. E.J. Sharpe, *Comparative Religion: A History*, 131.
106. Gore's support, in the midst of his opposition to certain Oxford scholars over their concept of miracles, also suggests that institutional considerations were perceived distinctly from contemporary methodological disagreements in the faculty.

It was without a doubt a bold and decisive programme for change. Logical, fair, and springing from the liberal catholicism and social radicalism of the *Lux Mundi* essayists, it was always likely to have been met with some anxiety by the English clergy beyond the university. The authors themselves seem to have been aware that the memorandum as it stood in June 1911 required moderation. Walter Lock, the Dean Ireland professor, warden of Keble, and, crucially, a member of the Hebdomadal Council, was tasked with redrafting Scott Holland's memorandum in language acceptable to the Council so that it might be easily assimilated into draft legislation for Congregation. His memorandum, dated 31 July 1911, succinctly identified the condition of theology at Oxford:

> There are two different principles on which Theology may be studied; the one assumes no religious presuppositions of true or false and studies facts of experience in a scientific spirit: the other assumes a standard of truth and a relation of knowledge to life. We believe that the latter is the only complete method of a Church instructing members: the former is the method of a University teaching and testing students.[107]

In writing this, Lock committed himself to a theological method quite distinct from his earlier pronouncements upon the intrinsic connection between theology and a living religious community. In response to the further unravelling of the Church of England's bonds to the university in the previous forty years, however, he now stated that

> [I]t has become very doubtful (a) whether the University has any longer a right to act on behalf of any religious body as giving or even seeming to give an authentication of the orthodoxy of its members; (b) whether it ought to do this on behalf of one religious body to the exclusion of

---

107. Bodl. MS. Eng. misc. d.124 (ff.182–85): Draft memorandum of W. Lock, sent to William Sanday, 31 July 1911

others; and (c) whether the right of access to its highest degrees ought to be denied to any of its students.

Although he affirmed Scott Holland's belief that "the Examinations and degrees are only tests and symbols of knowledge and are entirely independent of membership in any religious body," Lock nonetheless did not go so far as to advocate the separation of the divinity professorships from the canonries at Christ Church and commented that although he desired there to be no limitation upon the religious subjects studied in the school of theology, "practical considerations will naturally operate to confine the subjects mainly to those connected with the Christian Religion."[108]

Nonetheless, there was no doubt that Lock affirmed the methodological changes implied within this redescription of university theology; he recommended that as an expression of the faculty's openness to the study of other religions, the honour school of theology should be renamed as a 'School of Sacred Learning'. After some further redrafting during Michaelmas Term of 1911, a memorial was signed by the entire professoriate and the Dean of Christ Church and it was approved by the faculty board on 27 January 1912.[109]

The final memorial was slightly more hesitant than the drafts of Scott Holland and Lock. Gone is the suggestion of renaming the school of theology or, indeed, any mention of the study of other religions other than Christianity. However, the memorialists asked the vice chancellor to remember that "the Honour School is...in form, only an avenue to a Degree in Arts, and should be as free as

---

108. *Ibid.*
109. The *Memorial on Theological Degrees and School* can be found in Oxford University Archives FA 4/19/2/1: Theology Reports, 48. The faculty board's association with 'the general purport' of the Memorial can be found in OUA FA 4/19/1/2: Minutes of the Board, 125.

other avenues to the same Degree," and accordingly restrictions on its examiners should be removed.

With regard to the opening of the Divinity degrees (the BD and the DD) the language is more restrained, noting that such reform "implies a considerable change of principle, for these Degrees have hitherto presupposed dogmatic theology, and, nominally, convey the right of teaching authoritatively. They have had, moreover, a traditional connexion with the Church of England for many centuries." Reflecting the ambiguous status of the degrees, the Memorial proceeds to note that

> Some of us would prefer that the change should take the form of Concurrent Faculties, such as exist in some Continental and American Universities, under which system the University would delegate to members of each recognized religious denomination the duty, not only of testing knowledge, but of giving a Degree which would carry an accredited attestation and status within the body to which the candidate belongs.

Yet

> If our own conditions at home should make some such scheme impossible, then it would seem to us advisable that these Degrees also should be treated as simply representing a test and standard of scientific knowledge, and should be, in this character, open to all without restriction.

When pressed by the Hebdomadal Council for a definitive opinion about the future of the higher theological degrees, the Board agreed that "the Degrees should be treated as representing a test of scientific knowledge and should be open to all without restriction."[110] The

---

110. The Hebdomadal Council wrote to the assistant registrar on 9 March 1912 accepting the removal of restrictions on the honour school but inferring mild confusion as to which suggestion the board wanted the Council to consider regarding the Divinity degrees. (OUA FA 4/19/2/1: Theology Reports, 49). The faculty's reply can be found in OUA FA 4/19/1/2: Minutes of the Board, 14 March 1912.

complicated nature of the professorships as attached to canonries in a cathedral chapter, however, is "a matter of which…[the signatories] can make no suggestion, and with which, moreover the University has no power to deal [it being the prerogative of the Church of England]." Lock nonetheless wrote that the canon professorships "may be regarded as a contribution made by the Church of England towards the religious learning in the University, more especially in view of the needs of its own members. This contribution is more than is sufficient for the needs that it serves; and the Theological Faculty might well be strengthened by the addition of new Professorships, whether unrestricted by special conditions, or attached to other Religious Bodies."[111]

Beyond the abolition of restrictions, the Committee on the Degrees in Divinity also decided that the statutes should read the degrees as being "in facultate Theologica" or "in studiorum Theologicorum" rather than "in facultate *sacrae* theologiae."[112] The faculty was being 'de-sacralized' since "that special designation implied a view of revelation; it contemplated a formal profession of belief in that view; and the University acted on behalf of the Church of England in requiring such profession to be made."[113] Moreover, "the theses will not be limited to subjects belonging to Christian Theology," and no longer limited to "dogmatic or critical subjects (for the B.D.) and to exegesis of the Bible (for the D.D.)."

111. *Memorial on Theological Degrees and School,* 7 February 1912, Theology Reports, 48.

112. The report of the Committee on Degrees in Divinity, Minutes of the Board, 16 May 1912 (Italics added). This controversial move might be seen as the outcome of Scott Holland's desire that theology should include the study of all religions and Lock's suggestion that the Honour School be renamed.

113. Letter of the Board of the Faculty of Theology to the Hebdomadal Council, in response to a query regarding the Board's decision to change the name of the faculty, Theology Reports, 26 October 1912.

Anticipating the Hebdomadal Council's concern that such a proposal would incite the wrath of Convocation's ecclesiastical members, the Board replied that they had

> [T]he strongest grounds for believing that these considerations will appeal forcibly to many of those members of Convocation who are most likely to be interested in the subject. They will be more willing to accept the change in substance, if it is made clear that the title with its cherished associations and its confessional implications has been altered too…strengthened by the fact that that change will place our degrees in line with the similar degrees at Cambridge and in the Scotch and Modern English Universities.[114]

Naturally, the Hebdomadal Council was not averse to the proposed reforms, having long sought out a more equitable arrangement for Nonconformists in the university. Rumours of reform began to surface: in early March 1912, *The Times* reported of "important reforms… of an interesting and far-reaching kind", the principles of which included the belief that "the University can no longer to act on behalf of the Church of England in the character of its official representative".[115] When legislation was duly prepared and eventually promulgated in the Congregation in December 1912, it was clear that the statutory alterations to the faculty of theology would invoke far greater interest beyond Oxford than Scott Holland had anticipated.

The initial legislative procedures were successfully navigated by Scott Holland and his board colleagues. The statutory changes needed first to be debated by Congregation, the body of resident MAs in the University. There was some degree of opposition. Charles Oman, the Chichele Professor of Modern History, asked whether a person who had shown a "good general knowledge of Christian

---

114. *Ibid.*
115. *The Times,* 8 March 1912, 3, quoting the *Oxford Magazine* of 7 March 1912.

theology" and who had submitted to the board a thesis of purely destructive and anti-theistic tendencies, but of a high degree of intellectual merit, would be permitted to take the degree in theology under the Statute. Walter Lock, as mover of the statute, could only reply in the affirmative.[116] This followed logically from Scott Holland's assertion that "the University was an educational institution, and therefore any section of their educational action must be open to all, whether Christians or not Christians, and could not rest any longer on any dogmatic position."[117] Nonetheless, at a further vote in Congregation on 4 March 1913, the abolition of restrictions on examinerships in the honour school and candidates for the BD and DD were approved, *nemine contradicente.*[118]

Beyond the university, however, the proposals of the board were met with opposition. As the vote in Convocation approached, an external campaign sought to bring a swift end to what was seen as a symptomatic moment in the creeping disestablishment of the Church of England. The letters that began to appear in the *Times,* the High-Church *Guardian,* and the *Church Times* all signified worry among many conservative-minded clergy, who were already distressed by the Liberal government's plans to disestablish the Church in Wales. The Dean of Canterbury, Henry Wace, led the opposition to the statute, vigorously asserting the Christian character of the Oxford faculty. The reforms, he believed, were based on a principle which "if accepted, [will] endanger *any* corporate recognition by the University not only of the Church of England but even of any definite form of Christianity."[119]

116. Although an amendment was attached after the first meeting of Congregation that stipulated that the thesis "must bear some definite relation to some department of Christian theology".
117. The *Times,* 4 December 1912, 9.
118. *The Gazette,* 5 March 1913.
119. The *Times,* 7 March 1913, 4. Other than the Dean of Canterbury, signatories were from a varied group of Churchmen. They included the Dean of Windsor, Canon Knowling (Professor of Divinity at Durham), Canon B.W. Randolph, Archdeacon W.H. Hutton, Lord Halifax,

To opponents of the statutory changes, the faculty existed to teach and examine in the articles of revealed truth and, accordingly, if restrictions were removed there would be nothing to ensure that a non-Christian could not become an examiner in the honour school or take a BD or DD. As a correspondent to the *Guardian*, Oscar Watkins, commented:

> That science of Divine truth which is accepted by the Church as the Faith once delivered to the saints...it is for the teaching of this revealed truth that the Chairs of Theology proper were founded, and for which they still exist. It is no less for the same end that the Faculty of Theology exists. The various other studies in sacred learning are ancillary.[120]

For the opponents of reform, this conception of theological endeavour, "which had [at Oxford] weathered such storms as the Papal Schism, the Protestant Reformation, the Puritan Rebellion, and the onslaught of James II . . . the Divinity Professors themselves [now] calmly propose[d] in the course of a morning's work to throw . . . to the winds."[121]

The *Church Times*, which was likewise opposed to the reforms, echoed the memorialists' anxiety in its editorial of 14 March:

> If the Statute passes, there is no reason why the Buddhist and the aggressive agnostic should not in time materialise. It is true that the Statute provides that a thesis shall "bear a definite relation to some department of Christian theology," but it would not be open to anyone to say what is or is not Christian theology, at least if we accept Dr. Holland's position that it is no business of the University to decide such a question.[122]

Athelstan Riley, the President of Corpus Christi College, the President of St. John's, the Principal of Hertford, the Principal of St. Edmund Hall, the Censor of Non-Collegiate Students, Professor Margoliouth, Professor Oman, Mr Falconer Madan (Bodley's Librarian), Dr. W. Hatchett Jackson.

120. Oscar D. Watkins, letter to the *Guardian*, 15 March 1912. Watkins quoted Newman's description of theology as "notional apprehension." (*Grammar of Assent*) Such a reflection upon theological methodology was generally extraordinary in the debate that surrounded reform.

121. *Ibid.*

Criticism was not confined to Anglican circles. Even the Roman Catholic *British Review* wrote that

> [I]n effect, and probably in invention also, it is not so much the distinctive Church that is being thrown overboard as the idea of doctrine in the abstract. Ostensibly it is the Thirty-nine Articles that are being put on one side. Really the Westminster Confession and the Tridentine Decrees are being no less flouted . . . the attack is against formularies as such. It is an exhibition of Modernism in one of its worst forms, and it ought to be most strenuously resisted.[123]

The faculty's statutory bonds to the Church of England had a significance that clerics beyond the university seemed unwilling to surrender; despite being an institution that had seen steady detachment from the Church of England over the preceding seventy years, the opening of the faculty in the manner proposed by Scott Holland and the board was considered to be beyond the pale by the conservative rump of the Church.

Such acute and persistent critique of the proposed statutory reforms in the ecclesiastical press and in the letter columns of the *Times* and *Guardian* fuelled fervent opposition to the divinity professors' aims. When Convocation met on 29 April, almost 1300 MAs arrived at the Sheldonian Theatre where, the *Church Times* reported, "some two hundred MAs had to stand outside, whence their cries of impatience from time to time penetrated within."[124] Lords, bishops, "a large number of priests in the arena, and many well known lay Churchmen...brought up by a genuine alarm and resentment" crammed into the auditorium. During the debate, in which many of

---

122. Editorial, *Church Times*, 14 March 1913. Scott Holland's reference to the 'turbaned Buddhist' taking a DD in the Congregation debate struck all the wrong chords with those who perceived the Faculty to be a preserve of the Church and was frequently cited by his opponents in the press, especially in the *Church Times*, to stress his radicalism (if not his limited knowledge of Buddhism).
123. *Obiter Dicta* in the *British Review*, March 1913.
124. "The Divinity Question at the Universities: The Vote at Oxford," *Church Times*, 2 May 1913.

the arguments and concerns previously expressed in the newspapers were represented, the Magdalen lay theologian, Cuthbert Turner, announced himself a convert to the opposition to both statutes, believing that 'The Professors . . . had thrown all principles away, and all that remained was their own Chairs.'[125] Believing, reportedly, that "the Professors were imperilling the influence of Oxford on the religious life of England" and, with Dr Wace asserting that "the statutes would permanently deprive Oxford University of its Christian character," a majority of 426 voted to keep restrictions for examiners in the honour school and a majority of 429 to keep restrictions upon the degrees in Divinity. With the vice chancellor's *'Dissolvo hanc Convocationem',* the board's reforms had come to an undignified end.

A Faculty in Transition

In Michaelmas Term 1913, William Selbie, the principal of Mansfield, welcomed a young history graduate into the college by the name of Constance Todd. She was of the second generation of women to enjoy the full benefits of a university education (if not the actual degree) at Somerville College. Near the end of her Oxford course, Constance had become aware of a call to Christian ministry but, understanding that her own Presbyterian Church would have no sympathy with those instincts, she went to talk to Selbie, who welcomed her readily into the College. Constance was quickly accepted by the other students at Mansfield and read for the Bachelor of Divinity at London University over three years (London, unlike Oxford, already granted women degrees) before being ordained as a

---

125. *Ibid.* Between 1906 and 1910, Turner was Speaker's Lecturer in Biblical Studies; from 1914 to 1920 University Lecturer in Early Christian Literature and History; and in 1920 he was elected Ireland Professor of the Exegesis of Holy Scripture. Cf. W. Lock, *Oxford Memories* (London: Oxford University Press, 1932), 110–112.

Congregationalist minister with her future husband, Claud Coltman (another Mansfield student), on the evening of 17 September 1917. She was the first woman to be ordained to Christian ministry in Britain.[126]

Constance Todd's period at Mansfield and subsequent ordination in London witnesses to how Mansfield and its tutors adopted altogether different approaches to ecclesiology and theological education from the Anglican faculty at Oxford. Considering the long and painful history of women's ministry in the Church of England, the decision to include a woman in preaching classes and other ministerial training at Mansfield during the First World War is testament to both Selbie's courage and the much looser structures of authority found within the Congregational church.

Although the momentous decision to invite Todd to study at Mansfield is largely peripheral to the practice of theology within the University (as Todd matriculated in London), the radicalism of Mansfield and Selbie was clearly not to be integrated into the faculty at this stage of its development. The defeat of Scott Holland's legislation in Convocation in 1913 was a pivotal moment for the development of theology as a modern discipline at Oxford. While the reformers' plans were themselves remarkable for Oxford when laid out in the summer of 1911, and testament to a bold, trans-denominational, theological approach that typified Oxford theology prior to the First World War, perhaps equally significant for the history of modern English theology was their failure to be passed by Convocation. Whereas in 1904 William Ince had rallied the clergy to Oxford to vote down the liberalizing measures introduced by the Hebdomadal Council, the rejection of the statutes in the spring of 1913 signified a clear divide between how theology was perceived

---

126. Elaine Kaye, Janet Lees and Kirsty Thorpe, eds., *Daughters of Dissent* (London: United Reformed Church, 2004), 20-21, 55ff.

by academic theologians at Oxford (both in the colleges and in the Nonconformist halls) and in the rest of the Church of England.

This divide, interestingly, was not so prevalent at Cambridge, where measures opening the Divinity degrees to Nonconformists had been approved by the Senate on 22 November 1912. Cambridge, like Oxford, had accepted that a modern faculty of theology could no longer function purely as an arm of the Church of England; provision had to be made for Nonconformist theologians and students. How a faculty might be redefined had clearly exercised the minds of the Cambridge professors and, as in Oxford, their thinking had raised obvious questions about the boundaries of theology as such: without creeds, Articles, or the requirements of ordination, were there to be any boundaries to the practice of theology in the 'secularized' University? At Cambridge, however, there was no suggestion that their faculty would cease to be a Christian institution. W. Emery Barnes, the Hulsean Professor, repudiated the suggestion that the professors were seeking to 'dechristianize' the degrees. In a contribution to the *Cambridge Review,* he emphasized that the BD and DD would not practicably be extended to theses on non-Christian subjects ("The thing is unworkable"), commenting that, "One professoriate (whether five or fifty strong) cannot possibly represent Mahommedanism (and its languages), Buddhism (and its languages), &c., in addition to Christianity with its Hebrew, Greek, and Latin."[127]

Scott Holland, by contrast, failed to register fully the complex investment of the Church, historically and politically, in the life of the two 'ancient' English universities, and the overriding – and regularly obstructive – influence of Convocation in university matters. There were clear limits to what could be achieved. Whereas Cambridge professors worked pragmatically with its ecclesiastical partners, Scott

---

127. *Cambridge Review,* 2 May 1912.

Holland never recovered from his indelicate words at the promulgation of statutes in Congregation and successive writings. He wrote to his sister-in-law, Alice Holland, after the decisive vote in Convocation:

> I had got to accepting the blow before it came. It was inevitable: we had asked too much of the outsiders, who cannot understand the situation here. But I did not think that it would be quite so downright and smashing. And I do think that they might have shown some faint trust in our not being mere weak betrayers. It was too stupid of them. Our whole record seems to go for nothing. Their timidity shames me: and their total lack of generosity towards those outside the Church, in their rejection of the statute about the examiners. Up here, that hardly needed discussing. Everybody knew it was a mere matter of equity. We are 'done' for a time.[128]

Yet, "mere equity" had been the clarion call of the Cambridge professors, and reform had been approved there. Scott Holland's radicalism went beyond this, and his surprise that the defeat would be "quite so downright and smashing" suggests the naïveté of one unfamiliar, or at least out of touch with, the abiding ecclesiastical bonds of the faculty. Although his plans for an 'undenominational' faculty were arguably logical and cognizant of the changing shape and methodology of theology in the multidenominational University, its total rejection of dogmatic boundaries for the theological task proved to be a step too far. Oxford, in short, was not Manchester.

Although Convocation's influence was evidently frustrating for Scott Holland and his peers, its veto nonetheless ensured that Oxford could not totally 'secularize' its theological life by erecting an 'undenominational principle'. Early in the programme of reform, there was evidently some appetite for the study of religion "simply

---

128. Letter of Henry Scott Holland to Mrs Spencer Holland, quoted in S. Paget, *Henry Scott Holland: Memoir and Letters* (London: John Murray, 1921).

as a body of fact and experience which can be defined, classified, examined, compared", as Scott Holland had described it. The clear rejection of the faculty's proposals ensured that, whenever reform was proposed again, the faculty would not be allowed to abandon its Christian character, nor its historic commitment to the training of clergy in the Church of England. Despite the movement towards a 'scientific' theology in collaboration with Nonconformist theologians in the decades since 1882 among Oxford theologians, the faculty was not permitted to forget its confessional responsibilities, nor its basic commitment to theology as a response to revelation and the explication of a definite Creed. The role for the faculty that was crafted by Pusey and his colleagues at the outset of the honour school in 1868-69 was, as we have seen, echoed in the arguments against Scott Holland's reforms in 1912-13. Whatever Oxford theology would become in the years after the war in the search for "mere equity", the voice of Convocation announced clearly that it could not successfully be a department of 'comparative religion'. The settlement that was secured for Oxford theology came only in the aftermath of the Great War and in the form of a new Regius Professor of Divinity.

4
———

An Ecumenical Theology: The Makings of an English Paradigm, 1918-45

Introduction: the Abolition of 'Divvers'

On 9 February 1932, Congregation assembled in the Sheldonian Theatre, beneath Robert Streater's ceiling-fresco of Truth descending upon the Arts and Sciences to dispel ignorance in the university. The university's governing assembly had convened to determine the future of Responsions, the examinations that school-leavers sat prior to matriculation. Ostensibly, it was a debate sterile of any interest beyond what sorts of knowledge ought to be considered as preparatory to a university education. This meeting of Congregation was, however, a seminal moment in the history of the University of Oxford's foundational relationship with Christianity and the history of higher education in Britain. The *Oxford Magazine* went on to describe it as "a minor landmark in the cultural development of the country."[1] For, within an hour of the vice chancellor opening the assembly, Congregation had decided by a majority of nineteen to abolish the oldest remaining element in a common Oxford education: divinity.

As we have observed in earlier chapters, this examination had been the object of student ridicule for some years and many considered it to be performing a disservice to its title since the middle of the previous century. It had been introduced in 1800 as a means of a guaranteeing the religious affiliations of Oxford men in an era of political, philosophical, and social revolution, but by the middle of the twentieth century it was perceived not so much as a harmless survival of Oxford's ecclesiastical heritage, so much as an unnecessary obstacle to undergraduate education.

Prior to its abolition as a compulsory examination in 1932, what has come to be one of the most infamous episodes in divinity's history was the failure of the young John Betjeman to pass the examination in early 1928. He satisfied the examiners after being rusticated for the duration of Trinity Term, but he returned to Magdalen only to find himself re-classified as a Pass degree candidate by his tutor, C.S. Lewis. Annoyed, he took his vengeance by helping to publish a 'Divvers' edition of the student satirical magazine, *The University News,* in December 1928. Apart from 'cut-out and keep' Old and New Testament cribs in the style of shirt cuffs to be worn by candidates, it included pieces such as 'A Straight Talk to Candidates for Divinity Examinations: How "Divvers" Helped Me' by the fictional 'Brig[adier]-Gen[eral]. Sir John Alcock, V.C., D.S.O., C.B., B.F., etc., etc.':

> "Divvers" is an examination which jogs up your memory of the best parts of the Grand Old Book. I remember my tutor, old Tommy ("Tosspot" we called him) Littletap, when I was up at Brasenose – and it was brazen in my days, by gad – saying to me: "Jock" – I was always

1. *The Oxford Magazine,* 11 February 1932.

known as "Jock," "Jock" Alcock of the "Buffs" – "Jock," he says, "you'll have to take Divvers." "Be blowed for a yarn," I said. "Well, if you don't" he said, "you'll be sent down." Well, I had a date with little Eva Dishful, who was touring in "The Gaiety Girl" – none of your Playhouse stuff when I was up – and I couldn't afford to be sent down. So I brewed a pretty stiff peg – and by G—, Sir, our pegs were pretty stiff in my time – and I sent out for a Bible; and I read slap through it that night. When I went up for my Viva – Old Gutty Guggeberg vivaed me – "What happened to Judas?" he asked. "He hanged himself," I said, "and a d—d good job too." On the parade ground and in the barrack-room I have always relied on the sound Christian grounding that I got from "Divvers." [...] My creed has been simple: treat your rifle as your would your wife, treat your wife as you do your rifle, never mix your drinks, keep a stiff upper lip, remember women are the weaker sex, and that your stomach is bigger than your fist. And don't forget the Bible. I haven't got much time for Groups, but no nonsense about "Divvers."[2]

Satire was a natural response for undergraduates, for whom the peculiar roll-call of biblical facts required in the examination would have been an odd prerequisite for an Oxford degree in the post-war years. Some questions from a 1930 examination paper could almost have featured in the celebrated parody of English historical writing, *1066 and All That:*

Explain, with reference to the context: –
(a) The gates of Hades shall not prevail against it.
(b) Of a truth, Master, thou hast well said that he is one.
(c) Wist ye not that I must be in my Father's house.
(d) How can a man be born when he is old?

Describe *two* miracles of our Lord where fish are mentioned in the narrative.
(Questions 1 and 6, *The Four Gospels English,* Hilary 1930)

2. *The University News,* Vol.1, 229 (No. 7, 1 December 1928). cf.. J. Priestman, "The Dilettante and the Dons" in *Oxford Today* Vol. 18, No.3 (Trinity 2006); also, B. Hillier, *Young Betjeman* (London: John Murray, 1998).

Describe in detail the events which occurred between St. Paul's landing at Tyre and his arrest at Jerusalem. Make plain the cause of arrest.

Write brief notes on the following phrases: 'Grecian Jews', 'the Italian band', 'the days of unleavened bread','these that have turned the world upside down', 'the baptism of John', 'grievous wolves'.
(Questions 6 and 7, *Acts of the Apostles*)

Give a detailed account of the peril with which Jerusalem was threatened during the reign of Hezekiah, and of how that peril was averted.

Outline the song of 'my beloved touching his vineyard', and draw out its meaning.
(Questions 4 and 8, *2 Kings IX to the End, Amos, Isaiah I-XII*)[3]

The promulgation of the statute removing the Examination in Holy Scripture from the First Public Examination was passed in Congregation on 24 November 1931. Mr Parker of Magdalen, the *Oxford Magazine* tells us, spoke in favour, and the Provost of Oriel opposed, to no avail. In the months between the promulgation and approval of the statute, there was some debate over the examination's continued existence in *The Oxford Magazine*. An unnamed contributor offered an article in *The Oxford Magazine* on 21 January 1932, entitled "Holy Scripture: The Real Case Against a Compulsory Examination". The contributor believed that the approaching debate in Congregation would be so limited, or so carefully managed, that the "real case" against the examination would not be offered. "For the real case," he wrote, "is bound up in the end with the distinction

---

3. First Public Examination: Holy Scripture, Hilary Term 1930 (Oxford: Clarendon Press, 1930). The 'Divvers' edition of *The University News* offered its own array of 'useful' information in the 'Did you know?' section: '1. That Psalm xviii, verse 8, divides the Bible in two exact halves? 2. That the shortest chapter in the whole Bible is Psalm cxvii- which is also the middle chapter of the whole book? 3. That the shortest verse in the Old Testament is I Chronicles, i, 25 – "Eber, Peleg, Reu"; and in the New Testament, St. John xi, 35 – "Jesus wept"? 4. That the Old Testament contains 929 chapters, 31,173 verses and 693,503 words? Whereas the New Testament has only 260 chapters, 7,059 verses and 181,253 words? And that the whole Bible contains 3,566,480 letters? NO? Then go and take Divvers again.' (*The University News*, 1: 226)

between religion and theology, and the question whether and how it is possible or desirable to teach either."[4] In the article, the contributor attacks the principal argument of the examination's defenders ("the seven"), namely "the cultural argument", which emphasizes the literary and historical importance of the texts in question.[5] Despite claiming the examination as an important element in cultural formation, the defenders of the statute still described it as "religious education". Here, the contributor claimed, is the problem, for

> . . . it is plain that the study of the documents vital to the Christian religion, as conducted in our schools by professed or convinced Christians (sometimes by clergymen), cannot possibly be merely literary or historical or cultural; in effect, even if not directly, the truth of that religion, or rather theology, will be inculcated or suggested.

The element of inculcation in "religious education" was, the contributor claims, accepted by the university when it allowed conscientious objection to the examination on religious grounds. Yet, "No one has conscientious objections to the study of what is of prime merit in literature or importance in history." Accepting this as understood, the contributor proceeded to state a standard objection to religious education, aware that many in Congregation hoped to make the examination compulsory for school-leavers in Responsions, if not in Moderations:

> One objection to the teaching of religion is that religion cannot be taught. What can, in a sense, be taught is theology, but schoolmasters are not competent to teach it. The schoolboy is at a time of life when the emotions are strong and critical intellect is weak. It is not obviously desirable to utilise this situation in order to commend, however unconsciously, the acceptance of beliefs which everyone with even the rudiments of scientific or philosophic culture knows to be highly

---

4. *Oxford Magazine,* 21 January 1932. I presume that the correspondent was male only because the respondents do.
5. It has not been possible to find the article of the 'seven'.

doubtful, even when they are intelligible. Nor is it obviously desirable to suggest that there is some connection between the acceptance of such beliefs and the attainment of moral excellence.

This argument should not, he reassures, be construed as a plain "opposition to Christianity. This would be a serious misunderstanding." Rather, that "so far as possible, an acceptance of Christian tenets which is irrevocable, or hard to revoke, should not precede the comparative maturity of the intellect."[6]

The following week saw two letters in response to the 'real case': the first from a Christian ('C.M.F.') and the second ('Quo Vadis') seemingly from an agnostic or atheist. Both respondents express a concern with what they perceive to be the proposed vacuum of religio-philosophical thought for the schoolboy prior to his arrival at the University implied by the previous week's contributor. 'C.M.F.' queried how the professed Christian, who supposedly admits to religious education being "not an unmixed blessing...a danger to intellectual integrity and sound morals", might "keep the child from all hint of religious suggestion until he reached maturity."[7] For these parents would "feel some apprehension, if they fail to put those in their care in possession of the basic facts, that they will leave them prey to any casual and misleading influence." 'C.M.F.' asserted that

> . . . advocacy of such a course implies a view of human nature completely static. Are we to suppose that religion has no value for the intellectually immature, that they are thus to be deprived of it? Life does not wait for intellectual maturity to present its problems. . . . The category must be small of those who would sacrifice the real claims of human care and responsibility to a timid and mistrustful agnosticism that in the name of intellectual integrity cries Hold!

6. *Oxford Magazine,* 21 January 1932
7. *Oxford Magazine,* 28 January 1932.

Similarly, 'Quo Vadis', queried the postponement of a Christian conversion which through "some unhealthy admixture of enthusiasm . . . would degrade what should be an act of pure and perfect reason," asking whether

> [I]t really be possible to keep the growing boy unspotted from the taint of imperfectly proven theological hypotheses? Would there not always be a danger that he would exclaim inopportunely at a lunch party, 'Father, what are the Acts of the Apostles?' only to be sent away amidst the blushes of the ladies and looks of carefully sustained unembarrassment by the men, to see whether it was still raining? Can we be sure that his mind would still be conveniently blank when, having attained intellectual maturity the lad of twenty-five is led into his father's study to be told, 'My boy, there is something which I think you ought to know.' . . . the result would be to give the Mystery Religion a strange and terrible fascination to the youthful mind most unsettling to the intellect.

Instead, 'Quo Vadis' suggested that undergraduates ought to grapple with "the facts of religious experience" as were beginning to be understood by advances in psychology, suggested as the "antidote" to such religious concepts as "the conviction of sin". To suppose, however, "that the problem can be left to the age of maturity is to close our minds to facts that constitute the most relevant data of the problem."

The *Oxford Magazine* article and the accompanying correspondence suggest that Congregation was caught in a debate not about such urbane issues as the undergraduate level of study or secondary education, but about the place and role of religious education in an academic environment otherwise committed to the 'objective' pursuits of reason. If the *Magazine* was indeed accurately representing university opinion, then we must presume that the majority of Congregation agreed with 'Quo Vadis' and the initial contributor's characterization of 'religious education' as the propagation of unsatisfactorily established beliefs to supple minds; the university, as a centre for rational debate and enquiry, could no longer occupy itself with the claims of religion.

There is good reason, however, to think that the approach to divinity's abolition was more complex than these two contributors suggest. A further debate, about which we have more knowledge thanks to the *Magazine,* took place in Congregation on 10 February, 1932. Although the statute removing 'Divvers' from Moderations had been approved *nemine contradicente* in the Sheldonian, significant amendments had been tabled for the Responsions Statute. Since 1926 Responsions had been the university's entrance examination, and amendments had been attached to a statute passing through Congregation so as to make Holy Scripture a compulsory component of the school-leavers' examination.

The Lady Margaret Professor of Divinity, N.P. Williams, moved the amendment reminding Congregation that while the previous debate had discussed the place of divinity in the First Public Examination, the principle of a compulsory examination had yet to be settled. "The question," the professor asserted (according to the *Magazine*), "went right to the roots of our ideal of education. The University, unlike a technical school, presented an ideal of a complete life – it did not merely teach specialised knowledge."[8] Williams argued that the University of Oxford had always striven to establish an education that created "a scholar and a gentleman." Thus, to prepare men (and it was men he had in mind) to be citizens and rulers, a knowledge of the classics and basic divinity was essential. He attacked the belief that a boy could grow up "unbiased" by dogmatic knowledge: "If authorities abolished scripture study then the minds of the young were biased by the knowledge that it was

8. *Oxford Magazine,* 11 February 1932.

'to be abolished.'" He urged the university to adopt a position of "benevolent neutrality" towards the Christian religion, as the state had done. Being "at the apex of the educational pyramid", Williams inferred that schools would eventually stop teaching scripture unless Oxford continued to recognise the importance and value of knowledge about the Christian tradition.

Williams's opponent in Congregation was a young lecturer from Christ Church, a 'Mr. G. Ryle'. Gilbert Ryle, who had received a strict evangelical upbringing but was himself without religious belief, did not offer his own thoughts on religious education in the debate. He apparently claimed that "it was . . . one of those issues in the discussion of which the real motives were not mentioned and only *ad hoc* reasons given." Ryle, rather, desired only to give his real reasons which was the concern of schools for those "less-gifted" boys who were coming up to Oxford for Responsions and had not taken the relevant certificates exempting them from Scripture examinations. In particular, Ryle identified Scottish boys as those having no opportunity to study divinity prior to Responsions and thus at an obvious disadvantage to the English public schoolboy. To Williams's claim that schools would eventually omit Scripture from their curricula, he believed that "by a tacit understanding between parents and schoolmasters" Scripture was not in danger of being removed from secondary education. And although schoolmasters "were ready to teach Scripture as much as ever", yet they were "hostile" to the Williams's amendment because it "would only lead to cramming and the study of scripture in a useless and undignified manner."

The *Magazine* goes on to record that

> It was almost three o'clock by the time that Mr. Ryle was entering on the concluding portion of his speech. It might have been held that in a matter of this importance, in taking a decision which will remain, at the

very least, a minor landmark in the cultural development of the country, one hour was no excessive period for reflection or debate. There must, however, be some doubt about this assumption, for some of the scholars and gentlemen present saw fit to express impatience by shuffling and interruption. The House divided shortly after three o'clock and there voted: For the Amendments, 108; against, 127. The amendments were therefore defeated by 19 votes. [9]

The account of the *Magazine* almost complicates as much as it clarifies our understanding of the debate. Whilst Williams, as an ecclesiastical figure, confirms one side's anxiety about divinity's removal as indicative of a secularist advance against an established benevolence towards Christianity in the university, Ryle almost expresses indifference for the secularist-Christian debate, concerned solely with those schoolboys who would be placed at an obvious disadvantage in Responsions. On the one hand, the debate signals a "minor landmark in the cultural development of the country"; on the other, the scholars and gentlemen were unexcited by the debate, expressing their impatience "by shuffling and interruption." On the one hand, this was a debate about the removal of Christian knowledge from the University, the final 'nail in the coffin' for the 'queen of the sciences'; on the other, it was a largely insignificant step in the broadening and improvement of Oxford's curriculum.

Despite Williams' attempts to conserve divinity however, the decision of Congregation and commentary – in both student and university magazines – does suggest that, by 1932, the Examination in Holy Scripture existence was an anomalous and anachronistic feature of Oxford's theological life. As a remnant of the role of theology in the university as an 'architectonic science' dispensing 'necessary knowledge' to young minds, it belonged more properly to the idea of the university that was swept away in the mid-nineteenth

9. *Oxford Magazine,* 11 February 1932.

century. For students, it was a curious remnant of an earlier curriculum and a burden within the timetable. Despite the debate in Congregation revolving almost entirely around young men, the burden of the examination was well known to Margot Collinson, who was a Modern History student at the women's college, St Hilda's, before the end of the First World War. Clearly more conscientious than Betjeman, she wrote home in Michaelmas 1917, recounting revision sessions in her college:

> This place is almost quite untenable at present. Half the Hall is working either for Divvers or Smalls, and is like nothing so much as a bear with a sore head. There is something extra on every night – particularly now we are out of quarantine. Last night it was Cannon [sic] Streeter, who came to conduct a very interesting discussion which would up our study circles on Job. We made up "pours" for him to answer, mostly concerned with the Devil, that part of the question seeming to leave an extraordinary attraction for most people.[10]

Despite Williams' comments during the debate in Congregation, however, it does not seem as if there was enormous enthusiasm for the examination in the theological faculty itself. In 1919, the first Oriel Professor of the Philosophy of the Christian Religion, Clement C.J. Webb, can be read as treating the nomination of examiners for divinity as akin to committing a practical joke; in his diary for 23 January 1919 he wrote: "After luncheon to Nominating Committee for Exam in H[oly] S[cripture]. Nominated A.C.H.! [Arthur Cayley Headlam]" The new Regius Professor of Divinity would no doubt have been delighted by his nomination, considering the rate of *viva voce* examinations.[11] The vacation after being compelled to examine in the subject, Headlam called a meeting to discuss the future of 'Divvers':

10. St Hilda's College Archives: Collinson Papers.
11. Bodleian MS. Eng. misc. e. 1164 (f19): Diaries of C.C.J. Webb, 23 January 1919.

After luncheon to Headlam's for meeting to discuss the future of 'Pass Divinity'. Headlam, Walker, Prichard Cambridge, Warden of New College, Genner, Rawlinson, Brooks, Leonard Hodgson, Moberly, Streeter and J. All deemed its reform necessary except Rawlinson and Moberly who wanted to abolish it altogether. General agreement that it would come better at the beginning of a man's course and that Divinity in the Certificate examination should exempt from it.[12]

The continuation of the examination was perplexing and, many felt, damaged the position of theology more generally in the university. While undergraduates were being asked about Jesus' miracles involving fish, undergraduates being examined in the honour school of theology were being asked, by contrast:

How far is it possible to infer the pre-literary history of the traditions of the life and teaching of Jesus from the various forms in which the material is presented in the Gospels? (Question 7, *The Holy Scriptures*)

and

Discuss the view that the Ritschlian attempt to state a theology independent of metaphysics has hindered the development of a Christian philosophy. (Question 5, *The Philosophy of Religion*)[13]

By 1930 theology at Oxford was now a discrete and specialized subject within the university. It possessed its own honour school, its own faculty board, its own seminars and research students, and its members published learned monographs on biblical and dogmatic history. Although compulsory divinity had endured as a compulsory element of learning longer than even Greek, its abolition did mark

12. MS. Eng. misc. e. 1164 (f39): March 7 1919.
13. *Second Public Examination: School of Theology,* Trinity Term 1930 (Oxford: Clarendon Press, 1930). Examination reports, lecture lists and bibliographies suggest that the Philosophy of Religion was a popular subject amongst students for the first three decades of the twentieth century, and was a vehicle for the Modernists' interests in Continental philosophy.

the end of theology as an aspect of general education in the University of Oxford.

Despite being integrated into the aims and methods of the research university, Oxford theologians and the wider university did not simultaneously assert the need for the 'de-confessionalization' of the subject, nor desire its conversion into a department of religious studies or comparative religion. Although important elements of Oxford theology's historic bonds to the Church of England remained in place (the senior professorships, in particular, remained tied to canonries at Christ Church) the inter-war faculty was also reformed in such a way to accommodate plural Christian traditions and institutions. What emerges, as we shall see, is what became the hallmark of English university theology by the mid-twentieth century: a faculty that was not purely professional in its offering of education (as in many continental universities), that was not demarcated from the rest of the university as a graduate theological hall (as in the United States), nor defined purely by one Christian denomination (as in Germany and Scotland), but which was confidently multi-confessional, ecumenical in tone, committed to liberal education as well as professional, and situated firmly within a globally influential research university.

It is too much to suggest that this settlement for Oxford theology emerged from any single vision for the faculty's life and practice in the aftermath of the First World War. Indeed, like so much of Oxford's *ad hoc* development, both as a university and in its theological life, change was late in arrival and was invariably half as transformative as reformers had hoped. However, the key statutory reforms that formed the basis for Oxford theology's ecumenical character can be attributed, in large part, to the principles and energy of the man who succeeded Scott Holland as Regius Professor of

Divinity after he died in his rooms at Christ Church on 17 March 1918: Arthur Cayley Headlam.

A.C. Headlam as Regius Professor of Divinity

Arthur Cayley Headlam is more usually remembered for his infamous defence of the German Reichskirche during the 1930s when he was Bishop of Gloucester. As Principal of King's College London (1903-1913) and then as Regius Professor of Divinity at Oxford (1918-23), however, Headlam acted as one of the most formidable influences in shaping the practice of English theology as a university discipline in the early twentieth century.

When he was chosen by the Crown to succeed Scott Holland, the faculty that he encountered was unreformed; war and the ill health of Scott Holland had inhibited any further attempts by the Board to change the theological statutes, but the death of the Regius professor naturally prompted the reconsideration of the faculty's role and purpose. Headlam was a shrewd political choice for Oxford, and the *Oxford Magazine* warmly praised his appointment.[14] Headlam had "been in close touch" with Oxford's "local controversies", it reported, his having regarding Scott Holland's statute in 1913 as "the continuance of this process of taking away the Christian character of the institutions of the country, and the opportunities which they give for religious influence". Headlam's arrival would have appealed to those who had resisted the "undenominational" principle they had perceived in Scott Holland's proposals.[15]

This is not to claim that Headlam was unbending on the question of reform. While critical of Scott Holland's reforms, he had accepted in 1913 that "the time has come when it will be only just and fair that Nonconformists who are students of the University of Oxford should

14. *The Oxford Magazine,* 3 May 1918.
15. A.C. Headlam, "Degrees in Divinity", *Church Quarterly Review,* 76 (1913): 357.

be allowed under certain conditions to obtain a Divinity degree", even if "nothing should be done which would destroy the Christian character of the degree, or unduly change its traditional place in the system of the University."[16] He argued that the explicit conservation of the Christian character of the faculty actually provided a more equitable settlement for the Nonconformists; Mansfield College, he considered, could never have tolerated a system whereby half the professorships were held by Unitarians and the other half by Roman Catholics, as this would have rendered them incapable of training people for the Congregationalist ministry. An undenominational faculty of theology "would be entirely useless, and would do nothing but shock the religious sense of the country."[17]

Coming from London, Headlam had been all too aware of the challenge of integrating different denominational bodies without sublating their theological traditions. Headlam had been a professor of dogmatic theology at King's College London between 1906 and 1916 and had served as principal of the College between 1903 and 1912. During this time at London he had separated the college into two parts; the secular faculties were controlled by the Delegacy, appointed by the Senate of the University of London, while the theology faculty at King's continued to belong to the Church of England, governed by its own council, and unable to be incorporated into the University of London.[18] Nonetheless, the six affiliated theological colleges of the University of London, which included that of King's, together contributed to the Board of Studies of the Faculty of Theology in the University of London. The University's faculty recognized the teachers in each of the individual colleges,

16. *Ibid.*
17. *Ibid.*
18. *London Theological Studies* (London, 1911); see also Lambeth Palace Library, Headlam MSS 2618, ff192–94; Letter of A.C. Headlam to the Bishop of London about the foundation of Cheshunt College.

two of which were Congregationalist (Hampstead New College and Hackney College), one was Baptist (Regent's Park College, soon to move to Oxford), a Wesleyan college in Richmond, and St John's at Highbury alongside King's as another Anglican institution.[19] The teachers of these various colleges in turn formed the separate Board of Studies that appointed examiners who were taken from each college and who formed a common syllabus.

Headlam considered the University of London model, largely shaped by his predecessor Archibald Robertson, to be an ecumenical success. He praised the fact that the system did not "force people into a common mould", the examinations being on "an historical basis, and not a dogmatic basis."[20] Commending this multi-denominational model for the study of theology within a university, Headlam had written to the Bishop of London in critical terms of the proposed Anglican adoption of the buildings of the Nonconformist Cheshunt College after it moved to Cambridge in 1905 (what would later become Bishop's College). He argued that there were already more than enough post-graduate theological colleges in the Church of England and instead advanced that, "What we want to do is to concentrate our efforts in making the Church strong in contact with the life and vigour of the new Universities, as well as the old."[21]

This insistence upon rejuvenating English theological faculties was rooted in a belief that the Church of England was suffering from its multiple centres for theological education across the country. Echoing Evangelical voices earlier in the nineteenth century, Headlam complained that these were often small, isolated institutions with few teaching staff. Later, he would describe it as one of the greatest tragedies of the Western Church that the education of the

19. St John's would move to Nottingham in 1970.
20. Lambeth Palace Library, *ibid.*
21. *Ibid.*

clergy had been steadily separated from the "atmosphere of the Universities", both in the Roman Catholic Church since the Council of Trent and increasingly in the Church of England of his own day. Later encouraging the University of Bristol to engage with theological study in 1923, he asserted that

> . . . what is important is that the religion which is taught to the nation should be, on the one side, true to all the traditions of Christianity and to the life and spirit of our Lord and Saviour Jesus Christ, but that, on the other side, it should be taught in the language of the day, with full knowledge of the scientific, philosophical and theological knowledge of the time, recognising the inspiration of the intellect as well as the inspiration of the spirit.[22]

If the Church of England were to become once again a "great spiritual organ of the country", he believed that it could only be through substantial investment in the building up of theological faculties in close proximity to the universities, new and old, and nurturing a new generation of clergy who could be conversant with modern thought and know their religion "'practically and devotionally', as laymen do, but they have no clear guidance or help to give as to what lies beyond, as to what practice and devotion may rest upon, and yet that very guidance as to the 'beyond' is what the professional or expert is set apart to provide."[23]

These convictions, learnt at London, were soon translated into clear priorities for the study of theology at Oxford. These Headlam outlined in his inaugural lecture as Regius Professor of Divinity in June 1918, entitled simply 'The Study of Theology'. He began with the assertion that theology "must be the interpretation of a deep and simple religious experience", for which "our academic Theology and

22. A.C. Headlam, *Universities and Religion: A Sermon preached in Bristol Cathedral, May 24th, 1923* (Bristol, 1923),
23. Lambeth Palace Library, *ibid.*

the religious teaching of our clergy have been found wanting in the stress of the present crisis."[24] Instead

> Our Theology has been too much concerned with subordinate questions and too little with fundamental facts. Our minds became absorbed in the history of ministry, or the dislocation of the canon, or the Chalcedonian Christology, and we have forgotten to speak and think of the being and nature of God, of life and death and judgment.[25]

Headlam accepted that religion "had become confused with the conception of material progress" in the pre-war period, with people coming to believe that "sin had no real existence"; Christianity, he claimed, "was identified in many minds with the shallow contemporary political thought, and when the breakdown came the disillusionment was terrible." The source of our answers in the present crisis and the first condition for the study of theology, Headlam argued, was the teaching of Christ, and the "academic theologian must never allow the interest of intellectual problems to make him forget the realities of personal religion, or to centre his thought on any other point but the revelation of God through Christ."[26]

The second condition must be the "recognition of the full stream of Christian tradition, that throughout the centuries the Christian Church has been taught by the Spirit who will lead us into all truth." Striking a clearly ecumenical tone to theological practice, Headlam announced that

> We must be ready to learn from the whole Christian tradition – Patristic, Mediaeval, Reformation, Latitudinarian, Rationalist, Evangelical – and we must be ready also to learn from all Christian churches. We must correct the idiosyncracies of Anglicanism by the

24. A.C. Headlam, *The Study of Theology, An Inaugural Lecture* (Oxford: Oxford University Press, 1918).
25. A.C. Headlam, *The Study of Theology*, 5-6.
26. A.C. Headlam, *The Study of Theology*, 8.

study of Nonconformity. We must correct the Roman tradition by the Eastern. We must not despise Calvinism or Lutheranism. We must study Episcopalianism in the light of Presbyterian and Congregationalism and find out the defects of its presentation.[27]

The third condition for theology, Headlam suggested, is freedom, and he believed that the western Catholic tradition offered a generous space for development within the canon. "The reality of the atoning death of Christ has been always the life of Christianity," he said, "but the interpretation of that belief has been conditioned by the spiritual needs of each Christian generation." There was, for example, no single Catholic explanation for the Atonement and the Articles of the Church of England, he suggested (with echoes of Thomas Arnold) were "articles of comprehension, not exclusion". This "liberty" has allowed the Church of England to confront and deal with the problems presented by "modern biology" and biblical criticism.

This broadly liberal and ecumenical portrait of Christian theology was accompanied by his fourth condition for theology, which he described as "reverent criticism".[28] He classed this as not simply the "literary composition and the historical witness of the Bible and the Early Church", but also the psychology of religion and the history of modern theology. By being "reverent", this solidly English criticism nonetheless avoided the more speculative and radical work one found in much continental writing. He took as a positive example of such criticism S.R. Driver's work on the Old Testament. Driver avoided the "vagaries" and "guess-work" that seemed to characterize much – largely German – criticism, Headlam claimed, and the same could be said for Sir John Hawkins on the Synoptic Problem or Lightfoot on the Apostolic Fathers. British theology was marked by its desire for

27. *Ibid.*, 10.
28. *Ibid.*, 16.

"objective proof" and sound foundations, as opposed to what were seen as "plausible guesses" and "conjecture" abroad.[29]

How did these four conditions for the study of theology work practically, not least in a university that still demanded that one had to be in holy orders of the Church of England to supplicate for a Divinity degree or to be an examiner in the honour school? How could it bring about a more rigorous, yet reverent, criticism among its practitioners while still providing for the education of the clergy, a challenge that had perplexed theologians since the honour school was introduced in 1869?

Headlam compared the theological faculty in his inaugural lecture to one of the post-graduate professional faculties, such as Law or Medicine. Unlike in the United States, these faculties were not institutionally distinct from the rest of the university as professional divinity schools. As with medical students, Headlam asserted that the faculty existed within the university to offer professional training for future clergy, and in particular the clergy of the Church of England. However, just as medical professors could not be content with "repeating the traditional medical formulas", so every teacher "must be ready to enter on new fields of thought, and every clergyman must be trained to wrestle with new religious problems, because the thoughts of those to whom he is to minister will be continually changing."[30] And as a faculty of medicine will be staffed by doctors, so "the suggestion that the teachers of theology should not be required to be ordained could only be made by those ignorant of what a Theological Faculty means". As the medical faculty has a close relationship to the General Medical Council and the Royal Colleges, so the theological faculty has a "double-relation" to the University and to religious opinion in the public realm:

29. *Ibid.,* 19–20.
30. *Ibid.,* 22.

The University must have in its mind the practical demands of the religious society, just as it has to consider the requirements of the General Medical Council, but on the other side its duty is to correct the intellectual inadequacies of the Church and the weakness of popular religion.[31]

In order to address the "inadequacies" of the Church as a body of critical thinkers, the faculty thus needed to be in "a position of independence". The bishops of the Church of England should not, in Headlam's opinion, be allowed to exercise management in the faculty, just as the university at large could not be subject to the national Board of Education. The faculty existed as a point of contact, and the means of a critical partnership, between the university and the churches.

Reforming the Faculty at Oxford

The new Regius professor's insistence that a faculty of theology ought to remain staffed by practising clergymen and must be dedicated to the education of future clergy as a medical faculty is dedicated to the education of future doctors would have reassured those who had been disturbed by Scott Holland's disestablishmentarian instincts in 1911-13. Under Headlam's aegis, there was no suggestion that Oxford was about to abandon its commitment to the Church of England or, more generally, Christianity.

Headlam's principles outlined in 1918 were vigorously pursued in the faculty. As Headlam had written in his inaugural lecture, although Oxford had been "one of the most famous schools of Theology in the world, and its religious influence, direct and indirect, has been perhaps wider and more permanent than any other single University . . . by a curious anomaly as a University Faculty it is completely

31. *Ibid.,* 23.

unreformed."[32] He lamented the failure of the faculty to reform the Divinity degrees ("still distinguished by that absence of merit which, as in the case of the [Order of the] Garter, is so dear to the English heart") or to offer its own course of education for the clergy. Oxford was "probably no better place . . . better fitted to be a home for training the clergy", and Headlam suggested that strong recommendations were to appear shortly for the creation of courses for the training of the clergy within the university, not least "in order that we may be ready for the time after the war when the Church will have to recuperate her strength."[33] For Headlam, the university must once again reclaim its role from the theological colleges as the primary educator of the clergy, "enabling the student to construct his own system of thought and life", whilst avoiding the "seminary method" where the ordinand is moulded by a carefully defined, and often partisan, theological and devotional life.

Headlam was hesitant about recommending too strongly theological honours, although by no means did he wish to discard the course. However, he believed that

[A] clergyman, however thorough a knowledge of theology he may have, who is below the general standard of culture, and does not know how educated people think, is a danger to the Church. That is why I believe that for most men the best course is a good degree in arts and science, followed by a proper training in theology.[34]

Nonetheless, theological honours would be the right course for some, not least because, as he would admit,

[A] thorough theological training in the University [for honours] has a more broadening influence on the mind than the proposed alternative of a second-rate knowledge of Modern History obtained without any

32. *Ibid.,* 24.
33. *Ibid.* 25.
34. *Ibid.,* 26.

great exertion in the University followed by a second-rate acquaintance with Theology obtained without any great exertion in a Theological College.[35]

Alongside an ordination course at Oxford, Headlam also asserted that the reform of the Divinity degrees was necessary. "It is our first duty to make these degrees a reality," he said, demanding, "a thesis showing original investigation and thought."[36] He also argued they should be opened to non-Anglicans, believing there to be "no danger to be apprehended" in so doing.

Relating his own cooperation with Nonconformists in London ("no difference of principle has arisen"), he argued that the Divinity degrees might reasonably be extended once the quality of them had been ensured, not least because "theological difficulties at the present day are as much between Churchman and Churchman as between Churchman and Nonconformist, and the same theological divisions are found in all the different religious bodies."[37]

Headlam was not unaware of the "certain difficulties of organization" that extension of the faculty to Nonconformists presented. The Divinity degrees would have to be explicitly "in Christian theology", but Headlam believed that an English faculty of theology did not, like its continental counterparts, need to be denominationally aligned:

> Such an arrangement is not necessary with us because the distinction in theology between ourselves and the Nonconformist bodies is not so great but that we can work together in the same Faculty. The arrangement that should, I believe, be adopted is to recognize different 'schools' of theology (if I may use the term) in one Faculty. The Divinity Professors and other teachers of the Church of England should be recognized as the Church of England 'school'. Mansfield College should

---

35. A.C. Headlam, *Theological Education in the Universities* (Oxford: Blackwell, 1921), 7.
36. *The Study of Theology*, 27-28.
37. *Ibid.*, 28.

be recognized in the same way, and its Professors and teachers be given a proper status in the University. They should have an adequate representation on the Faculty Board.[38]

By suggesting such denominational 'schools' could be incorporated within the one – previously exclusively Anglican – faculty, Headlam seemed to be aiming at a similarly pluralist constitution for theology to that which had been procured for the theological faculty in the University of London. It was a proposal not borne of dissatisfaction with the compromises or injustices of Establishment, as had been the case with Scott Holland's initial proposals, but out of a more positive account of ecumenism. Such a settlement for theology was not simply about satisfying the expectations of Nonconformists in the University, but was, for Headlam, crucial to the longer-term goal of reunion:

> The closer union will come when the different religious bodies are united – a consummation which many of us devoutly desire, but which will not be hastened by ignoring the differences which at present exist.[39]

Headlam offered these suggestions as purely "tentative" and his priority was, above all, the raising of standards for the Divinity degrees. However, in his inaugural lecture he had articulated a positive account of how different denominations might live together under the one 'Christian' umbrella of the faculty that, for 1918, was boldly ecumenical.

The Board did not delay in seeking reform. As the *Magazine* noted in October 1918, "Our new Regius Professor, we are glad to see, does not intend to allow himself to enjoy the dignified ease which used to be associated with the academic chairs of Oxford" and by the end of the year, the faculty board had appointed a committee to

---

38. *The Study of Theology*, 29.
39. *Ibid.*, 31.

consider the reform of the Divinity degrees.[40] While the committee initially put to one side the question of opening the degrees to those not in holy orders, it demanded that supplication for the DD required the candidate to offer a thesis which "must contain an original contribution to the study of Christian theology."[41]

What did an "original contribution" entail? An answer can be found in Hastings Rashdall's material submitted in support of his candidacy for the BD and DD jointly. As an examiner of Rashdall's work, Headlam described an "original contribution" as "to mean that the writer has gone to the original sources, that he has studied them with thoroughness and independence and that the conclusions that he arrives at, whether or not they are novel, are the result of original independent and first-hand investigation."[42] Unsurprisingly, there was no doubt that Rashdall had displayed such originality.

A further committee of the board advised that it was no longer appropriate to hand out doctorates in Divinity *iure dignitatis* to cathedral deans and public school headmasters if the faculty hoped to sustain the "intellectual standard" expected of the degree. More radically, the committee now suggested "that on suitable occasions the Degree should be conferred on members of the University who are not members of the Church of England."[43]

Headlam's broader aim of extending the degree to those not in Anglican holy orders was also successful. On 24 February 1920, the BD and the DD were opened to non-Anglicans, and from 16

---

40. *The Oxford Magazine,* 18 October 1918.
41. OUA FA 4/19/2/2, Theology Reports 1917-32, p11: Report of the Committee appointed to consider the question of the Divinity Degrees (no date, but late 1918)
42. OUA FA 4/19/2/2, Theology Reports 1917-32, p32: Report on Hasting Rashdall's application for the BD and DD (no date).
43. OUA FA/4/19/2/2, Theology Reports 1917-32, p31: Report of the Committee on Divinity Degrees conferred *iure dignitatis.* The committee consisted of Headlam, B.H. Streeter, and C.F. Burney. In relation to awarding DDs *iure dignitatis* to non-Anglicans, the committee gave as an example whomsoever was appointed as President of the Free Church Council.

May 1922, one no longer needed to be in Anglican holy orders to be an examiner in the honour school of theology.[44] Both proposals were passed *nemine contradicente* in Congregation, thus removing the necessity that the proposals should also be put to Convocation. William Selbie, the Principal of Mansfield and successor to Fairbairn, became the first Nonconformist to be awarded the DD by decree, and in 1924 the first Nonconformist to be an examiner in the honour school. In 1923, the board even asked the Registrar what steps it would need to take to open the Divinity degrees to women, which was itself a sign that the faculty no longer saw itself as an Anglican seminary; if it was "an original contribution to Christian theology" that was the mark of the qualification, then why indeed could a woman not be a candidate?[45] Despite the board's enthusiasm, a statute granting women Divinity degrees would not be passed until 1935.

In large part these measures were easily passed because there was a widespread conviction that reform was long overdue. The success in legislating these reforms can also, however, be attributed to the tact and care with which Headlam presented the statute. As H.B. Cooper of Keble College wrote in a letter to the *Magazine*,

> The main difference is that we are happily no longer confronted, as we were in 1913, with the grim alternative of all religions or none. When the earlier statute was introduced, it was authoritatively stated that a work e.g. on the Buddhist doctrine of Nirvana, or even an anti-theistic treatise, if showing sufficient learning, might have to be accepted as the qualifying thesis for the D.D. degree, though it is true that by a later amendment (tolerated rather than welcomed by the authors of the statute) any such subject would have to be dealt with in relation to Christian Theology. The wording of the present statute (which is

---

44. Headlam had introduced the statute 'with an excellent speech' and the statute's promulgation was passed *nemine contradicente,* according to Clement Webb in his diaries (Bodleian Special Collections MS. Eng. misc. e. 1164, f28v: Diaries of Clement Webb, entry for 4 February 1920).
45. OUA FA/4/19/2/2, Theology Reports 1917-32, p132: Letter of E.S. Craig, on behalf of the Board of the Faculty of Theology, to the Registrar of the University of Oxford regarding the admission of women to the Divinity degrees.

understood to be mainly the work of our new Regius Professor) show from first to last that the D.D. degree will remain one in Christian Theology and *nothing else*.[46]

Understood as "mainly the work of our new Regius Professor", these changes to the theological statutes were no small achievement by Headlam. Clearly, he had succeeded where Scott Holland had not and, while this must be in part due to the changed circumstances and atmosphere of post-war Oxford, the reforms were also the result of Headlam's tact and clear vision for how a theological faculty might remain confidently Christian in its focus whilst being inclusive of denominations other than the Church of England. While Cambridge had passed similar reforms with ease in 1913, the difference at Oxford in the early 1920s was that the reforms were presented as part of a positive ecumenical account of how theology might operate in practice in the modern English university. The denominational pluralism that was introduced into the Oxford faculty by Headlam would, in its essence, endure for the rest of the twentieth century.

The Oxford Ordination Course

Less successful was Headlam's other initiative during his brief tenure as Regius professor: the Oxford Ordination Course. Even before war had ended, Arthur Headlam had convened a group within his rooms at Christ Church to discuss the possibility of a new course for Anglican ordinands that would operate from within the faculty. It would be directed at postgraduate students but would be a course that benefited from the theological teaching on offer within the faculty, as well as Oxford's libraries. It was a distinctly alternative approach to ministerial training from what was available in the theological colleges and the *Magazine* suggests that his proposals were not

---

46. *The Oxford Magazine,* 20 June 1919.

unanimously greeted. In a letter to the *Magazine,* Headlam corrected what he thought was the periodical's one-sided account of the meeting. Headlam admitted that that opinion that theological colleges would still be necessary had been expressed, but he also told the *Magazine* that

> [T]here was an equally strong expression of opinion by others who also had practical experience that the reverse was true – that residence at a Theological College was not necessary or desirable for the majority of candidates for Orders.[47]

For the man who enjoyed claiming descent from Peter the Great and Oliver Cromwell, such opposition was not enough to disrupt his plans. Despite a further letter by 'a correspondent' to the *Magazine* who suggested that the Regius professor's "impressions get the better of his memory of the facts of his own meeting," Headlam proceeded with the Course.[48] With a committee that consisted of all the professoriate as well as other influential theologians in the university, Headlam produced regulations for the new course. Aimed at graduates and demobilized servicemen, it required .candidates to reside in one of the theological colleges or colleges of the university and to sit papers in the Old and New Testaments, Church History, Liturgies, the Study of Religion, Christian Doctrine, and engage in practical training in voice training, music, education and child psychology, and the composition and delivery of sermons.[49] He wrote to the bishops of the Church of England, commending the course as an ideal means of ensuring their desire that every candidate for orders should possess a degree from a recognised university or college.[50]

47. *The Oxford Magazine,* 25 October 1918.
48. *The Oxford Magazine,* 1 November 1918.
49. Bodleian G.A. Oxon, 80 884 (7): Regulations for the Oxford Ordination Course, no date (probably early 1919).

There is little evidence for how many students embarked upon the course, although examination papers are to be found in the Bodleian for the years 1919-24, and it was praised by the *Oxford Magazine* upon Headlam's departure in 1923.[51] In the end, however, the course disappeared. There is no clear account for why it failed. One might suspect, however, that it was simply unsustainable, and unattractive, when placed alongside the provision for ordinands that was already on offer in the four Anglican theological colleges in or near Oxford.

What, however, might be deduced from the course's failure for the development of English theology after the First World War? In one sense, it is not at all surprising that the Course was unsustainable; it was a long time since the universities had been perceived as the primary locations for ministerial training. Since the Oxford University Act 1854 (following the Royal Commission), there had been discontent with the universities as locations for training for orders, as can be seen in the foundation of Cuddesdon Theological College. Likewise, the further dissolution of the universities' ecclesiastical character with the Universities Tests Act 1871 encouraged the foundation of Wycliffe and St Stephen's House in Oxford and Westcott House and Ridley Hall in Cambridge. These later extra-mural institutions had been founded at the same time as the honour school of theology was failing to attract students by styling itself as a seminary-within-the-university. Accordingly, while the theological colleges on the periphery of the university would use the resources of the faculty (chiefly, having ordinands read for the

50. Lambeth Palace Library Headlam MSS 2622, f241: Memorandum of Walter Lock as Secretary of the Executive Committee on the Ordination Course, no date.
51. *Oxford Ordination Course Examination Papers* (Oxford, 1921-24). The first examination papers seem to date from October 1919. The first examination paper includes the note: "Candidates have this year been examined on work done during two terms only. The papers therefore do not cover all the subjects which are studied in the Course and will be a matter of examination in future years." Thus, we can presume that the first candidates for the ordination course began their studies in Hilary of 1919, the second term of Headlam's as Regius Professor of Divinity.

honour school as postgraduates), it is reasonable to conclude that by the middle of the twentieth century the faculty of theology at Oxford (as at Cambridge) was, first and foremost, a department of humanistic study and not a professional department of the Church of England.

Such a view of the faculty had actually been articulated by the Church of England long before Headlam had introduced the Ordination Course. As early as 1900, a Church committee on 'the Supply and Training of Candidates for Holy Orders' had stated in its report to the Convocation of Canterbury that

> [T]he real function of the University teaching of the Theological Faculty will always be misunderstood, unless it is distinctly realised that a Board of Theological Studies is an academic body, and not the servant of the Church. It is responsible to the University and not the Episcopate, and its members have to do with theology, or criticism, or hermeneutics as branches of learning…To use a sentence of Bishop Westcott (*Cathedral Foundations in relation to Religious Thought,* 'Essays on Cathedrals,' p.118) while "it would be disastrous to separate clerical education generally from the highest literal education of the country, the theological education at a University (in the case of candidates for Holy Orders) is only preparatory.[52]

A report was published eight years later at the request of Randall Davidson, archbishop of Canterbury, which became definitive for the Church in the first two decades of the twentieth century. Likewise, it had also expressed the Church of England's commitment to the belief that "a University course should be regarded as a preliminary to, not as an alternative for, a Professional Training."[53] In the evidence of the report, the Dean of Christ Church, T.B. Strong, opined "the University, as the Commission left it, is essentially a secular institution. The Divinity professorships are still held by Priests, but

---

52. *Convocation of Canterbury, Report of the Committee on the Supply and Training of Candidates for Holy Orders, May 1900* (London, National Society, 1900).
53. *The Supply and Training of Candidates for Holy Orders* (Poole: W.H. Hunt, 1908), 34.

the University is not concerned as such, either with maintaining, or developing, or arousing a desire for Holy Orders."[54]

In post-war Oxford, Headlam was rowing against the tide by trying to reintroduce ordination training as a core element of the faculty's duties. This is not to claim that the faculty was inimical to ordination training *per se*. For most of the twentieth century, the faculty would remain largely clerical in terms of its teachers, and a large proportion of theology graduates would enter some form of Christian ministry. Nonetheless, the positioning of ordination training within a university theological faculty that Headlam had desired was comprehensively shown to be impracticable and generally unwanted both within the university and the Church of England by the early twentieth century.

From 'Seminary of the Anglican Communion' to 'Ecumenical High School'

If it had been finally accepted that a university theological faculty was no longer primarily a school of ordination training and that undergraduate courses were merely "preparatory" to professional training, then what was a modern theological faculty for? In this final section, we examine how theology settled into a pattern of life and work at Oxford that it would sustain for the rest of the twentieth century. It is in many respects an account of *ad hoc* compromise and adjustment; Headlam was atypical amongst his peers in the early twentieth century in setting out a clear account the role and responsibilities of a theological faculty.

At the outset of this section, however, it is worth reflecting that the most celebrated figure of Oxford theology in the mid-twentieth century was not, in fact, a professional theologian. Several months

54. *Ibid.*, 9.

after Congregation had dismissed divinity from the list of compulsory subjects for undergraduates at Responsions, a Magdalen fellow of English was holidaying in Northern Ireland, writing what in due course would be published as *A Pilgrim's Regress*. It was C.S. Lewis's first allegorical work, and related the author's own conversion in 1929. That experience had occurred less than a year after Lewis had relegated Betjeman to a pass degree course having failed 'Divvers'. *A Pilgrim's Regress,* however, was the first of many books about Christian theology and apologetics, including *The Screwtape Letters* (1942), *Mere Christianity* (1952) and *Letters to Malcolm* (1964). His series of wartime broadcasts would also influence many; among others, a young Margaret Roberts, would later recount "the power of his broadcasts, sermons and essays" for their "combination of simple language and theological depth".[55] This combination made Lewis a publishing phenomenon. He sold almost a million paperbacks by 1963 and his life and thought continues to be the object of controversy and fascination internationally in a way incomparable with any other Oxford theologian, with the exception of John Henry Newman.[56]

Although Lewis occasionally is known to have helped examine theses in the faculty, and was friends with several Oxford theologians, he otherwise had no other responsibilities towards Oxford's theology faculty.[57] When Lewis was awarded an honorary doctorate in Divinity from the University of St Andrew's, the dean of their faculty, Donald Baillie, commented that

55. Roberts was the maiden name of Margaret Thatcher. See M. Thatcher, *The Path to Power* (London: Harper Collins, 1995), 40.
56. See Alister McGrath, *C.S. Lewis: A Life: Eccentric, Reluctant Prophet* (London: Hodder & Stoughton, 2013); *The Intellectual World of C.S. Lewis* (Oxford: Wiley Blackwell, 2013).
57. Oxford University Archives FA 4/19/2/5: Reports of the Board of the Faculty of Theology, 50. Lewis judged R. Sencourt's application for the BD and DD by accumulation in June 1940.

With his pen and with his voice on the radio Mr. Lewis has succeeded in capturing the attention of many who will not readily listen to professional theologians, and has taught them many lessons concerning the deep things of God. For such an achievement, which could only be compassed by a rare combination of literary fancy and religious insight, every Faculty of Divinity must be grateful.[58]

However, Lewis's contribution to his own faculty of divinity at Oxford was negligible. He perceived the faculty as a clerical body, and it is only in very recent years that professional theologians have begun to consider Lewis as a serious conversation partner.[59] During his period of celebrity at Oxford, however, the interests of academic theology were rarely aligned with the currents of popular religion, either nationally or within the university.

Compare, for instance, Lewis's publications with his friend and theology faculty member, Austin Farrer. Farrer has, like Lewis, enjoyed a revival among theologians in the past decade, but the influence he wielded does not even begin to compare with that of Lewis. Farrer was a fairly typical example of the mid-century professional theologian at Oxford. After a curacy, he had returned to the university in 1931 as chaplain and tutor at St Edmund Hall, before becoming chaplain and fellow in theology at Trinity College in 1935. He was ordained (the faculty was staffed entirely by men at this point) and combined his academic writing and research with pastoral care within his college. He has been widely considered as one of the greatest Anglican theologians of the twentieth century and yet his books were written for an altogether different market from those of Lewis. *Finite and Infinite* (1946) and *The Freedom of the Will* (1958) are densely written tracts of philosophical theology that

---

58. *St Andrew's Citizen*, 29 June 1946; quoted in W. Hooper, *C.S. Lewis: A Companion & Guide* (London: Harper Collins, 1996), 46. Lewis was awarded the DD on 28 June 1946.
59. J.F. and B.N. Wolfe, eds., *C.S. Lewis and the Church: Essays in Honour of Walter Hooper* (Edinburgh: T&T Clark, 2011).

would have been largely impenetrable to the average churchgoer. Even his popular works – *Saving Belief* (1964) and *Love Almighty and Ills Unlimited* (1962) – employ a method of argumentation that would have been understood only by a theologically articulate audience.[60]

The sales of Farrer's theological works do not, evidently, begin to compete with those of Lewis. Farrer's theological work was the fruit of academic specialization. Just as most of Lewis's writings on medieval English literature are not known beyond university departments, so it is unreasonable to expect the same reception for Farrer's work beyond theologians. What this comparison does suggest, however, is that the research and publications of the theological faculty at Oxford during the inter-war period and beyond had become those of the academic guild. There was to be no publishing sensation from Oxford comparable to *Essays and Reviews* or *Lux Mundi* in the twentieth century. Rather, the publications of professional Oxford theologians in the middle of the twentieth century tended to continue the nineteenth-century Oxonian interests in biblical study, philology, philosophical theology, patristics, and church history.

For example, Henry Leighton Goudge, the Regius Professor of Divinity from 1923 until the outbreak of the Second World War, published commentaries on the letters to the Corinthians, wrote on the authority and interpretation of the Bible and theological methodology. This was alongside the publication of his sermons delivered in the university and at Christ Church, ecumenical papers, and occasional papers on contraception, pacifism, and the possibility of a Jewish state.[61] Walter Lock, a contributor to *Lux Mundi,* was

60. See P. Curtis, *A Hawk among Sparrows: A Biography of Austin Farrer* (London: SPCK, 1985).
61. H.L. Goudge, inter alia, *The Second Epistle to the Corinthians,* (London: Methuen, 1927), *The Admission of Nonconformists to Communion: A Paper* (London, 1932), *The Church and the Bible* (London: Longmans, Green & Co., 1930), *The Authority and Value of the New Testament* (London: Mowbray, 1935).

appointed the Lady Margaret Professor of Divinity from the end of the war until 1927, and his work was similarly focussed on biblical study and Christian history. His cautious approach to biblical criticism – the 'reverent' criticism that typified Oxford – was seen in his *Critical and Exegetical Commentary on the Pastoral Epistles,* published in 1924.[62] He had earlier published a biography of John Keble as the sub-warden of Keble College, and prepared new editions of his poetry.

Likewise, younger scholars in the faculty of the period sustained Oxford's interest in the biblical and historical material and only tended to address contemporary theological questions in pamphlets, which were often transcripts of sermons. Frank Leslie Cross was in due course the first editor of the magisterial *Oxford Dictionary of the Christian Church* (1957), but began his studies as a chemist before developing interests in the philosophy of religion. He was a university lecturer in the philosophy of religion from 1934, having written *Religion and the Reign of Science* in 1930. He became the Wilde lecturer in natural and comparative religion in 1936, by which point he had developed a strong interest in the church fathers. His subsequent editions of ancient texts, his carefully researched articles for the *Journal of Theological Studies,* and his extensive work for the invaluable *Patristic Greek Lexicon* (co-edited by Darwell Stone and Geoffrey Lampe, and published in 1961-68), all epitomized a model of patristic scholarship for which Oxford was becoming justifiably famous, and which would be sustained in later years by, among others, Henry Chadwick (1920-2008) and Maurice Wiles (1923-2005).

The professionalization of theologians at Oxford (as elsewhere) encouraged the increasing desire among students to take

---

62. Walter Lock, *A Critical and Exegetical Commentary on the Pastoral Epistles* (Edinburgh: T&T Clark, 1924).

postgraduate research degrees. These were a relatively late phenomenon at Oxford and Cambridge by comparison with the continental universities and emerged in part out of a desire to nurture the kind of research culture that was bearing fruit – especially for the sciences – in Germany; the BLitt was introduced in 1895, and the DLitt and the DSc degrees were introduced in 1900 as a means of recognizing research. In 1917, Congregation approved the introduction of its own Doctor of Philosophy degree, the DPhil. Given an English title, in opposition to the German PhD, the degree was supervised by the newly created Committee for Advanced Studies, and required students to produce an unpublished dissertation after five terms, if an Oxford BA, or eight terms if a graduate of another university.[63] To many these degrees were a peculiar addition to the university's duties, as in the opinion of a large proportion of Oxford tutors the specialized character of the honour schools diminished the need for the pattern of study that was encouraged by a PhD course. The traditional higher degrees (such as the DD) were awarded in response to academic achievements later in life and had seniority over the MAs in the university. Accordingly, grafting a German-American model of postgraduate doctorates and research-based Master's degrees onto Oxford's undergraduate-focussed education was, for many, unnecessary and undesirable. Indeed, very few academically able Oxford graduates proceeded to the BLitt, and were instead encouraged by their college tutors to enter for prize essays or to go to the continent to gain language and research skills.[64]

63. *History of the University,* 8:125; *The Oxford Magazine,* 23 February 1917. A DPhil could also be awarded to a student who had been given advanced student status by the new Committee and pursued a supervised course of study over no less than six terms, with the results of that work being embodied in a published dissertation. This route to the DPhil was not popular and was abolished in 1925.
64. *History of the University,* 7:620.

However, by 1943, 1000 students had successfully qualified for the DPhil (in all subjects) in the university, and the examination of faculty reports from 1932 show probationary research students submitting to the faculty board working titles for their theses such as "The adaptation of pagan rites to Christian beliefs and practices in South Africa" and "Chinese Religious Ideas and Experience in the light of the New Testament."[65] On the whole, research students mirrored the interests of their supervisors and most theses were biblical and historical in their focus. J.L. Morrison, for instance, submitted his BLitt thesis of "over 300 pages" on "The structure of the Gospel according to St Mark approached from the standpoint of Formgeschichte (with special consideration of (a) Mark ii.1-iii.6, and (b) Mark xi.15 – xii.40)." His thesis, the examiners record, "gave evidence of much painstaking work and study, and shewed a very full knowledge of modern German work upon his subject."[66] Employing the methods of Dibelius and Bultmann, and showing knowledge of a wide range of French, German, and English literature on the matter, Morrison had offered what was considered an exemplary thesis.

The work of Mr Morrison, his professors and the expectations they had of those taking honours evidently reflected a model of academic practice that was now *de rigueur* at Oxford. They were standards that were not just expected, but also increasingly prized by theologians and others across the university. Even before the First World War had ended, Reginald Macan (by then master of University College) had offered his reflections on Oxford's theological and religious developments over the previous fifty years to the Society of Historical Theology. The man who had struggled through Henry Liddon's

---

65. *History of the University*, 8:52. OUA FA 4/19/2/5: Reports of the Board of the Faculty of Theology, 1932-36, 27 October 1932. These were the applications of G.R.W. Beaumont (Exeter College) and F.A. Smalley (St Edmund Hall) respectively.
66. *Ibid.,*104. It is interesting to note in this respect that the Board of the Faculty had stressed to the theology librarians "the need of a full provision of foreign theological periodicals" (69).

lectures on the Pastoral Epistles now proudly reflected upon "the extraordinary Palingenesis of Theology at Oxford", remarking upon the "steady growth of Natural Science in Oxford, the marked development of Historical Studies, the recognition of Anthropology, the rise standard of Scholarship, the growing seriousness of students and teachers who had adopted study and teaching as a life's vocation."[67] While the "elder generation of Churchmen, almost despairing of the academic *Res Publica,* had been gathered to its fathers", now a

> younger generation, more philosophic, more hopeful, more socialistic perhaps one may dare say – developed the new Apologetic just about the time when Criticism itself was ready to attempt reconstruction, adaptation, re-interpretation, making the Bible the most interesting and vivid literature in the world, and converting Theology itself at last to a scientific, as distinguished from merely logical, mood.[68]

Macan was in no doubt that the changes to the study of theology at Oxford had been for the benefit of both the English churches and the university. For him, the growing critical study of theology allowed those who had seen the devotional substituted for the intellectual reconciled to their faith. In place of the sharp divisions that had marked Oxford in his youth – between the Puseys and Liddons and "the Stanleys, and Jowetts, and Pattisons, and Hatches" – there was now this "younger generation" that was turning against both liberals and conservatives who stated that there was "a formula ... possible which expresses the truth, the whole truth, and nothing but the truth."[69] Confidence in such formulae, whether atheistical or

---

67. R.W. Macan, *Religious Changes in Oxford during the Last Fifty Years. A paper read before the Oxford Society for Historical Theology,* 37.
68. *Ibid,* 37-38.
69. *Ibid,* 27.

Christian, had dissipated because Oxford had opened its doors to all and sundry with the Tests Act. There had been a

> trans-substantiation of a small, select, homogenous, celibate, clerical community of theologians, classicists, and mathematicians of a sort, into a multitudinous, open, colluvial, diversified and predominantly lay society, of men, women, and children, with a welcome for every branch of study and research, and for every sort of student and researcher, has made of Oxford a larger and a better, but also a much more complicated and difficult, world to live in...[70]

This dilution of Oxford's theological *coterie* had complicated the binary approach to truth and criticism that had marked Oxford in the 1860s and 1870s. For Macan, to practise theology at Oxford near the end of the First World War engendered an acceptance that discerning the truth was more complicated than it had seemed a century earlier, but that the pursuit of theological study was enriched by such an acceptance. "Criticism", he wrote, "is everywhere and always a question of Principle, and of Method, not a question of this or that datum or conclusion." Rather, criticism "discards finality, whether of thought, or of expression, while more and more fully appreciating the historic value of the institutions, the formulas, the life of the past."[71]

Macan wrote in 1917 to celebrate this 'liberalization' of the modern faculty, which celebrated the complexity and curiosities of history, of anthropological study, and of greater philological knowledge. This critical approach surely, Macan suggested, offered hope in the face of the "inadequacy of the official and traditional presentation of Christianity amid the searching realities of war". In this "hour of her visitation", Macan called upon Oxford to reach a "synthesis of institutional and evangelical ideas" that united practical religion with

70. *Ibid.,*29.
71. *Ibid.,* 27.

the results of criticism. He was hopeful, and one can hear the passion with which he must have addressed the assembled in Christ Church's common room:

> Is not the present note of Oxford Religion a demand for a synthesis of institutional and evangelical ideas, subject to, nay rather, the product of, a criticism, as free as Science, as free as History and Philosophy, as free as Thought, and as honest; controlled, verified, and moralized by life in a community of friends and neighbours at home and abroad? Are not the changes which we have witnessed during these fifty years a good omen for the times to come? All the Christianity we have ever known has been, on its historical and theological sides, syncretic; and even as in the beginning, and on a large scale, Jewry, Hellas, and Rome combined to mould the nascent Christendom, so might in this twentieth century, and in Oxford, Evangelicalism, Criticism, Catholicism, unite to mould, for the whole company of faithful people, bonds of Union, not easily broken, whatever problems of thought, or of practice, may yet be to solve.[72]

Macan wrote in large part to advance that "syncretic" model of theologizing. He was speaking, at that time, to a faculty that retained confessional and professional restrictions upon the Divinity degrees and its honour school. Nonetheless, his words in 1917 do indicate the more irenic theological life that had emerged in the early twentieth century that was a source of both pride and hope in a period of conflict. "Oxford," he wrote, "has grown out of the condition of an appanage, preserve, and seminary of the Anglican Communion into a national, an imperial, one might say an ecumenical, High School."[73]

In early 1920, a student of Oxford wrote to the *Modern Churchman* questioning whether the honour school "affords its students an adequate equipment for meeting the difficulties of the modern situation . . . armed with a positive answer to the intellectual

72. *Ibid.,* 39.
73. *Ibid.,* 17.

difficulties of the first or five centuries, and a largely negative answer to the biblical difficulties of the twentieth century."[74] Another student replied in the following edition that, on the contrary, the skills learnt at Oxford were essential for theological work in the world. "To know one's J, E, D, and P, &c.," he wrote, "should be nothing but a source of pleasure in the insight and enlightenment that comes of reading an intelligible text and an historically interpreted literature":

> I do not deny that at times we encounter criticism for criticism's sake, rather than criticism for truth's sake. Delicate hands only should reverently remove the coverings from the truth we believe to be concealed under old traditions. The task becomes sacrilegious in the hands of the irreverent, careless and impudent. We should do well never to forget what it cost Our Lord to be a liberal. Unless and until, in acquiring new beliefs, "a sword has passed through our own soul also," we are not qualified to preach them to the world. In such a spirit each should endeavour to pursue critical studies. Such studies then can only strengthen, purify, and ennoble.[75]

The confidence of this student and Macan that liberal theology could have such a purifying role and strengthening role in the wider Church would contrast sharply with the highly critical attitude of dialectical theologians to Liberal Protestantism's inadequacies in post-war Germany, and it may read to many conservative theologians today as a characteristically Anglican defence of theological murkiness. This confidence was not confined to the more Protestant members of the faculty. Goudge, in 1923, was in no doubt that the Church had nothing to fear from reason and the force of criticism:

> The removal of "those things that are shaken" is "that those things that are not shaken may remain"; and just in so far as error disappears, truth shines more brightly. The criticism does not create truth; the truth is there before the criticism begins; but criticism removes what

74. *The Modern Churchman*, 9 (1920): 551.
75. *Ibid.*, 603-04.

overshadows it, or draws attention away from it; and so in effect may be little less than creative.[76]

"What", Goudge asked, "has criticism not done for Old Testament prophecy?" Whereas the early and medieval Church understood little, biblical criticism provided "a fountain of authoritative teaching" opened to the Church that had been closed before.

The ecumenism that Macan valued and which was secured by Headlam in statute evidently contrasted with the statutory confessional restrictions on the German faculties. In the context of global war, the denominational diversity and collaboration that was prospering at Oxford and Cambridge seemed to offer genuine opportunities for interreligious reconciliation that were few elsewhere and it is not impossible to understand how the unusual constitution of the faculty seemed to offer a hopeful model for post-war Christian life.

Dry and Scientific?

The ideal of a faculty that brought about a "synthesis of institutional and evangelical ideas", which subjected the Christian religion to the purifying and ecumenical razor of a 'scientific' criticism, did mean that the faculty could sometimes seem positioned uncomfortably between the competing impulses of the churches and the university.

During 1930, a series of articles was published in the *Oxford Magazine* that reviewed the status of various disciplines within the University. B.H. Streeter, by this stage the Provost of Queen's, wrote on "Theology" and identified that the honour school of theology had been perennially subject to criticism "from directly opposite quarters":

76. H.L. Goudge, *The Methods of Theology: An Inaugural Lecture Delivered in the Chapter House of Christ Church, Oxford, Friday, June 8, 1923* (London: Mowbray & Co., 1923), 19-20.

Many an undergraduate, who intends to enter the ministry of the Church, has to listen to grave warnings from some country adviser that, if he reads Theology in Oxford, he runs the risk of infection from the poison of Higher Criticism – and might, indeed, so far succumb to it as even to become a Modernist. On the other hand, if a freshman consults a lay tutor as to what the School he shall read, as often as not he gets the reply: "Read something which will give you a mental education; you can get all the theology you want at a year at theological college."[77]

Considered too broad by some, too professional by others, and likely to lead the faithful undergraduate astray, the theology school was an institution in need of defence from both academic and ecclesiastical quarters and Streeter wrote "to raise the question of the value of the Honour School of Theology as a purely mental and educational discipline alongside the other Honour Schools." Following Burgon in 1875, and Scott Holland in 1913, Streeter sought to emphasize that theology was no longer a professional activity at Oxford, but was an admirable means of a liberal education.

Indeed, it bore a close resemblance, Streeter suggested, to the most respected of the honour schools, *Literae Humaniores*. In fact, undergraduates would pursue Theology only after Moderations, having already studied classics in their first two years. From there, they would move to study the texts of the Christian faith: the Old and New Testaments, Streeter wrote, form the "principal original authorities for the study of a period of history extending over upwards of a thousand years, exhibiting a wide variety in cultural development – ranging from that implied in the battle of song to Deborah to the tribal war god up to the Platonizing philosophy that underlies the prologue to the Fourth Gospel." Literature as historically and philosophically rich as this is "studied in exactly the same way as the literature, history and thought of Greece and

77. B.H. Streeter, "Theology", *The Oxford Magazine,* 12 June 1930.

Rome are studied for Greats." Indeed, "by the better men attention is given to Textual Criticism, for which in the New Testament the materials – in antiquity, variety, abundance and complication – afford far better training than those which exist for the Greek and Latin classics." Streeter thus claimed that this range of literature and history, combined with the Philosophy of Religion, meant that "the Honour School of Theology is literally a *miniature* Greats."[78]

Streeter was not, however, blind to the course's difficulties. He admitted that the ground covered by a theologian was less than that of a Greats student, "due, less to the nature of the subject, than to the intellectual and educational standard of the average candidate". Undergraduate theologians were generally weaker, Streeter suggested, because they had usually failed to secure scholarships in open competition that were usually reserved for classics and, if they were not reading theology after taking some other honour school, they were probably pursuing the subject after a "winnowing" at Moderations (second year examinations). If senior tutors thought their students were unlikely to perform well at Greats, theology would sometimes be suggested as an alternative. The number of firsts was maintained in the honour school, Streeter averred, because of the number of candidates who already had a first degree (invariably ordinands, many from the theological halls).

The poorer quality of candidate accepted, it is nonetheless noticeable that by 1930, the nature of the course was still sufficiently ambiguous for Streeter to feel the need to defend it within the university by comparing it to Greats. Theologians could no longer presume theology's automatic privileges within the university but, like every other discipline, had to prove their worth through demonstrating theology's educational opportunities and the quality

78. *Ibid.*

of their research. Clearly still understood as a professional course by many (not least by undergraduate handbooks to the university) since so many of its graduates took holy orders, Streeter's defence of the school as a 'mini-Greats' protests perhaps a little too much.[79]

It is true, however, that theology's development as an academic discipline in the first half of the twentieth century and its retention as a discipline within the faculty of arts meant that, despite being read by those intending to become clergymen, it was still resolutely not directed towards the practical – what Newman had described as the "general and superficial knowledge as is necessary for work in the world."[80] This is evident in the reminiscences of an undergraduate theologian at Queen's, resident in Oxford during the Second World War.

Robert Ewbank, later the Anglican dean of Bulawayo, read Greats at Queen's and then Theology (whilst also being attached to Cuddesdon Theological College), before being ordained in 1948. He described Oxford as a "religious place" at the time with a lively Student Christian Movement (SCM) group and Inter-Collegiate Christian Union (OICCU). Evensong at the University Church "was always packed."[81] As a theology student, Ewbank shared tutorials with Hugh Montefiore, later the Anglican bishop of Birmingham. For the philosophical papers, they went to Keble for tutorials with Donald MacKinnon "who taught in a bare room with a table covered by books and a single chair"; the great philosophical theologian, Ewbank recorded, "liked to sit under the table". For their theology,

79. "This School is taken mainly by students who intend to enter the Christian ministry, but it offers a varied and substantial course of study to other students interested in the study of the Bible and of Theology in general." *The Oxford University Handbook* (Oxford: Oxford University Press, 1939), 155.
80. Bodl. MS Eng. th. d. 136-7, J.H. Newman to J.W. Burgon, 6 March 1875.
81. The Queen's College Archives, Ewbank MSS. These reminiscences formed part of a university-wide collection that contributed to the writing of the eighth volume of the *History of the University of Oxford* (ed. Brian Harrison).

they were taught by the "radical" chaplain of Queen's, Dennis Nineham, whose much-quoted aphorism was "if your faith can stand up to the Honour School, it can stand up to anything." Montefiore, Ewbank recalled, "absorbed the Nineham ethos better than I". However, Ewbank found that

> [T]oo much Oxford had left me over-intellectual...I could make no real contact with my parishioners, and accordingly abandoned parochial ministry for teaching . . . too bookish to make an effective pastor . . . . Oxford left me with a love of book-learning and simultaneously a feeling that it is "escape".

Although Ewbank is obviously not representative of every Oxford undergraduate theologian, his remarks about the tension between the theological learning he encountered at Oxford and the demands of parish life are suggestive of how the interests of the faculty were felt to have diverged from the work of the priest.

Of course, Ewbank's frustrations in the parish were entirely reasonable. How, we might reasonably ask, had learning the philosophy of religion from Donald MacKinnon as he sat under his table helped Ewbank to meet the urgent social and religious demands of post-war Britain, let alone colonial Rhodesia? Evidently, the content of the honour school and theological research at Oxford was no longer directed towards the practical in this way. Indeed, even before the Second World War had ended, the Bishop of Durham wrote to the Board as chairman of a church commission on ordination training stating that, "we ought to do everything possible to strengthen the connection of training for Ordination with those Universities where Theological Faculties exist."[82] Repeating a long-standing tradition of thinking in the Church of England, the bishop nonetheless asserted

---

82. Oxford University Archives, FA 4/19/2/5 (Faculty Reports, 1932-36), Letter to the Chairman of the Board from the Bishop of Durham (Alwyn Williams), 28 January 1943 (126).

[I]t is most desirable, too, that part at any rate of their theological training, whether before or after graduation, should be received at a University whose teaching resources are, and are always likely to be, far greater than those of any isolated Theological College.

The Church of England commission recognized that "the University teaching of Theology cannot and ought to be mainly, or even largely, 'vocational'". It must, Williams admitted, "be academic in the best sense." Nevertheless, if the bonds between ordination training and the universities were to be strengthened, the Commission urged that the faculties be "prepared to lay more stress, in their arrangement of teaching and examination, on the study of Systematic Theology." Although they desired that ordinands should have a sounder "grounding in Historical Theology", yet "they are to be entitled to a coherent and integrated grasp of the Faith which they are presently to teach". Unless increased attention was given to systematizing the fruits of all this historical study, the Commission warned that "the succession of students . . . was likely to diminish dangerously".[83]

This plea from the central Church of England for a greater focus within the nation's theological faculties on doctrine such that ordinands would be better enabled to teach the Christian faith – rather than just the historical expressions of it – to some degree confirms Ewbank's recollections. An undergraduate embarking upon the honour school after Moderations would study the Old and New Testaments, the development of doctrine in the early Church, Hebrew, the Philosophy of Religion, Liturgies, Sacred Criticism, and Archaeology. The approach to all of these subjects, with the exception of the Philosophy of Religion, was unremittingly historical; this was, after all, a "miniature Greats". Although William Sanday had written at the turn of the century that "Christianity is so much bound up with history that the first duty of the student [of

83. *Ibid.*

theology] is to ascertain, as nearly as may be, what were the historical facts", this allying of "the scientific impulse, proceeding largely from the study of Ancient History . . . with the religious temper" was clearly leaving some by the mid-twentieth century dissatisfied and feeling unprepared for the practical work of ministry.[84] Possibly, the apologetic enthusiasm for historical-critical study promoted by Sanday, Driver and Hatch after Pusey's death (itself an echo of the passions of Arnold, Jowett and Stanley) faded as a result of two global wars that provoked entirely different theological questions from those posed in Oxford during the 1880s.

Certainly, the faculty was very slow to respond to the desires of the Church of England commission, but this was not necessarily the result of any sort of embarrassment that the study of systematic theology might provoke from the secular colleagues of Oxford theologians. As the Lady Margaret Professor, N.P. Williams, commented in his 1939 essay 'What is Theology?' in Kenneth Kirk's compendium, *The Study of Theology,*

> It may help the existing situation if we point out that what is understood by 'Theology' in the *curricula* of the ordinary, secular universities of Europe and America is almost exclusively 'Historical Theology,' [i.e., *Dogmengeschichte*] and that the teaching of 'Systematic Theology' [i.e., *Dogmatik*] is (owing to the divisions of Christendom, and the absence of any universally 'agreed' version of the Christian Faith) confined, for the most part, to seminaries and other institutions under direct ecclesiastical or denominational control.[85]

For Williams just before the outbreak of the Second World War, it was the denominationally plural character of theology in the university that directed its practitioners towards the purely historical;

---

84. W. Sanday, "The Historical Method in Theology", *Expository Times* 9 (1897): 84.
85. N.P. Williams, "What is Theology?" in *The Study of Theology,* ed. Kenneth Kirk(London: Hodder & Stoughton, 1939), 14.

'constructive theology' was the preserve of the theological college or Nonconformist hall. Even when modern theology was introduced to the syllabus, it was largely through the writings of specific theologians. It was not until 1962 that a paper on contemporary theology would be introduced to the honour school, and this built upon the introduction of optional papers on modern theologians that were introduced in 1955 (including Brunner, Berdyaev, and Kierkegaard). Maurice Wiles would comment in his inaugural lecture as Regius Professor of Divinity in 1971 that, "while it may no longer be possible to study theology as if the world came into existence in 4004 BC, it is still possible in Oxford—by a judicious, or rather injudicious, selection of papers which is fortunately not very common—to do so as if the world went out of existence in ad 461".[86]

The case against the faculty as a location for practical ministerial training can be overstated, however. It is clear that, despite concerns about theology's historical focus, Oxford still remained an attractive location for the churches on account of its considerable resources. The liberal Anglican theological college, Ripon Clergy College, moved from Leeds to a site on Parks Road in 1919 and was renamed Ripon Hall.[87] The London Baptist divinity hall, Regent's Park College, relocated to Oxford in 1927 and its first principal, the leading Old Testament theologian Henry Wheeler Robinson, was

---

86. M. Wiles, *Jerusalem, Athens, and Oxford: An Inaugural Lecture Delivered before the University of Oxford on 18 May, 1971* (Oxford: Oxford University Press, 1971), 21. Quoted in F. Turner, 'Religion', *History of the University of Oxford*, viii, 307. Wiles' attempts in the early 1970s to remove Greek from the undergraduate syllabus (as it was supposed to be making the subject inaccessible to school-leavers) was voted down in Congregation, supposedly with the argument, "if Galilean fishermen could cope with lots of New Testament Greek, how much more could Oxford undergraduates." ('Maurice Wiles', obituary by Robert Morgan, *The Guardian,* 10 June 2005, accessed 20 November 2013, http://www.theguardian.com/news/2005/jun/10/guardianobituaries.obituaries)
87. The college then moved to Berkeley House at Boar's Hill, just outside Oxford in 1933. It subsequently merged with Cuddesdon Theological College in 1975, the two colleges becoming Ripon College Cuddesdon on the Cuddesdon site.

immediately involved in faculty life and administration as a popular lecturer, supervisor, examiner, and member of the faculty board.[88]

The later twentieth century would see Roman Catholic involvement in faculty – as opposed to purely university – life after the Second Vatican Council, the introduction of new university degrees aimed at ordinands (the Bachelor of Theology (BTh) and Master of Theology (MTh) degrees), and the greater inclusion of the theological halls within the statutes of the University as 'Permanent Private Halls' (PPHs) from 1918 onwards. This meant that the theological halls were granted a licence from Convocation to matriculate students in the university, under the supervision of the vice chancellor and the proctors. Campion Hall and St Benet's, Roman Catholic institutions of the Jesuits and the Benedictines respectively, were granted such licences by the University in 1918.[89] Mansfield College became a PPH in 1955 and a full college in 1995. Manchester (later Harris Manchester) College became a PPH in 1990 and a college of the University – catering primarily for mature students – in 1996. The Franciscan house, Greyfriars, received its licence in 1957 along with Regent's Park, the Dominican house of Blackfriars in 1994, Wycliffe Hall in 1996, and St Stephen's House in 2003. Even more so than Cambridge, Oxford was arguably more inclusive of the various theological institutions within its borders during the twentieth century than it had been during the nineteenth. The denominational pluralism that Headlam had imagined in his inaugural lecture in 1918 had in many respects been realized,

88. E.A. Payne, *Henry Wheeler Robinson, Scholar, Teacher, Principal: A Memoir* (London: Nisbet, 1946); R.E. Cooper, *From Stepney to St Giles': The Story of Regent's Park College, 1810-1960* (London: Carey Kingsgate Press, 1990).
89. It should be noted, however, that the Roman Catholic halls were initially founded at Oxford in order that Roman Catholic students and members of religious orders might read for 'secular' degrees, rather than the theology school or the Divinity degrees.

although this settlement has faced severe challenges in more recent years.[90]

Although the University of Oxford certainly offered a credibility and gravitas to education that would have been hard to find as an isolated theological institution elsewhere, the life of the faculty was evidently not so divergent from wider English religious life that the churches looked elsewhere to resource their theological teaching.

A Discipline of Facts?

By the end of the Second World War, a distinctive paradigm for the practice of theology had been established at Oxford. Had Pusey been alive in 1945, he may have despaired that his conception of theology as the foundational discipline in the university had been so comprehensively abandoned. The abolition of divinity as a compulsory element of undergraduate education one hundred years after the beginning of the Oxford Movement signalled the termination of that idea of theology in the university.

On the other hand, Newman may have been less surprised by what had emerged at his *alma mater*. His own celebrated *Idea of a University* expected that theology should emerge as a distinctive discipline in its own right and, as in his correspondence with Burgon in 1875, Newman exhibits recognition that theology would always struggle to be 'scientific' and critically rigorous while retaining provision for

90. The theological colleges of Cambridge (Wesley House (Methodist) and Ridley Hall and Westcott House (Anglican)) formed an ecumenical Federation in 1972, sharing teaching and resources. However, their relationship to the University of Cambridge is more distant than the Permanent Private Hall status at Oxford. This relationship has not been without its tensions, and a review in 2007 (in part, prompted by internal problems at Wycliffe Hall) challenged the governance of these small institutions and recommended, *inter alia,* that if "*any Hall shall be shown to be departing from the values of a liberal education conducted in the spirit of free and critical enquiry and debate to which the University holds*" then the Council of the University was permitted to review its licence to remain a PPH (*Review of the Permanent Private Halls associated with the University of Oxford: Report to the Council of the University* (Oxford University internal document, 2007), 7).

ordination training. What neither could have imagined (or at least tolerated) was how Oxford theology had incorporated into its life the denominational pluralism that characterized the wider university; for the conservatives of the 1860s, theology could only guard its 'deposit of faith' so long as it remained protected by the credal boundaries of subscription or a clerical hierarchy. What was evident in Oxford by the Second World War was, instead, a self-governing and multi-denominational faculty that reported to the General Board of the Faculties rather than the episcopal bench of the Church of England.

The settlement for theology at Oxford that was secured in the inter-war period was thus a mixed economy of academic research, liberal, and professional education that served both university and the churches. The tensions of being caught between their – not always congruent – expectations were well documented by the chaplain-fellow of The Queen's College, David Jenkins, in an article on Oxford's "Anglican tradition" in the book *Theology and the University: An Ecumenical Investigation* in 1964. It testified that, to be in the university and to be a location where a range of confessional bodies might be involved in work together, theology had to justify itself in terms different from those that had been so crucial to Pusey:

> There is now nothing 'sacred' about Theology, as far as the general opinion of the university is concerned. Consequently, amid the surviving evidences of the lingering effects of 'the character of Oxford as a Church university' (such as Canon Professors, admission to senior degrees by a formula which includes the name of the Trinity, and university sermons statutorily required), the teaching members of the faculty are acutely aware that the 'justification' of their subject matter is important historically and culturally, whatever personal view of the Christian *faith*, and in the preservation and practice of a rigorous academic discipline, which allows no question to be foreclosed by faith, and which requires them always to be open to all available facts and challenges.[91]

In the "now secularised university", the basis of the faculty's "data" ought, Jenkins asserted, to be "as 'hard' as possible, i.e. which believer and unbeliever alike will agree are indeed 'given', however much they may disagree about the significance of givenness." In this way, theologians were inclined to "get back" to the hard facts of the texts, the history, and the knowledge of the philosophers. The discipline was not about "faithful believing, which is an intrusion of bias", but "the discipline of facts". Jenkins argued that in this almost Harnackian account of theology in the university – no doubt, influenced by the analytic philosophy that dominated Oxford – theologians were left seeming "on the whole to be unfaithful underminers of the faith", while the theologians believed that "the rigorous analysis of sound learning cannot but contribute in the end to the firmer establishment of true religion."[92] Capturing the ambiguous position of the theology faculty in relation to the churches and the university, Jenkins commented that "our present practice in the Theology faculty at Oxford is not constructive enough for believers and not open and relevant enough for unbelievers."[93]

Jenkins' portrayal of Oxford theology in 1964 captures how the modern faculty was caught between the two poles of Christians unsettled by perceived heterodoxy and academics who reckoned theologians to be wedded to metaphysical dogma. N.P. Williams, writing in 1939, had spoken of how in England, the dominance of Anglican and Presbyterian models of theological work ("where a close control of theological and critical speculation does not exist"), had resulted in what he term "the Critical Orthodoxy". This was distinguished from the Harnackian, "Liberal Protestant" view that historical Christianity was a collection of false accretions upon the

91. John Coulson, ed., *Theology and the University: An Ecumenical Investigation* (London: Darton, Longman & Todd, 1964), 149.
92. *Ibid.,* 152.
93. *Ibid.,* 159.

original words of Jesus, and the "naïve orthodoxy" that was wilfully ignorant of historical and textual criticism. Rather, the critical orthodoxy, which was typified in the English learning of Bishop Lightfoot, C.H. Turner of Magdalen, and Sir William Ramsey,

> would hold indeed that the substance of historical Christianity is the eternal truth of God, expressed in such forms as the human intellect is capable of receiving; but, precisely because it believes the Catholic Faith to be true, it is convinced that that Faith has nothing to fear from the most candid and open-minded scrutiny of all the evidence, and it is, consequently, able to meet the 'Liberal Protestant' scholars on their own ground, to argue with them on the basis of common premises, and to co-operate with them in the pursuit of what is the common goal of all scholars as such, the establishment and vindication of the truth.[94]

The Anglican-Nonconformist theological approach that Williams promoted, and which he knew from his own experience at Oxford, would decline to surrender to the 'Liberal Protestants' that the birth-narratives of Matthew and Luke were purely mythological, while at the same time demanding the fundamentalists to explain "the existence and practically universal diffusion of the belief in the miraculous Birth, other than the simple explanation that it really happened."[95] To what extent this perceived English *via media*, to coin a phrase, endured into the more theologically radical ambiance of 1960s Oxford is beyond the chronological limits of this survey. Both Williams in 1939 and Jenkins in 1964, however, testify to a distinctive character for English theology that to a considerable degree was the result of its peculiar institutional evolution in the universities of Oxford and Cambridge (and particularly Oxford).

Oxford theology's transition from being an Anglican seminary under the strict supervision of High Churchmen into an ecumenical

---

94. N.P. Williams, *ibid.,* 34–35.
95. For a good example of this 'mediating' biblical criticism, see H.L. Goudge, *The Authority and Value of the New Testament* (London: Mowbray & Co., 1935).

faculty of the humanities was, as we have observed, unpredictable, controversial, disappointing to many, and lengthy. The late introduction of the honour school in 1868-69 – long after ordination training had migrated to theological colleges – meant that theology would never have quite the same strength that has generally marked the continental faculties. As an undergraduate discipline, it was pursued by the interested and by those ordinands deemed sufficiently able intellectually by their bishops or churches. The multi-denominational context perhaps, as N.P. Williams suggested, prospered the less controversial elements of theological work (in which Oxford already excelled), namely the historical and textual; despite the attempts of some, not least the disciples of T.H. Green at the beginning of the century, constructive theology never really became a significant element of Oxford's theological life. The dominance of classical study in the university, and its concomitant emphasis upon close textual study, set alongside the Protestant inheritance that theology *was* the study of Scripture, all inhibited the exploration of the speculative. Coupled with a strong post-Kantian antipathy towards metaphysics from Mansel onwards and the rise of analytic philosophy in the early twentieth century, there was no impetus to alter these disciplinary commitments.

The resulting paradigm for theological life at Oxford has always had its malcontents and critics, and one might reasonably suspect that, for as long as there are those unwilling to countenance the critical examination of faith, there always will be. Nonetheless, the assertion here has been that the structures of English university theology are distinctive as a result of their unusual provenance. Theology has developed at both Oxford and Cambridge in a way that marks it out from other faculties as a result of their ecclesiastical foundations, their relative independence from the state, their collegiate structures, the retention of their endowments, and their avoidance of political revolution. The most serious threat theology faced in a nation with a securely Established Church through most of the nineteenth and twentieth centuries was probably from theologians themselves who, despairing for the spiritual dilution of their institutions, relocated the professional training of the clergy to extra-mural colleges. At Oxford, in particular, the abiding influence of Christ Church upon the life of the theology in the university has also shaped the ethos of the faculty and – largely for financial considerations – kept the senior professorships tied to cathedral canonries. This marks Oxford out from Cambridge, where the formal attachments to Ely Cathedral have been much weaker.[96]

By the Second World War this distinctive development shaped a pattern for university theology that was rooted in the heritage and worshipping life of the Church of England, yet was not subject to episcopal control; which was denominationally plural, yet ecumenically collaborative; that was critically rigorous as a discipline in the faculty of arts, yet always closely conversant with the churches. Its development was haphazard and almost derailed at points by personal animosities and religious controversy, yet theologians were skilful in renewing their discipline, especially in the inter-war period. The resulting constitution for theology in the university at Oxford was an ambiguous legacy and, as can be seen, has perennially had its critics. In a society that was religiously vibrant, however, theology survived at Oxford in an ecumenical form that mirrored the increasing religious diversity of city, university, and nation. In contrast to the genealogies of the confessional and professionally orientated faculties of the state universities on the continent, the Scottish faculties, and the post-graduate divinity schools of North America, Oxford's distinctive genealogy, this study has hoped to

96. At the time of writing, it must be noted, the Lady Margaret professorship and its associated canonry have just been opened to laypersons.

demonstrate, clearly merits greater recognition and reflection in contemporary debate.

Epilogue: From 'Sacra Theologia' to 'Theology and Religion'

As this book is written, one hundred years after Henry Scott Holland and the faculty board attempted to 'disestablish' divinity and introduce a 'school of sacred learning' in the university, the theological faculty at Oxford has just rebranded itself as a 'Faculty of Theology and Religion' and, soon, undergraduates will be examined for the first time in the 'Honour School of Theology and Religion'. This decision has been taken to reflect how, over the past twenty years, Oxford's theology faculty has diversified to include the study of other world religions and the nature of religion itself. It was also a change that, according to the faculty board, while "reflecting the Faculty's pride in and continuing commitment to its longstanding traditions in Christian theology" will also "be helpful in attracting new undergraduate and postgraduate students, as well as affirming the intellectual range of Faculty members' interests."[1] Unlike Scott Holland's reforms, however, this statute was passed with barely a murmur of dissent. No letters flooded into *The Times* or the *Church Times* in protest from the country clergy of the Church of England,

---

1. "Faculty of Theology Name Change", from the faculty website, accessed 12 November 2013, http://theology.nsms.ox.ac.uk/news/untitled-resource.html.

long since denied a veto in Convocation. The current Regius Professor of Ecclesiastical History, unlike her predecessor Charles Bigg, was not shouted down in the Sheldonian Theatre as a "Judas" or "Anti-Christ" for the alteration.[2]

The faculty has indeed changed considerably since 1945. At the end of the Second World War, Oxford's faculty was a predominantly clerical, male, collection of scholars focussed on the study of Scripture and patristic theology and engaged in teaching – in the main – young men who were to enter Christian ministry (either in the Church of England or in the Free Churches). The faculty of the early twenty-first century is a far more diverse body. Perhaps most significantly, half of the faculty's undergraduates, a large minority of its graduates, and a smaller percentage of its senior members are female.[3] The teaching posts of the colleges have almost all been separated from college chaplaincies, and despite the persistence of the canon-professorships, there are far fewer faculty members who are ordained members of the Church of England. In terms of academic interests, while still nurturing its historic strengths in biblical study and history, there is also a growing number of people at Oxford studying and teaching other world religions, Continental philosophy of religion, the relationship between science and religion, and theology's relationship to the secular public square. Undergraduates may also read Theology and Religion in the honour school in conjunction with Philosophy or Oriental Studies. And while many of Oxford's students are taking courses as part of their training for ministry, many are also exploring theological questions or religion as non-believers, and will go on to work in a range of professions, from banking to the BBC, education, law, or management consultancy.

2. Prof. Sarah Foot has been the chairman of the Board of the Faculty responsible for implementing these changes.
3. Of the university-funded posts in the faculty, still only six out of the twenty-four members are women.

Theology and Religion is now more unambiguously a department of the humanities than at any point since the institution of the honour school in 1869.

None the less, the quietly momentous alteration to one of Oxford's most ancient faculties is worthy of reflection at the end of this historical survey. From the outset, it must be noted that Oxford's faculty, characteristically, is very late in changing its name. Cambridge's Faculty of Divinity, while not changing its title, renamed its tripos 'Theology and Religious Studies' before the millennium, and Durham, King's College London, Leeds, Nottingham, Manchester, Birmingham, Kent, and many other English theological faculties have also long since embraced what the Regius Professor of Divinity at Cambridge, David Ford, has called "new theology and religious studies". This is how he describes the new paradigm that was established in response to the government's desire for a national "benchmarking statement' in 2000. It is a paradigm that, Ford tells us, combines theology's questions of "truth and practice, including normative practice" alongside (in what is a remarkable echo of Scott Holland exactly a hundred years earlier) the "particular phenomena of the field" being "richly and rigorously described, analysed, and explained in ways that are often not possible where theology is studied apart from the range of academic disciplines that come under the heading of religious studies."[4] Ford celebrates this evolution of the discipline as it avoids the pitfalls of, simultaneously, a rigid confessionalism that might characterize a faculty solely committed to theology and an aggressive secularism that too often defines departments of religion. This 'new' combination of theology *with* religious studies in the university context reflects, Ford stresses

---

4. David Ford, 'New Theology and Religious Studies: Shaping, Teaching, and Funding a Field' in *The Future of Christian Theology* (Oxford: Wiley-Blackwell, 2011), 151.

[T]he legacy of a difficult history in which religious studies had to fight for its existence in the face of theological (often church-led) domination, and later theology sometimes had to fight for its existence in the face of secularist domination.[5]

With the "waning" of church domination in England, however, Ford suggests that "power relations within the field are far less susceptible to a simplistic dichotomy".[6] Rather, the "new ecosystem" nurtures a creative tension between the two disciplines will be to the benefit of the "main stakeholders": the churches (and other religious communities), pluralist democracies, universities and students. This "new ecosystem" is in contrast to Germany where the faculties of theology are still firmly under the confessional control of the denominations, or the United States where the divide between private institutions with religious roots and the state universities invariably keeps theology and religious studies as entirely discrete disciplines.[7]

Ford's assessment of the UK's contemporary pattern of theology and religious studies is hopeful, asserting that the flexibility inherent in the British context allows for a range of conversations within the university that challenge, inform, and promote dialogue among theologians, scholars of religion, seminarians, and the wider public and government. Grounded in the "*ad hoc,* diverse, experimental, locally negotiated settlements" of institutional evolutions in Britain, the faculties today offer a distinctive paradigm for scholarly practice that has much to offer to the rest of the West, whose structures remain more straight-jacketed by the political and institutional orthodoxies of the Enlightenment.

---

5. One of the most famous British centres of a 'pure', secular religious studies was established by Ninian Smart at Lancaster University in 1967. See N. Smart, *A New Look at Religious Studies: the Lancaster Idea* (London: Routledge, 1967).

6. D. Ford, *ibid.,* 153.

7. D. Ford, *ibid.,* 156-161.

As indicated in the introduction, Ford has been unusual in articulating the institutional distinctiveness of British theology. Although Oxford has been one of the last English faculties to rebrand itself, has not this study suggested that the paradigm described by Ford has a long pedigree? Oxford's approach to the institutional development of theology has, certainly, given support to Ford's description of British theology's development as *ad hoc,* diverse and experimental. In sharp contrast to the foundation of the University of Berlin in 1810, decisions were invariably taken tardily, often in reaction to a perceived threat from either within the university or Parliament, and negotiated between the colleges, professors, tutors, Congregation, Convocation, and the churches with varying degrees of rapidity and ease.

Oxford's own explanation for its recent name-change reflects this pattern of development. Rather than expressing an agenda for the faculty's future that is grounded in an explicit vision for the discipline, a key motivation appears to be the recruitment of postgraduate and undergraduate students, many of whom are – it is presumed – not always madly enthused by the faculty's "longstanding traditions in Christian theology". At Oxford, at least, there has been no English equivalent to a Schleiermacher shaping his or her philosophically pungent 'occasional thoughts' on theology in the university; as in 1875, when Burgon wrote his *Plea,* a primary concern for the faculty remains to attract bright students who will win first-class degrees. In the collegiate university, the nineteenth-century English premium upon a good liberal education rather than grand philosophical visions remains strongly in evidence.

Secondly, the press release for the faculty's name-change also reflects the delicate balance that Oxford has long since been compelled to find between Christian theology and the 'scientific' study of religion in its various forms. The confessional model of theology that was promoted by Pusey and Liddon proved to be unsustainable in a university that had become open to all denominations and none, and which also desired universally coherent reasoning for Christian belief. On the other hand, of course, those who had desired a purely 'scientific' approach to religion, notably Henry Scott Holland in his thinking about reform at Oxford in 1911–13, were rebuffed; neither Convocation nor the wider Church of England could countenance theology's extrication from the life of the churches, and throughout the twentieth century the faculty's engagement with the life of the English churches has not weakened. With the inclusion of the theological colleges as Permanent Private Halls of the University and the introduction of degrees specifically catering for Christian ministry, the faculty's involvement with the churches has arguably been strengthened since 1945. Far from being an aspect of the new "ecosystem" of theology and religion, it seems Oxford has long been finding ways of satisfying all its stakeholders during the twentieth century.

What, however, can be made of the more concerted effort to include religious studies in the faculty? This development is obviously, in one sense, a more recent aspect of British universities seeking to engage more convincingly with what is now a multi-faith society. This growing interest in other world religions and, at Oxford, the creation of a new professorship (in "Abrahamic Religions") and lectureships to cater for the study of religion does signal a departure from the exclusively Christian and clerical character of Oxford's faculty for much of the twentieth century. This is combined with the growing influence of the various "Oxford Centres" for Hebrew and Jewish Studies, for Islamic Studies, for Hindu Studies, and for Buddhist Studies.[8]

---

8. These are defined as "recognized independent centres" that are not part of the University of Oxford, but which work with the University in delivering research and teaching.

Can the involvement of different religious groups be regarded as that novel, however? Since the last two decades of the nineteenth century, Oxford theology (as at Cambridge) has been accommodating religious pluralism. It is easy to forget how the arrival of Nonconformists in Oxford was deemed as deeply threatening to many; compare, for instance, emotions surrounding the building of the Unitarian Manchester College a matter of yards away from New College in the late 1880s with the building of the new Centre for Islamic Studies on the edge of Magdalen in the first decade of the twenty-first century. In 1893, the Regius professor had been deeply fearful of how Oxford theology would be endangered by the presence of this non-credal form of Christianity, and had warned his deputy professor, William Sanday, not to attend the opening of the college. Fifty years later, however, and Oxford had become Reginald Macan's "ecumenical high-school": a collection of scholars from a variety of denominational backgrounds with a shared commitment to seeking theological truth. That denominational pluralism was, however, hard won, and achieved through personal friendships, the determination of several Regius professors, and the unavoidably high quality of the non-Anglicans' scholarship. The involvement of Roman Catholics in the faculty since the Second Vatican Council has only bolstered what became one of the most important ecumenical institutions of the twentieth century. Emotionally, at least, the pluralism that Ford celebrates is not so new, and has its origins in the faculties' – often painful – negotiation of religious differences over the past one hundred and fifty years. There may, of course, still be Christians who are reluctant to share an ancient faculty once dedicated to the service of the church with those of other faiths. Looking back at Oxford's history, however, is there not hidden within it the promise of rich rewards for religious communities, wider society, and the university, through the basic collegial friendships that have accompanied religious pluralism?

Recognizing the long history of such negotiation may not change the sense of many theologians, such as John Webster, Stanley Hauerwas, or John Milbank, that theologians are subject to a Babylonian captivity of an unrepentant, nihilistic, secularism in our universities. While the histories of Oxford and Cambridge offer firm evidence that theology's duties to the churches have not been neglected and that their theologians' focus on history rather than 'constructive' theology was not unambiguously the result of theologians trying to 'please' their secular colleagues, there are still plenty theologians on both sides of the Atlantic who feel compromised by the secular university.

For such as these, the history of Oxford's theology faculty may provide as much support as challenge. The idea of the university that was cherished by Newman and Pusey in the 1830s – theology as a *habitus* that enculturated wisdom and formed character – was not, in the end, an idea that persisted in the nineteenth-century university. The Tractarian approach to the university was steadily marginalized in the process of reform and the triumph of a more utilitarian politics in national and academic life. Where that 'idea' was consolidated in a somewhat reactionary fashion from the corner of the university (or, at least, from Pusey's own lodgings in Christ Church), theology effectively doomed itself to obsolescence. Theologians clearly had to work within what Christopher Harvie has termed the '*polis*' of the post-reform university where many different groups were seeking to advance their own interests and agenda, often using highly polarizing strategies.[9]

9. C. Harvie, "Reform and Expansion, 1854-71" in *History of the University,* 6:702.

However, as Nigel Biggar, the Regius Professor of Moral and Pastoral Theology at Oxford, indicated in a 2009 lecture ("What Are Universities For?"), weeping for a lost era when theology reigned supreme and people pursued knowledge in an entirely disinterested way for "sheer *amor scientiae*" is, to some degree, an exercise in nostalgia. From their medieval beginnings, universities have clearly served private and practical purposes; a university began to emerge in Oxford in the late twelfth century probably out of a need to train lawyers to serve the ecclesiastical courts that had been set up in what had become a seat of royal administration.[10] Even if those practical purposes have changed considerably over the succeeding eight centuries, to pretend that the disciplines of the university have always operated in a purely disinterested way in obeisance to the 'queen of the sciences' is to be wilfully ignorant of the historical realities, not least, as noted, in the rigidly confessional university of the early nineteenth century where theology was very weak in institutional terms.

Moreover, it is worth remembering that theologians who are anxious about their place in the university are not unique among the humanities. Many outside theological faculties feel oppressed by the government's obsession with the 'usefulness' of academic knowledge, and especially the latest research assessment category of 'impact', introduced by the Labour government in 2009 and sustained by the current Coalition government since 2010.[11] While this new category is in large part aimed at encouraging universities to be more directly

10. Nigel Biggar, 'What Are Universities For? A Christian View' in M. Higton, J. Law, and C. Rowland, eds., *Theology and Human Flourishing: Essays in Honor of Timothy J. Gorringe* (Eugene, OR: Cascade, 2011), 239–50.
11. The Research Councils define impact in terms of "Academic Impact" (defined as "a demonstrable contribution that excellent research makes to academic advances") and "Economic and Societal Impacts" (such as "fostering global economic performance, and specifically the economic competitiveness of the United Kingdom"); from "Excellence with Impact: What do Research Councils mean by Impact?", Research Councils UK Website (http://www.rcuk.ac.uk/kei/impacts/Pages/meanbyimpact.aspx), accessed 10 December 2013

focussed on exploiting the 'knowledge-economy', demonstrating the societal and economic impacts of studying the fourteenth-century motet is as challenging as 'evidencing' the same from an article on child sacrifice in the Hebrew Bible. As Biggar rightly indicates, 'usefulness' "connotes a shrunken, materialistic, utilitarian understanding of human goods – an understanding that has sunk deep into the Anglo-Saxon mentality." The understanding of the usefulness of knowledge sought by the late-capitalist society is "pinched, anaemic, and degrading."[12] If the humanities are to survive, Biggar suggests that they need to rediscover a "moral vocation", which he engagingly describes as the ability of the Arts and Humanities "to introduce us to foreign worlds" and "to treat them well":

> They teach us to read strange and intractable texts with patience and care; to meet alien ideas and practices with humility, docility, and charity; to draw alongside foreign worlds before we set about – as we must – judging them. They train us in the practice of honest dialogue, which respects those distant from us in time or place as potential prophets, who might yet speak a new word about what's true and good and beautiful – about what makes for human flourishing.[13]

Universities do not exist as adjuncts to the Government's Department of Business, Innovation, and Skills (which assumed responsibility for British higher education in 2009). Rather, as Neil MacGregor has described the purpose of museums, universities are in the business of "giving people their place in things."[14] This must be as true for

---

12. Biggar, *ibid.,* 245.

13. Biggar, *ibid.,* 247.

14. MacGregor is the Director of the British Museum. Quoted in S. Collini, *What Are Universities For?* (London: Penguin, 2012), 11. On the basis of MacGregor's remark, the historian David Wootton has written that the purpose of the discipline of history is "to give the past its place in us." (David Wootton, "Formal Feelings for History", *Times Literary Supplement,* 24 September 2010, p.17).

history, theology and religion, or literature, as it is for astronomy, biochemistry, or psychology.

And is not the 'theology and religion' paradigm now prevalent in British universities well placed to be instrumental in such a renewal of the humanities? The discipline invites us to read ancient and often strange texts, now in the company of those from very different traditions.[15] The new paradigm clearly aspires to nurture 'honest dialogue' between different communities of faith, even as those traditions are in a critical conversation with the historical, psychological, anthropological, and sociological phenomena of religious practice. In a nation that is increasingly complex with regard to religion, 'spirituality', and what constitutes a 'good life', which other discipline is more concerned, especially at a practical level, with establishing what is good, true, and beautiful? Moreover, as a discipline that enjoys such close proximity to the religious communities of the nation, is there any other in the humanities that is able to have a more tangible social 'impact' than 'theology and religion'?

Theologians may retreat into Puseyite reactionary poises in the face of these often challenging paradigm shifts. In the face of the cantankerous 'new atheists', a Barthian posture of bold defiance may understandably appear to have more integrity for some, not least in universities where the centralized administration is fiercely secularist. For those who remain in the 'new' faculties of 'theology and religion' (and perhaps especially in those universities that still retain strong links to confessional communities), however, there do seem to be signs of a hopeful and imaginative reconfiguring of the discipline. Are there not in the words of David Ford echoes of Benjamin Jowett

---

15. The 'Scriptural Reasoning' project in the University of Cambridge is a good example of this, encouraging Jews, Christians and Muslims to read passages from their Scriptures together. This is part of the Cambridge Inter-Faith Programme, of which Prof. David Ford is the director.

and Arthur Stanley in 1848, Henry Scott Holland in 1911, or Arthur Headlam in 1918? The passion that Ford or Biggar, among others, have for renewing our universities and faculties, and the desire they share for theologians and scholars of religion to be protagonists in seeking public wisdom for the flourishing of society, is surely to be commended. Such passion will find inspiration in their faculties' histories, where theologians can be seen to have been reimagining their discipline for the benefit of church, society, and university over several generations. Unless one agrees with Dr Pusey in 1878 that "the battle as to all outward things is lost", may such imagination continue to fire the minds of theologians and scholars of religion, in Oxford and across the West.

Bibliography

Manuscript Sources

Balliol College Archives
Green MSS
Jowett MSS
Scott Holland MSS

Bodleian Library
Bright MSS
Bryce MSS
Burgon MSS
Liddon MSS
Max Müller MSS
Pusey MSS
Rashdall MSS
Sanday MSS
Thompson MSS
Vaughan MSS
Webb MSS

Cambridge University Archives
Minutes of the Board of Theological Studies

Christ Church Archives
Sanday MSS

Harris Manchester College Archives
Minute Book of the Society of Historical Theology

Lambeth Palace Library
Headlam MSS

Mansfield College Archives
Minute Book of Spring Hill College and Mansfield College
Reports of the Committee of Management of Mansfield College

Oxford University Archives
Minutes of the Board of the Faculty of Theology
Minutes of the Hebdomadal Council
Register of Congregation
Reports of the Board of the Faculty of Theology

Pusey House Library
Pusey MSS
Liddon MSS
Scott MSS
Stanley MSS

The Queen's College Archives
Ewbank MS

St. Hilda's College Archives
Collinson MSS

Books and Other Material

Abbott, E. and Campbell, L., eds., *The Life and Letters of Benjamin Jowett*. 2 vols., London: John Murray, 1897.

Academicus (pseud.), *To members of Convocation. Is the University in her new position, called upon to abandon in any case her theological instruction, and its proper evidence at the public examination? Or, if any modification as to the latter be required, is the proposed mode of substitution the desirable one?* Oxford, 1855.

Allen, W.C. *The Clergy and the Honour School of Theology*. Oxford: Parker and Son, 1904.

An appeal to the statutes [concerning the powers of the Regius Professor of divinity in divinity degrees]. Oxford, 1844.

Anson, H. *T.B Strong: bishop, musician, dean, vice-chancellor*. London: SPCK, 1949.

Arnold, Matthew. *Essays in Criticism*. London: Macmillan, 1865.

_____. *Schools and Universities on the Continent*. London: Macmillan, 1868.

Arnold, Thomas. *Principles of Church Reform*. London: Roake & Varty, 1833.

_____. "The Oxford Malignants and Dr Hampden", *Edinburgh Review* 63 (1836).

_____. "Revival of the Faculties at Oxford," *Dark Blue* 2:380-86, 493-509.

Atherstone, Andrew. "Benjamin Jowett's Pauline Commentary: An Atonement Controversy", *Journal of Theological Studies* 54 (2003).

_____. "The Founding of Wycliffe Hall, Oxford", *Anglican and Episcopal History*, 73 (2004): 78-102.

_____. "Robert Baker Girdlestone and 'God's own Book,'" *Evangelical Quarterly* 74 (2002): 4, 313-33.

Authorized Report of the Church Congress, held at Nottingham October 10, 11, 12, & 13, 1871. London: W. Wells Gardner, 1871.

Barth, Karl. *Ethics.* Grand Rapids: Eerdmans, 1981.

_____. *The Word of God and Theology.* London: Continuum, 2011.

Bateman, J. *The Tractarian Tendency of Theological Colleges.* London, 1853.

Biggar, N. "What are Universities for? A Christian View" in Higton, M., Law, J. and Rowland, C., eds. *Theology and Human Flourishing: Essays in Honor of Timothy J. Gorringe.* Eugene, OR: Cascade, 2011.

Bill, E.G.W. *University Reform in Nineteenth-Century Oxford: A Study of Henry Halford Vaughan.* Oxford: Clarendon, 1973.

Bishop, Morris. *A History of Cornell.* Ithaca, NY: Cornell University, 1962.

Brent, Richard. *Liberal Anglican Politics: Whiggery, Religion, and Reform.* Oxford: Oxford University, 1987.

_____. "Hampden, Renn Dickson (1793–1868)", *Oxford Dictionary of National Biography.* Oxford: Oxford University, 2004.

Bosworth, C.E. *A Century of British Orientalists, 1902-2001.* Oxford: Oxford University, 2001.

Brooke, C.N.L. *A History of the University of Cambridge* (4 vols.). Cambridge: Cambridge University, 1988-2004.

Bryce, J. and Fairbairn, A.M. "Nonconformity and the Universities: The Free Churches and a Theological Faculty", *British Quarterly* (April 1884).

Buckland, William. *Geology and Mineralogy.* London: William Pickering, 1836.

Bullock, F.W.B. *A History of Training for Ministry of the Church of England in England and Wales from 1800 to 1874.* St. Leonards-on-Sea: Budd & Gillatt, 1955.

_____. *A History of Training for the Ministry of the Church of England in England and Wales from 1875 to 1974.* London: Home Words Printing and Publishing, 1976.

Burgon, J.W. *The Disestablishment of Religion in Oxford, the Betrayal of a Sacred Trust: Words of Warning to the University: A Sermon.* Oxford: Parker and Co., 1880.

_____. *Plea for a Fifth Final School.* Oxford: Parker & Co, 1868.

_____. *A Plea for the Study of Divinity at Oxford.* Oxford: J.H. Parker, 1875.

Burney, C.F. "Samuel Rolles Driver", *Oxford Magazine,* 5 March 1914.

Burns, A. *The Diocesan Revival in the Church of England c.1800-1870.* Oxford: Clarendon, 1999.

Butler, Joseph. *The Analogy of Religion.* London: William Tegg, 1859.

Butler, Perry, ed. *Pusey Rediscovered.* London: SPCK, 1983.

Caldecott, A. ed. *London Theological Studies.* London: University of London, 1911.

Cambridge Review

The Cambridge University Reporter. 1871-1876. Cambridge: Cambridge University

Campbell, Lewis. *On the Nationalization of the Old English Universities.* London: Chapman and Hall, 1901.

Carpenter, H.J. "Beresford James Kidd, 1864-1948", *Oxford Magazine,* 27 May 1948.

Carpenter, S.C. *Church and People, 1789-1889: A History of the Church of England from William Wilberforce to 'Lux Mundi'.* London: SPCK, 1959

Catto, Jeremy, ed., *Oriel College: A History.* Oxford: Oxford University, 1932.

Aston, T.H., Brock, M., Catto, J.I., Curthoys, M.C., Evans, T.A.R., Harrison, B., McConica, J., Mitchell, L.G., Sutherland, L.S., Tyacke, N., eds. *The History of the University of Oxford* (8 vols.). Oxford: Clarendon, 1984-2000.

Chadwick, Owen. *The Founding of Cuddesdon Theological College.* Oxford: Oxford University, 1954

_____. *The Victorian Church* (2 vols). London: A&C Black, 1966, 1970.

_____. *Westcott and the University.* Cambridge, 1963.

Chandler, M. *The Life and Work of Henry Parry Liddon.* Leominster: Gracewing, 2000.

Chapman, Mark. "Newman and the Anglican Idea of the University", *Journal for the History of Modern Theology*, 18 (2011): 212-22.

_____. "The Socratic Subversion of Tradition: William Sanday and Theology, 1900-1920", *Journal of Theological Studies*, 45 (1994).

Chapman, Mark, ed. *Ambassadors of Christ.* Aldershot: Ashgate, 2004.

Chase, D.P. *The de-Christianising of the Colleges of Oxford.* Reprinted from the *Standard* of 27 October 1868. London, 1869.

_____. *To members of Congregation* [On the effect of the proposed new regulations affecting theological examinations and Dissenters. Signed D.P.C.] Oxford, 1855.

Cheyne, T.K. *Book of Isaiah.* London: Macmillan, 1870.

_____. *Essays on the Endowment of Research.* London: Henry S. King, 1876.

_____. *The Prophecies of Isaiah,* 2 vols. London: Kegan, Paul, Trench & Co., 1886.

_____. "Reform in Old Testament Teaching", *Contemporary Review* 56 (1889).

Church Quarterly, 10 Feb. 1890.

Church Times, 1863-1945.

Clark, Elizabeth A. *Founding the Fathers: Early Church History and Protestant Professors in Nineteenth-Century America.* Philadelphia: University of Pennsylvania, 2011.

Clark, J.C.D. *English Society, 1688-1832: Ideology, Social Structure and Political Practice during the Ancien Régime.* Cambridge: Cambridge University, 1985.

Clements, K.W. *Lovers of Discord: Twentieth-Century Theological Controversies in England.* London: SPCK, 1988.

Cobb, P.G. *A Brief History of St Stephen's House, 1876-1976.* Oxford, 1976.

Collini, Stefan. *What are Universities for?* London: Penguin, 2012.

Conington, J. *The Theological Statute.* Oxford, 1869.

Convocation of Canterbury, Report of the Committee on the Supply and Training of Candidates for Holy Orders, May 1900. London, National Society, 1900.

Conybeare, William. *Analytical Examination of the Character, Value, and Just Application of the Writings of the Christian Fathers during the Ante-Nicene Period.* Oxford: J.H. Parker, 1839.

Cooke, G.A. "Driver and Wellhausen", *The Harvard Theological Review* 9 (1916).

Cooper, R.E. *From Stepney to St Giles': The Story of Regent's Park College, 1810-1960.* London: Carey Kingsgate, 1960.

Copleston, E. *An Enquiry into the Doctrines of Necessity and Predestination.* London: John Murray, 1821.

————. *A Reply to the Calumnies of the Edinburgh Review against Oxford.* Oxford: J. Parker, 1810.

Cooper, R.E. '*From Stepney to St Giles': The Story of Regent's Park College, 1810-1960.* London: Carey Kingsgate, 1990.

Coulson, John. ed. *Theology and the University: An Ecumenical Investigation.* Baltimore, MD: Helicon, 1964.

Cunliffe, Christopher. ed. *Joseph Butler's Moral and Religious Thought: Tercentenary Essays.* Oxford: Clarendon , 1992.

Curtis, Philip. *A Hawk among Sparrows: A Biography of Austin Farrer.* London: SPCK, 1985.

Dale, A.W.W. *The Life of R.W. Dale of Birmingham.* London: Hodder & Stoughton, 1899.

Darbishire, R.D. *Theology and Piety: Alike Free: from the point of view of Manchester New College, Oxford. A Contribution to its Effort, offered by an Old Student.* London: Kegan Paul, Trench, Trubner & Co. Ltd., 1890.

Darwall-Smith, R. *A History of University College Oxford.* Oxford: Oxford University, 2008.

D'Costa, G. *Theology in the Public Square.* Oxford: Blackwell, 2006.

Degrees in Divinity. Oxford, 1868.

Denyer and Johnson Theological Scholarships Examination Papers. Oxford: Clarendon, 1866.

"The Divinity Question at the Universities: The Vote at Oxford." *Church Times* (2 May 1913).

Dowland, D. *Nineteenth-Century Anglican Theological Training.* Oxford: Clarendon,1997.

Driver, S.R. *The Book of Daniel, with Introduction and Notes.* Cambridge: Cambridge University, 1912.

————. "Canon Bright: an appreciation," *Oxford Magazine,* 13 March 1901.

————. *Sermons on Subjects Connected with the Old Testament.* London: Methuen & Co., 1892.

Dwyer, Philip G. *The Rise of Prussia 1700–1830.* London: Longman, 2000.

The Ecclesiastic

Ellis, Ieuan, *Seven against Christ: A Study of 'Essays and Reviews'.* Leiden: E.J. Brill, 1980.

Engel, J. *From Clergyman to Don.* Oxford: Oxford University, 1983.

Essays and Reviews. 7th ed. London: Longmans, Green, 1861.

Espin, T.E., *Our want of clergy: its Causes and Suggestions for its Cure.* Oxford: J. Parker, 1863.

The Expository Times

Faber, G. *Jowett, a Portrait with a Background.* London: Faber, 1958.

Fairbairn, A.M. *Letter to the Regius Professor of Divinity on the School of Theology.* Oxford: Horace Hart, 1898.

_____. (and Bryce, J.). "Nonconformity and the Universities: The Free Churches and a Theological Faculty," *British Quarterly,* Apr. 1884.

Farley, Edward. *Theologia: The Fragmentation and Unity of Theological Education.* Philadelphia: Fortress, 1983.

First Public Examination: Holy Scripture, Hilary Term 1930. Oxford: Clarendon, 1930.

The First Report of Her Majesty's Commissioners, appointed 10 November, 1852, to inquire into the State and Condition of the Cathedral and Collegiate Churches in England and Wales. London: Her Majesty's Stationery Office, 1854.

Firth, Charles. *Modern History in Oxford, 1841-1918.* Oxford: Blackwell, 1920.

Forbes, D. *The Liberal Anglican Idea of History.* Cambridge: Cambridge University, 1952.

Ford, David. *The Future of Christian Theology.* Oxford: Blackwell, 2011.

Ford, D., Quash, B. and Soskice, J.M., *eds. Fields of Faith: Theology and Religious Studies for the Twenty-First Century.* Cambridge: Cambridge University, 2005.

Forrester, D. *Young Doctor Pusey: A Study in Development.* London: Mowbray, 1989.

Frei, Hans. *Types of Christian Theology.* New Haven, CT: Yale University, 1992.

Garbett, J. *University Reform: A Letter to the Reverend the Warden of Wadham College, Oxford by the Ven. J. Garbett M.A., Archdeacon of Chichester and Late Professor of Poetry.* London: T. Hatchard, 1853.

Garnett, J. "Bishop Butler and the *Zeitgeist*" in Cunliffe, C. ed. *Joseph Butler's Moral and Religious Thought: Tercentenary Essays.* Oxford: Clarendon, 1992.

Garnett, J. and Davies, C.S.L., *Tutorial Teaching at Wadham: A History.* Oxford: privately printed, 2008.

The Gazette, 5 March 1913.

Gentleman's Magazine, 1st ser., 99/1 London, 1829.

Girdlestone, Robert B. *The Training of the Clergy.* Oxford, 1880.

_____. *Wycliffe Hall: Its Nature and Its Object.* privately printed, 1878.

Gore, C. *The Basis of Anglican Fellowship in Faith and Organization.* London, 1914

_____. ed. *Lux Mundi: a series of studies in the religion of the Incarnation.* London: John Murray, 1920.

_____. *The New Theology and the Old Religion.* London: John Murray, 1907.

Goudge, H.L. *The Admission of Nonconformists to Communion: A Paper.* London, 1932.

_____. *The Authority and Value of the New Testament.* London: Mowbray, 1935.

_____. *The Church and the Bible.* London: Longmans, Green & Co., 1930.

_____. *The Methods of Theology: An Inaugural Lecture Delivered in the Chapter House of Christ Church, Oxford, Friday, June 8, 1923.* London: Mowbray & Co., 1923.

_____. *The Second Epistle to the Corinthians.* London: Methuen, 1927.

Gray, G.B. "S. R. Driver: the character and influence of his work," *Contemporary Review,* 105 (1914), 484–90.

Green, S.W. 'Sketch of the History of the Faculty' in *London Theological Studies.* London: University of London, 1911.

Green, V.H.H. *Religion at Oxford and Cambridge.* London: SCM, 1964.

The Guardian.

Haig, Alan. "The Church, the Universities and Learning in Later Victorian England," *The Historical Journal,* 29.1 (1986).

_____. *The Victorian Clergy.* London: Croom Helm, 1984.

Hampden, Henrietta. *Some Memorials of Renn Dickson Hampden Bishop of Hereford.* London: Longmans, Green and Co., 1871.

Hampden, Renn Dickson. *Observations on Religious Dissent.* Oxford: J.H. Parker, 1834.

_____. *The Scholastic Philosophy Considered in its Relation to Christian Theology.* Oxford: J.H. Parker, 1833.

Hansell, E.H. *The Margaret Professorship.* Oxford, 1856.

Hare, A.J.C. *Biographical Sketches.* London: George Allen, 1895.

Harvie, Christopher. *The Lights of Liberalism: University Liberals and the Challenge of Democracy, 1860-1886.* London: Allen Lane, 1976.

Hatch, E. *The Organization of the Early Christian Churches* (8th ed.). London, 1918.

Hatch, S.C. *Memorials of Edwin Hatch.* London: Hodder & Stoughton, 1890.

Hauerwas, Stanley. *The State of the University: Academic Knowledges and the Knowledge of God.* Oxford: Blackwell, 2007.

Hawkins, E. *An Enquiry into the Connected Use of the Principal Means of Attaining Christian Truth.* Oxford: J.H. Parker, 1836.

_____. *An inaugural lecture upon the foundation of Dean Ireland's professorship, Nov. 2. 1847; with brief notices of the founder.* London, 1848.

_____. *A letter...upon a recent statute of the University of Oxford with reference to dissent and occasional conformity. By the provost of Oriel.* Oxford, 1855.

Headlam, A.C. "Degrees in Divinity", *Church Quarterly Review*, 76 (1913).

_____. *The Life and Teaching of Jesus Christ.* London: Macmillan, 1923.

_____. *Memorandum on the Proposed Course of Training for Orders in Oxford.* Privately printed, 1918.

_____. *Memorandum on the Teaching Office of the Church in relation to the Universities.* Privately printed, 1918.

_____. "Report of the Royal Commission on Oxford and Cambridge Universities", *Church Quarterly Review,* 16 (1922): 322-51.

_____. *The Study of Theology, An Inaugural Lecture*. Oxford: Oxford University, 1918.

_____. *Theological Education in the Universities*. Oxford: Blackwell, 1921.

_____. *Universities and Religion: A Sermon preached in Bristol Cathedral, May 24th, 1923*. Bristol, 1923.

Helmstadter, R.J. and Lightman, B., eds. *Victorian faith in crisis: essays on continuity and change in nineteenth-century religious belief*. Stanford: Stanford University, 1990.

Hennell, S. *Essay on the Sceptical Tendency of Butler's 'Analogy'*. London, 1859.

Heurtley, C.A. *An Appeal to the Members of Convocation on the Proposal to alter the Statutes Relating to Theological Instruction and Examination*. Oxford, 1855.

Herbert, Lionel. *Memorials of Lionel Herbert*. London: Oxford University, 1926.

Higton, Mike. *A Theology of Higher Education*. Oxford: Oxford University, 2012.

Higton, Mike, Law, Jeremy, and Rowland, Christopher, eds. *Theology and Human Flourishing: Essays in Honor of Timothy J. Gorringe*. Eugene, OR: Cascade, 2011.

Hillier, B. *Young Betjeman*. London: John Murray, 1998.

Hinchliff, Peter. *Benjamin Jowett and the Christian Religion*. Oxford: Clarendon, 1987.

_____. *God and History: Aspects of British Theology, 1789-1914*. Oxford: Clarendon, 1992.

Holland, H.S. *A Bundle of Memories*. London: Wells Gardner, Darton & Co., 1915.

_____. "Historical Evidence for Miracles", *Report of the Church Congress, Middlesborough*. London (1912).

_____. *Pleas and Claims for Christ*. London: Longmans, Green & Co., 1892.

_____. ed., *Miracles*. London: Longmans, 1911.

Holroyd. M. ed., *Memorials of the Life of G.E. Corrie, D.D.* Cambridge: Cambridge University, 1890.

Hooper, W. *C.S. Lewis: A Companion & Guide*. London: Harper Collins, 1996.

Hort, A.F., ed. *Life and Letters of J.F.A. Hort.* London: Macmillan, 1896.

Houlden, J.L. *Connections: The Integration of Theology and Faith*. London: SCM, 1986.

Hoskyns, E.C. *The Fourth Gospel.* 2nd ed., London: Faber & Faber, 1947.

Howard, Thomas Albert. *Protestant Theology and the Making of the Modern German University.* Oxford: Oxford University, 2008.

Howarth, J. "Science Education in Late-Victorian Oxford: A Curious Case of Failure?" *English Historical Review* 102 (1987): 334-371.

How shall we examine Dissenters? Considerations suggested by clause xliv of the Oxford University Act, by an Examiner. Oxford, 1854.

Hussey, Robert. *An examination of the new form of the statutes Tit. IV. Tit. V.: With hints for establishing a system of professional teaching.* Oxford: J.H. Parker, 1839.

_____. *Remarks on Some Proposed Changes in the Public Examinations.* Oxford: J.H. Parker, 1848.

_____. *University Prospects and University Duties, a Sermon.* Oxford: J.H. Parker, 1854.

Illingworth, A.L., ed. *The Life and Work of John Richard Illingworth.* London: John Murray, 1917.

Ince, William. *The Past and Present Duties of the Faculty of Theology.* Oxford: James Parker, 1878.

Iremonger, F.A. *William Temple, Archbishop of Canterbury.* London: Oxford University, 1948.

Jenkins, D. "Oxford: the Anglican tradition" in Coulson, J., ed. *Theology and the University.* Baltimore, MD: Helicon, 1964.

Johnston, J.O. *Life and Letters of H.P. Liddon*. London: Longmans, Green & Co, 1904.

Jones, H.S. *Intellect and Character in Victorian England: Mark Pattison and the Invention of the Don*. Cambridge: Cambridge University, 2007.

Jones, John. *Balliol College: A History*. Oxford: Oxford University, 2005.

Jowett, Benjamin. *The Epistles of St. Paul to the Thessalonians, Galatians, Romans: with Critical Notes and Dissertations* (2 vols.). London: John Murray, 1855.

[Jowett, B. and Stanley, A.P.] *Suggestions for an Improvement to the Examination Statute*. Oxford: Francis Macpherson, 1848.

Kaye, Elaine. *Mansfield College: Its Origin, History, and Significance*. Oxford: Oxford University, 1996.

Kaye, Elaine, Lees, Janet and Thorpe, Kirsty, eds. *Daughters of Dissent*. London: United Reformed Church, 2004.

Kemp, E.W. *N.P. Williams*. London: SPCK, 1954.

Kenyon, F.G. *The British Academy: The First Fifty Years*. London: Oxford University, 1952.

Ker, I. *John Henry Newman: A Biography*. Oxford: Oxford University, 1988.

Ker, Ian and Merrigan, Terrence. eds. *The Cambridge Companion to John Henry Newman*. Cambridge: Cambridge University, 2009.

Ker, I., Tracey, G., Gornall, T. and McGrath, F., eds. *The Letters and Diaries of John Henry Newman*. (32 vols.) Oxford: Oxford University, 1978–2008.

Kerr, Clark. *The Uses of a University*. Cambridge, MA: Harvard University, 2001.

Kidd, B.J., ed. *The Selected Letters of William Bright*. London: W. Gardner, Darton & Co., 1903.

Kirk, Kenneth, ed. *The Study of Theology*. London: Hodder & Stoughton, 1939.

Knox, R. "Absolute and Abitofhell", *Oxford Magazine,* November 1912.

Lagarde, Paul de. *Über das Verhältnis des deutschen Staates zu Theologie, Kirche und Religion.* Göttingen: Dieterich, 1873.

Lancelot, J.B. *Francis James Chavasse.* Oxford: Blackwell, 1929.

Larsen, Timothy "E.B. Pusey and Holy Scripture," *Journal of Theological Studies* 60 (2009): 490-526.

_____. *A People of One Book: The Bible and the Victorians.* Oxford: Oxford University, 2011.

Lawson, F.H. *The Oxford Law School, 1850-1965.* Oxford: Clarendon, 1965.

"Letter of the Board of the Faculty of Theology to the Hebdomadal Council, in response to a query regarding the Board's decision to change the name of the faculty", *Theology Reports* (26 October 1912).

Liddon, H.P. *Dr Pusey and the Pusey House: A Sermon by Dr H.P. Liddon.* Oxford: Friends of Pusey House, 1974.

_____. *The Life of Edward Bouverie Pusey*, (4 vols.). London: Longmans, Green & Co., 1894-1898.

_____. "Recent Fortunes of the Church in Oxford", *Church Quarterly Review* 21 (1881).

Lightfoot, J.B. "Greek New Testament Lectures, Lent Term 1855" in Kaye, B.N. and Treloar, G.R. "J.B. Lightfoot and New Testament Interpretation: An Unpublished Manuscript of 1855," *Durham University Journal,* 82:2 (July 1990).

"List of the Professors' Lectures for the Present Term." *The Oxford Undergraduate's Journal*, 25 October 1869.

Livingston, James C. *Religious Thought in the Victorian Age: Challenges and Reconceptions.* Edinburgh: T&T Clark, 2006.

Lock, Walter. *A Critical and Exegetical Commentary on the Pastoral Epistles.* Edinburgh: T&T Clark, 1924.

_____. *Oxford Memories.* London: Oxford University, 1932.

_____. *To the Members of the Board of the Faculty of Theology.* privately printed, 1904.

Lyttleton, E. *The Mind and Character of Henry Scott Holland*. London: Mowbray, 1920.

Macan, R.W. *Religious Changes in Oxford during the Last Fifty Years*. London: Oxford University, 1917.

Magrath, John. *A Plea for the Study of Divinity in the University of Oxford: A Sermon preached before the University of Oxford on the Second Sunday after the Epiphany, January 19, 1868*. London: Rivingtons, 1868.

Marriott, C. *A few words to the resident members of Convocation on the subject of the statute [affecting theology and law] shortly to be proposed*. Oxford, 1844.

Marsden, George M. *The Soul of the American University: From Protestant Establishment to Established Nonbelief*. New York, NY: Oxford University, 1994.

Matheson, P.E. *The Life of Hastings Rashdall*. London: Oxford University, 1928.

Matthew, H.C.G. "Edward Bouverie Pusey: From Scholar to Tractarian," *Journal of Theological Studies* 32 (1981).

_____. "Hussey, Robert (1801-1856)" in the *Dictionary of National Biography*. Oxford: Oxford University, 2004.

_____. "Noetics, Tractarians, and the Reform of the University of Oxford in the Nineteenth Century," *History of Universities,* 10 (1990): 195-255.

McClellan, James E. *Science Reorganized: Scientific Societies in the Eighteenth Century*. (New York: Columbia University, 1985.

McGrath, Alister. *C.S. Lewis: A Life: Eccentric, Reluctant Prophet*. London: Hodder & Stoughton, 2013

_____. *The Intellectual World of C.S. Lewis*. Oxford: Wiley Blackwell, 2013.

"Memorial on Theological Degrees and School, 7 February 1912". *Theology Reports*, 48.

Memorial on Theological Degrees and School. Privately printed, 1912.

Milbank, J. "The Conflict of the Faculties: Theology and the Economy of the Sciences," in Nation. M.T. and Wells, S., eds. *Faithfulness and Fortitude: In Conversation with the Theological Ethics of Stanley Hauerwas.* Edinburgh: T&T Clark, 2000.

Minutes of Evidence taken by the Commissioner. London, 1878.

The Modern Churchman, 9. 1920.

Morgan, Robert. "Maurice Wiles". *The Guardian,* 10 June 2005. http://www.theguardian.com/news/2005/jun/10/ guardianobituaries.obituaries

Morgan, Robert, ed. *The Religion of the Incarnation: Anglican Essays in Commemoration of Lux Mundi.* Bristol: Bristol Classical, 1989.

Mozley J.B. and Mozley, A. *Letters of the Rev. J.B. Mozley.* London: Rivingtons, 1885.

Müller, Friedrich Max. *Chips from a German Workshop.* London: Longmans, Green & Co., 1868.

_____. *Introduction to the Science of Religion.* London: Longmans, Green & Co., 1873.

Müller, G., ed. *The Life and Letters of F. Max Müller.* 2 vols., London: Longman, Green & Co., 1902.

Neill, Stephen and Wright, NT.. *The Interpretation of the New Testament, 1861-1986.* London: Oxford University, 1988.

Nietzsche, Friedrich "On the Uses and Disadvantages of History for Life" in *Untimely Meditations*, trans. R. Hollingdale. Cambridge: Cambridge University, 1997

Neville, W.P. ed., *Addresses to Cardinal Newman with his Replies, 1879-81.* London: Longmans Green, 1905.

The New Degree of Candidate in Theology. Oxford, 1842.

The New Divinity Statute. Oxford, 1844.

The New Examinations for Divinity Degrees. Oxford, 1844.

The New Theological Statute. Oxford, 1860.

The New Theological Statute [Objections to]. Oxford, 1868.

Newman, John Henry. *Apologia pro vita sua*. London: Oxford University, 1964.

————. *The Idea of a University Defined and Illustrated*, ed. I. Kerr. Oxford: Clarendon, 1976.

————. *The Scope and Nature of University Education*. London: J.M. Dent, 1903.

Nietzsche, F. *Untimely Meditations.* Cambridge: Cambridge University, 1997.

Nicholson, Ernest, ed. *A Century of Theological and Religious Studies in Britain.* Oxford: Oxford University, 2002.

The Nonconformist.

Nockles, P. "An Academic Counter-Revolution: Newman and Tractarian Oxford's Idea of a University," *History of Universities* 10 (1991): 137-197.

————. *The Oxford Movement in Context.* Cambridge: Cambridge University,1994.

Nussbaum, Martha C. *Not for Profit: Why Democracy needs the Humanities.* Princeton: Princeton University, 2012.

Ogilvie, C. *The Divine Glory Manifested in the Conduct and Discourses of our Lord: Eight Sermons preached before the University of Oxford.* Oxford: J.H. Parker, 1836.

Outram, D. "Military empire, political collaboration, and cultural consensus: the Université imperiale reappraised: the case of the University of Turin", *History of Universities* 7 (1988): 287-303.

Overbeck, Franz. *Über die Christlichkeit unserer heutigen Theologie*, reprint of 2nd edn. Darmstadt: Wissenschaftliche Buchgesellsschaft, 1981.

Oxford and Cambridge Undergraduate's Journal. 25 November 1880.

Oxford Essays

Oxford Magazine.

Oxford Ordination Course Examination Papers. Oxford: Oxford University, 1921-24.

Oxford Ordination Course: Regulations for the Course. Oxford: Oxford University, 1919.

The Oxford Undergraduate's Journal, 10 December 1868. Oxford.

The Oxford University Handbook. Oxford: Oxford University, 1914, 1939.

Paget, S. *Henry Scott Holland: Memoir and Letters.* London: John Murray, 1921.

Paget, S. and Crum, J.M.C. *Francis Paget, Bishop of Oxford.* London: Macmillan, 1912.

Pattison, M. *Memoirs.* London: Macmillan, 1885.

————. "The present state of theology in Germany", *Westminster Review* 67 (1857): 246–62.

————. *Suggestions on Academical Organisation with Especial Reference to Oxford.* Edinburgh: Edmonton & Douglas, 1868.

Patrick, J., *The Magdalen Metaphysicals: Idealism and Orthodoxy at Oxford, 1901-1945.* Macon, GA.: Mercer, 1985.

Payne, E.A. *Henry Wheeler Robinson, Scholar, Teacher, Principal: A Memoir.* London: Nisbet, 1946.

Peake, A.S. ed. *Inaugural Lectures delivered by Members of the Faculty of Theology during its First Session, 1904-05.* Manchester: Manchester University, 1920.

Pelikan, J. *Religion and the University.* Toronto: Toronto University, 1964.

Pereiro, James. *'Ethos' and the Oxford Movement.* Oxford: Oxford University, 2007.

Perowne, J.J. Stewart. "Dr Pusey on Daniel the Prophet", *Contemporary Review* 1 (1866).

Powell, B. *Rational Religion Explained.* London: C. & J. Rivington, 1826.

Prestige, G.L. *The Life of Charles Gore: A Great Englishman.* London: Heinemann, 1905.

Priestman, J. "The Dilettante and the Dons" in *Oxford Today* Vol. 18, No.3 (Trinity 2006).

Prothero, Rowland E. *The Life and Correspondence of Arthur Penrhyn Stanley, D.D.* (2 vols.). London: John Murray, 1894.

Purver, Margery. *The Royal Society: Concept and Creation.* Cambridge, MA: MIT, 1967.

Pusey, E.B. *All Faith the Gift of God. Real Faith Entire.* Oxford: J.H. Parker, 1855.

_____. *The Board of Examiners for the Proposed Theological School.* Oxford, 1868.

_____. *Collegiate and Professorial Teaching and Discipline.* Oxford, 1854.

_____. *The Divinity School.* Oxford, 1868.

_____. *Daniel the Prophet: Nine Lectures, Delivered in the Divinity School of the University of Oxford, with Copious Notes.* Oxford: J.H. Parker, 1864.

_____. *Dr Hampden's Past and Present Statements Compared.* Oxford: J.H. Parker, 1836.

_____. *Historical Enquiry into the Probable Causes of the Rationalist Character Lately Predominant in the Theology of Germany* (2 vols.). London: C. & J. Rivington, 1828.

_____. *Of the 'Honours' proposed to be conferred in the new Theological Statute.* Oxford, 1860.

_____. *The proposed school of theology, Whit-Monday, 1869* [A reply to the observations of H.J.S. Smith]. Oxford, 1869.

_____. *The proposed statute for a theological school. May 12, 1869.* Oxford, 1869.

_____. *Remarks on the prospective and past benefits of Cathedral Institutions.* Oxford: J.H. Parker, 1833.

_____. *A Summary of Objections against the Proposed Theological Statute.* Oxford: J. Parker, 1854.

_____. *Toleration for members of the Church of England.* Oxford, 1868.

————. *Un-science, not science, adverse to Faith : a sermon preached before the University of Oxford on the twentieth Sunday after Trinity, 1878.* Oxford: J. Parker, 1878.

Quilibet (pseud.), *Is the University justified in omitting to instruction any of her members in theology?* [Arguments against clause vi of the proposed new statute.] Oxford, 1855.

Ramsey, A.M. *From Gore to Temple.* London: Longmans, 1960.

Reardon, B.M.G. *Religious Thought in the Victorian Age: A Survey from Coleridge to Gore.* London: Longman, 1980.

————. ed. *Henry Scott Holland: A Selection from his Writings.* London: SPCK, 1962.

Reasons for hesitating to vote in favour of the proposal to be made in Convocation on…March 17. [relative to the endowment of two new theological professorships]. Oxford, 1842.

Report and Evidence upon the Recommendations of Her Majesty's Commissioners for Inquiring into the State of the University of Oxford. Oxford: Oxford University, 1853.

Report of the Committee of Management of Mansfield College, Oxford, for the Session 1886-87. Birmingham: Hudson & Son, 1887.

Report of the Committee of Management of Mansfield College, Oxford, for the Session 1912-13. Oxford: Alden & Co, 1913.

Research Councils UK. "Excellence with Impact: What do Research Councils mean by Impact?" http://www.rcuk.ac.uk/kei/impacts/Pages/meanbyimpact.aspx.

Review of the Permanent Private Halls associated with the University of Oxford: Report to the Council of the University. Oxford: Oxford University internal document, 2007.

Richardson, Herbert, ed. *Friedrich Schleiermacher and the Founding of the University of Berlin: The Study of Religion as a Scientific Discipline.* Lewiston, NY: Edwin Mellen, 1991.

Roberts, David B. *The Church Militant: Interpreting a Satirical Cartoon*. Oxford: Magdalen College, 2013.

Rogerson, J. *Old Testament Criticism in the Nineteenth Century: England and Germany*. London: SPCK, 1984.

Rolleston, G. *The Proposed School of Theology*. Oxford, 1868.

Rothblatt, S. *The Modern University and its Discontents: the fate of Newman's Legacies in Britain and America*. Cambridge: Cambridge University, 1997.

_____. *Tradition and Change in English Liberal Education: An Essay in History and Culture*. London: Faber, 1976.

Rüegg, Walter, ed. *A History of the University in Europe* (4 vols.). Cambridge: Cambridge University, 2004.

Rumscheidt, H. Martin. *Revelation and Theology: An Analysis of the Barth-Harnack Correspondence of 1923*. Cambridge: Cambridge University, 1972.

Sanday, William. "The Future of English Theology", *Contemporary Review* 56 (1889).

_____. "The Historical Method in Theology" (a paper read to the Church Congress in Nottingham in 1897), *The Expository Times* 9 (1897).

_____. *The Life of Christ in Recent Research*. Oxford: Oxford University, 1907.

_____. ed., *Oxford Studies in the Synoptic Problem*. Oxford: Clarendon, 1911.

_____. *Outlines of the Life of Christ*. Edinburgh: T&T Clark, 1905.

Sanday, William and Williams, N.P. *Form and Content in the Christian Tradition*. London: Longmans, 1916.

Sanderson, Edgar. *The Creed and the Church: A Handbook of Theology*. Oxford: J. Parker, 1865.

Sandford, Ernest G. ed., *Memoirs of Archbishop Temple, by Seven Friends*. (2 vols.). London: Macmillan, 1906.

Sayce, A.H. *Reminiscences*. London: Macmillan, 1923.

Schüssler Fiorenza, F. "Theological and Religious Studies: The Contest of the Faculties" in Wheeler, B.G. and Farley, E., eds. *Shifting Boundaries: Contextual Approaches to the Structure of Theological Education*. Louisville, KT: Westminster, 1991.

Second Public Examination: Honour School of Literae Humaniores. Oxford: Oxford University, 1863.

Second Public Examination: Honour School of Theology. Oxford: Clarendon, 1877.

Second Public Examination: Honour School of Theology, Michaelmas Term 1873. Oxford: Clarendon, 1873.

Second Public Examination: Honour School of Theology, Trinity Term 1873. Oxford: Clarendon, 1873.

Second Public Examination: School of Theology, Trinity Term 1930. Oxford: Clarendon, 1930.

Seeley, J.R., "Liberal education in universities" in Farrar, F.W., ed., *Essays on Liberal Education*. London: Macmillan, 1867.

Selbie, W. *Fifty Years at Oxford*. London: Independent Press, 1936.

_____. *Life of Andrew Martin Fairbairn*. London: Hodder & Stoughton, 1914.

Sharpe, E.J. *Comparative Religion: A History*. London: Duckworth, 1975.

Shea, Victor and Whitla, William, eds., *Essays and Reviews: The 1860 Text and its Reading*. Charlottesville, VA: University Press of Virginia, 2000.

Sketch of a case prepared by Dr. Pusey. [A paper on technical points connected with the statute consisting of a new theology school: undated but apparently May, 1869.] Oxford, 1869.

Slee, P.H., *Liberal and a Liberal Education: The Study of Modern History in the Universities of Oxford, Cambridge and Manchester, 1800-1914*. Manchester: Manchester University, 1986.

_____. "The Oxford Idea of a Liberal Education 1800–1860: The Invention of Tradition and the Manufacture of Practice," *History of Universities* 7 (1988): 61–87.

Smart, Ninian. *A New Look at Religious Studies: the Lancaster Idea.* London: Routledge, 1967.

Smith, Barbara. ed. *Truth, Liberty, Religion: Essays Celebrating Two Hundred Years of Manchester College.* Oxford: Manchester College, 1986.

Smith, Goldwin. *Reminiscences.* New York: Macmillan, 1910.

_____. *The Reorganization of the University of Oxford.* Oxford: J.H. Parker, 1868.

Smith, Henry J.S. *The Proposed School of Theology.* Oxford, 1868.

_____. *The Proposed School of Theology* [observations against]. Oxford, 1869.

Smith, Robin Darwall. *A History of University College.* Oxford: Oxford University, 2008.

Sparrow, J. *Mark Pattison and the Idea of a University.* London: Cambridge University, 1967.

Special Report from the Select Committee on the Oxford and Cambridge Universities Education Bill; together with the Proceedings of the Committee, Minutes of Evidence, and Appendix. London, 1867.

Stacpoole, Dom Alberic, OSB. "The Return of the Roman Catholics to Oxford", *New Blackfriars*, 67 (1986).

Stanley, A.P. *The Life and Correspondence of Thomas Arnold.* London: B. Fellowes, 1844.

_____. "The late Dr. Arnold", *Edinburgh Review* 76 (1843).

Stoner, James, "Theology as Knowledge: A Symposium," *First Things* 163 (May 2006).

Storr, Richard J. *Harper's University: A History of the University of Chicago.* Chicago: University of Chicago, 1966.

Streeter, B.H. ed. *Foundations.* London: Macmillan, 1912.

_____. "Theology", *Oxford Magazine* (12 June 1930).

Stuchtey, Benedikt. and Wende, Peter, eds. *British and German Historiography 1750-1950: Traditions, Perceptions, and Transfers.* Oxford: Oxford University, 2000.

The Student's Handbook to the University and Colleges of Oxford. Oxford: Clarendon, 1901.

Suggestions respectfully addressed to graduates in divinity connected with the coming election [of the Lady Margaret Professor of Divinity].Oxford, 1853.

The Supply and Training of Candidates for Holy Orders. Poole: W.H. Hunt, 1908.

Tait, Archibald Campbell. *Hints on the Formation of a Plan for the Safe and Effectual Revival of the Professorial System in Oxford.* Oxford: J.H. Parker, 1839.

Tamarkin, Elisa. *Anglophilia: Deference, Devotion and Antebellum America.* Chicago: University of Chicago, 2008.

Thatcher, Margaret. *The Path to Power.* London: Harper Collins, 1995.

Theissen, M.T. and Wells, S., eds. *Faithfulness and Fortitude: In Conversation with the Theological Ethics of Stanley Hauerwas.* Edinburgh: T&T Clark, 2000.

The Theological Statute. Case submitted to Mr. George Mellish, Q.C., and Mr Charles Bowen, Q.C., with their Opinion. Privately printed, January 1869.

Thompson, David. *Cambridge Theology in the Nineteenth Century.* Aldershot: Ashgate, 2008.

Thompson, J.M. *Miracles of the New Testament.* London: Edward Arnold, 1911.

Thomson, John Cockburn. *Almae Matres by Megathym Spleme.* London: James Hogg & Sons, 1858.

The Times, 4 December 1912.

The Times, 7 March 1913.

Turner, F.H. *Between Science and Religion: the reaction to scientific naturalism in late Victorian England.* New Haven: Yale University, 1974.

_____. *John Henry Newman: The Challenge to Evangelical Religion.* New Haven, CT: Yale University, 2002.

_____. *Contesting Cultural Authority.* Cambridge: Cambridge University, 1993.

Turnbull, George H. *The Educational Theory of J.G. Fichte: A Critical Account, Together with Translations.* Liverpool: University of Liverpool, 1926.

University of London: address from the Senate to the [Privy] Council in support of the University for a charter. London: Richard Taylor, 1834.

University of Oxford Commission. London: Her Majesty's Stationers, 1881.

University of Oxford: Faculty of Theology and Religion. "Faculty of Theology Name Change". http://theology.nsms.ox.ac.uk/news/untitled-resource.html.

Vogan, Thomas. *The Principal Objections against the Doctrine of the Trinity.* Oxford: J.H. Parker, 1837.

von Harnack, Adolf. *Die Aufgabe der theologischen Fakultäten und die allgemeine Religionsgeschichte.* Giessen, 1901.

Wace, H. *Divinity Degrees and Theological Studies at Oxford.* Privately printed, 1912.

Ward, M.A. , "The New Reformation: A Dialogue", *The Nineteenth Century*, 25 (1889).

Ward, G.R.M. and Heywood, J. *Oxford University Statutes Translated*, Vol. II (1767-1850)

Ward, W.R. *Victorian Oxford.* London: Frank Cass & Co, 1964.

Watson, E.W. *Bishop John Wordsworth.* London: Longmans, Green & Co., 1815.

Webb, C.C.J. *A Century of Anglican Theology: and other lectures.* Oxford, Blackwell, 1923.

_____. *A Study of Religious Thought in England since 1850*. Oxford: Clarendon, 1933.

Webster, John. *Confessing God: Essays in Christian Dogmatics II*. Edinburgh: T&T Clark, 2005.

Whiting, C.E. *The University of Durham, 1832-1932*. London: Sheldon, 1932.

Whytcock, J.C. *An Educated Clergy: Scottish Theological Education and Training in the Kirk and Secession, 1560–1850*. Milton Keynes: Paternoster, 2007.

Wilberforce, H.W. *The Foundations of Faith Assailed in Oxford*. London: Rivingtons, 1835.

Wiles, Maurice. *Jerusalem, Athens, and Oxford: An Inaugural Lecture Delivered before the University of Oxford on 18 May, 1971*. Oxford: Oxford University, 1971.

_____."Jerusalem, Athens, and Oxford: An inaugural lecture as Regius Professor of Divinity in the University of Oxford" in *Working Papers in Doctrine*. London: SCM, 1976.

Wilkinson, J.T. *Arthur Samuel Peake: A Biography*. London: Epworth, 1971.

Witheridge, John. *Excellent Dr Stanley*. Wilby: Michael Russell Publishing, 2013.

Wolfe, Judith F. and Brendan N. eds. *C.S. Lewis and the Church: Essays in Honour of Walter Hooper*. Edinburgh: T&T Clark, 2011.

Woods, F.H. *A Guide to the Study of Theology, adapted more especially to the Oxford Honour School*. Oxford: James Thornton, 1880.

Wordsworth, John. *The Church and the Universities: A Letter to C.S. Roundell*. Oxford: Parker & Co., 1880.

Wootton, David. "Formal Feelings for History", *Times Literary Supplement* (24 September 2010).

Zachhuber, Johannes. *Theology as Science in Nineteenth Century Germany*. Oxford: Oxford University, 2013.

Index

Montefiore, Hugh, 267–78

Moore, Aubrey, 195

moral philosophy, 52, 58, 70, 87, 132, 191, 203

Morrison, J. L., 259

Mozley, James, 59, 137, 188

Müller, Karl Otfried, 75

natural science. *See* science

New College, 176, 234, 287

Newman, John Henry, 19–20, 24–28, 40, 46, 48, 51, 55–59, 63–66, 68–69, 74, 94–95, 143–44, 166, 215, 254, 267, 273, 288

Nicholas I, tsar, 26

Nicoll, Alexander, 47–48

Niebuhr, Barthold Georg, 75–76

Nietzsche, Friedrich, 12–13

Nitzsch, Karl Immanuel, 44, 49

Nockles, Peter, 51 n.15, 53–58, 68, 79

Nonconformists' Union, 184

Nonconformity, 27, 31, 37–41, 81–82, 106, 144, 158, 163, 166–74, 183–90, 195–221, 236–48, 271, 276, 287

Nottingham University, 283

Nutt, John, 128

Ogilvie, Charles, 51n16, 67, 84, 129

Oman, Charles, 213, 215n119

Ordination Course, Oxford, 245, 249–53

ordination training, 36, 65, 83–84, 89, 100, 138, 144–45, 178, 190, 245, 249–53, 268–69, 273–74, 277

Oriel College, 26, 46, 50–55, 59, 64, 68–69, 117, 137, 171, 178, 226,

Oriel Professor of the Interpretation of Holy Scripture, 171, 178

Oriel Professorship in the Philosophy of Religion, 233

Overbeck, Franz, 12–13

Oxford Inter-Collegiate Christian Union (OICCU), 267

Oxford, the University of: and the Church of England, 26, 29–30, 34–39, 49–50, 66, 79–94, 101–3, 112–14, 170–73, 223, 198; historiography of, 31–34; reform of, 24–28, 45–46, 70, 79–92, 106–12, 112–14, 121, 170–73, 198, 211–12. *See also* colleges; Congregation; Convocation;Hebdomadal Board; Hebdomadal Council

Ripon Clergy College, 271

Ripon College Cuddesdon,
271n87

Ripon Hall, 271

Roberts (Thatcher), Margaret, 254

Robertson, Archibald, 238

Robinson, Henry Wheeler,
271–72

Roman Catholic Church, 40, 50,
57, 68, 127, 148, 166–67, 216,
237, 239, 241, 272, 287

Romanes, Ethel, 200

Romanes, Ethel Georgina, 200

Rose, Hugh James, 47–48

royal commissions of inquiry, 40,
45, 80–84, 91, 95, 106–7,
116–18, 137n64, 142n78,
164–65, 170–71, 177, 251–52

Rudiments of Faith and Religion.
See divinity, examination in

Rugby School, 59, 69, 75, 97, 113

Russell, John, 1st Earl Russell, 65,
69, 84, 109

Russia, 26, 102n133

Ryle, Gilbert, 231–32

Salisbury Theological College,
100

Salisbury, Lord (Robert Gascoyne-
Cecil, 3rd Marquess of
Salisbury), 136

Sanday, William, 156, 168–69,
176–83, 187–209, 269–70, 287

Sayce, Archibald, 145, 147–48,
156, 176

Schleiermacher, Friedrich D., 3,
6–23, 46–47, 187, 285

Schmalz, Theodor, 6

Schweitzer, Albert, 13

science (natural and physical), 5, 8,
13, 16, 22, 28, 31, 36, 70, 80,
91, 93, 99, 108, 132, 140, 176,
191, 241, 258, 260, 262, 282

'scientific' theology, 3, 6n8, 9–15,
31, 37–41, 44, 47, 76, 86, 94,
111, 114–15, 122, 141–43, 152,
156, 168–70, 179–82, 187–90,
195–200, 203–11, 221,
260–262, 264, 270, 273, 285

Scotland, theological education in,
4, 26–27, 41, 63, 72–73, 101,
213, 235, 278

Scott Holland, Henry, 170,
191–95, 202–21, 235–36, 243,
246, 249, 265, 281, 283, 286,
292

Scott, Robert, 76n72, 75, 96, 135

scriptural reasoning, 291n15

Second Vatican Council, 272, 287

Second World War. *See* war

Selbie, William, 217–18, 248